A Modest Proposal and Other Prose

THE BARNES & NOBLE LIBRARY OF ESSENTIAL READING

A Modest Proposal and Other Prose

JONATHAN SWIFT

INTRODUCTION BY LEWIS C. DALY

BARNES & NOBLE
NEW YORK

THE BARNES & NOBLE
LIBRARY OF ESSENTIAL READING

Originally published (sometimes anonymously) between 1704–1736

This 2004 edition published by Barnes & Noble, Inc.

Barnes & Noble, Inc.
122 Fifth Avenue
New York, NY 10011

ISBN-13: 978-0-7607-6051-2
ISBN-10: 0-7607-6051-9

Printed and bound in the United States of America

3 5 7 9 10 8 6 4

Contents

INTRODUCTION

He had, early in life, imbibed such a strong hatred to hypocrisy, that he fell into the opposite extreme. . . .

—THOMAS SHERIDAN (*Life of Jonathan Swift*)

JONATHAN SWIFT (1667–1745) IS GENERALLY ACKNOWLEDGED AS THE finest satirical writer in the English language, and it is no exaggeration to say, as Harold Bloom does, that he is likely the most "savage and merciless satirist" as well. Although Swift is best known for his longest and most ambitious work, the allegorical fiction *Gulliver's Travels*, shorter works such as *A Modest Proposal* and *A Tale of a Tub*, among other important pieces collected here, are no less accomplished and in some ways are more revealing of his satirical genius. The surprising, sometimes perverse humour and stinging mockery, the complex stylistic interplay of rhetoric, argument, and meaning, and the superb ironic control displayed throughout these pieces are the hallmarks not only of a master satirist, but of a skilled controversialist and public spirit, someone intensely concerned with engaging pressing issues and affecting his audience in certain ways. The art of satire has rarely provoked more controversy and had such lasting effect.

Born of English parents in Dublin, Ireland, in 1667, Jonathan Swift lived in a time of unprecedented political and intellectual change. Liberal democracy, the scientific revolution, and the British Empire were all built on foundations laid during this period, and Swift's career and writing bear the marks of these momentous changes. His family was well connected in the Anglo-Irish settler circles that ruled Ireland during this period, and he received elementary and secondary training at the elite Kilkenny School, followed by Trinity College, Dublin, where he received his B.A. in 1686. Aspiring above his provincial station as an Irish native, Swift sought fame and power in London, shifting his political alliances according to a complicated mix of personal opportunism and iconoclastic principle. Although his professional life centered on the Church of England, where he was ordained a priest and aspired to be a bishop, it was his brilliance as a writer and controversialist that brought him, briefly, into the center of power as chief publicist for the Tory regime of Robert Harley (1710–1714). With the dissolution of the Harley regime, however, Swift was "exiled" back to Ireland, where he spent the remaining decades of his life as Dean of St. Patrick's Cathedral in Dublin.

Swift's writing career began in the 1690s, following his departure from Ireland amid the civil unrest unleashed by the Glorious Revolution (1688–89). Through a family connection, he found employment as secretary in the household of Whig party leader Sir William Temple, where he was based for nearly a decade. During this time he took his M.A. at Oxford and was ordained a priest of the Church of England in 1695. Although he held several clerical positions in Ireland after 1695, he traveled frequently to England on church business and spent significant time in Temple's vast library. By the late 1690s, he was at work on his first and possibly his greatest satirical masterpiece, *A Tale of a Tub.*

Although deeply conservative by the emerging liberal standards of his day, Swift was in many ways the most radical stylist and polemicist of his generation, and he suffered professionally as a result. Many of his most important works, including *Gulliver's Travels* and *A Tale of a Tub,* appeared anonymously or pseudonymously, although often to little effect in shielding him. Later in life, Swift took up his pen with particular force for the cause of Ireland, his birthplace, against English commercial policies. This culminated in *A Modest Proposal,* the darkest of all his satires and one that has secured his place in the annals of Irish patriotism. Although for this and other interventions Swift stood among the most important and widely read controversialists of his day, ultimately his satire remains as politically unclassifiable as it is stylistically recognizable. At heart Swift was a consistent, unsparing skeptic toward the "modern" spirit of his time, with its own brand of religious enthusiasm for rational system-building and scientific dominion over human nature and the natural world. If, as Henry Fielding noted, "the satirist is to be regarded as our physician, not our enemy," satire was, for Swift, a method finely tuned to the moral purpose of, as he put it, "dissect[ing] the carcass of human nature"—exposing the delusive assumptions and contradictions, and the potential destructiveness, of voiding the "nature" from human nature by an unfounded faith in self-reliant intellectual progress.

Swift wrote during the eighteenth-century "Augustan Age" in British literature, known especially for its refined stylistic qualities, its deep engagement with classical literary forms and techniques, and its argumentative public spirit. An ambitious, well-known controversialist and publicist throughout a literary career spanning four decades, Swift was ultimately denied high professional appointment in the Church of England, where he had sought fame and power above his station as a native of Ireland. From 1714 until his death, Swift lived in Ireland in what he felt was an exile. Toward the end of his life, Swift experienced frequent attacks of dizziness, likely suffering from what modern medicine calls Ménière's syndrome, and by 1742 his mental state had deteriorated to the point where associates placed his affairs under legal guardianship. This situation fueled rumors of madness his less inventive critics frequently exploited to explain away his difficult attitudes and style. In 1710, Swift began writing actively in support of the conservative Tory government of Robert Harley, and he was appointed editor of the main pro-government newspaper *The Examiner*. Although he considered himself a "balance-of-powers" liberal in the Old Whig tradition of the Glorious Revolution, Swift had grown disenchanted with Whig politics over attempts within the party to repeal the Test Act, which barred Presbyterians, Catholics, and others opposed to the Church of England from holding public office. Swift's one abiding institutional loyalty throughout his life was to the Church of England, and it was arguably this loyalty that shaped his political allegiances and the political goals of many of his writings.

Allying with the pro-Church Tories was something of a personal triumph for Swift as well, however, giving him access to the London audience and power base he had long craved but never attained under Whig patronage. With John Gay, Alexander Pope, and other Augustan luminaries, Swift formed the Scriblerus Club during this period, a kind of Tory united literary front to undertake collective works that would expose cultural degradation at the hands of modern pedants and "scribblers." As George Levine suggests, three of the greatest works of eighteenth-century literature, Gay's *A Beggar's Opera* (1728), Pope's burlesque verse masterpiece *The Dunciad* (1728), and Swift's *Gulliver's Travels* (1726), likely had their genesis in the Scriblerus Club.

Swift's time at the center of power was short-lived, however. In 1713, he was appointed Dean of St. Patrick's Cathedral in Dublin, and the following year, when the Harley government was dissolved, he returned to Ireland permanently. Swiftly partly attributed his Irish "demotion" to royal hostility fueled by lingering suspicions of irreligion in *A Tale of a Tub*, first published nearly ten years earlier. In any case, his long-nurtured ambition for high preferment in the Church of England went unrequited by Tories and Whigs alike. Swift's sense of exile was surely part of the backdrop to the remarkable patriotic campaign he later began against English policies in Ireland.

Swift's career as a literary controversialist was launched in 1704, with the anonymous publication of a miscellany volume containing *A Full and True Account of the Battel Fought last Friday, Between the Antient and the Modern Books in St. James' Library, A Tale of a Tub,* and *A Discourse Concerning the Mechanical Operation of the Spirit.* Although many consider this volume to be Swift's most brilliant work, in fact it haunted him throughout his career. The prefatory "Apology" to *A Tale of a Tub* was in fact written after the original publication to address accusations of anarchy and irreligion aroused by the book.

The Battle of the Books was Swift's entry into an aristocratic pamphlet war that erupted in the 1690s concerning the value of ancient versus modern learning. As contemporary scholarship has shown, this conflict was essentially between two types of criticism— an older literary humanism or cultural "letters" tradition, associated with the Renaissance and its revival of classical wisdom, and an emerging "scientific" criticism emphasizing texts and philology, rather than ideas and sentiments, as the starting point for scholarship. Swift's account of the battle was written in defence of his patron William Temple at the provocation of several "moderns," including Richard Bentley, Keeper of the Royal Library. Bentley had demonstrated that the ancient texts put forward by Temple in his 1690 essay "On Ancient and Modern Learning" (Phalaris' *Epistles* and Aesop's *Fables*) were in fact forgeries, or the product of later editors, thus reducing Temple's defence of the "ancients" to absurdity. Rejecting this textual focus as a gratuitous display of useless learning, Swift presents an Aesopian fable of his own, comparing the scholarly moderns to a lordly spider, "which feeding and engendering on itself . . . produces nothing at last but flybane and a cobweb." He contrasts this to the humanistic bumblebee, whose "universal range . . . brings home honey and wax."

While written during the same period, *A Tale of a Tub* is a far more original and independent work—perhaps even the "most powerful prose work in the language," as Bloom claims. It is also the first major expression of Swift's central preoccupation with the "New Philosophy" of his day—centered in the Royal Society and other highly positioned rationalist circles. Just as Temple's opponents said he had "treated with Contempt" the "Inventions and Discoveries of the present Age, especially by *Men of Gresham*" (where the Royal Society was based), Swift believed this philosophical vanguard threatened humanity with ruin by subsuming religious tradition and human nature in the mechanical framework of modern science. Isaac Newton had been appointed president of the Royal Society in 1703, marking an important intellectual turning point and greatly amplifying the changes Swift perceived.

A Tale of a Tub was certainly the most striking and disturbing contemporary satire on the new learning. Although a publishing success, it was attacked by establishment and dissenting figures alike. Samuel

Clarke, one of the leading Newtonians among Anglican divines, launched the first public attack in 1705, citing *A Tale* as the work of a "Profane and Debauched Deist," meaning someone who thinks God acts through natural processes rather than divine intervention, as held in the Bible and church teaching. In fact, Swift was anything but a Deist. His own *Argument Against Abolishing Christianity* from the same period (1708), although meticulously inlaid with ironic misdirections, was an unmistakable defence of the established church against Dissenters, Deists, and their Whig supporters. Moreover, John Toland, the controversial early Deist, is plainly attacked in *A Tale of a Tub*, where he is partly personified in the character of Jack. Clarke's misguided criticism gives us an idea, however, of the political confusion Swift's satirical methods caused. It also sheds light on the "leveling" persuasion Swift held toward virtually all the modernizing elements of his day, whether within or outside the established church and political system.

Even as the "Apology" published with later editions of *A Tale* sought to refurbish the religious standing of its author, Swift's *Tritical Essay upon the Faculties of the Mind* (1707) can be read as a kind of restatement of the satirical essence of *A Tale*, shorn of stylistic impediments in its juxtaposition of ancient wisdom with the "opinions of philosophers" that "have scattered through the world as many plagues of the mind as Pandora's box did those of the body." The hallmark of *A Tale*, in contrast, is a remarkable complexity and opacity of style, where speaker, narrative, genre, rhetoric, tone, and reference are consciously and purposefully deployed, but without clear boundaries as to authorial intent: At every turn the satire and the thing satirized are blurred or doubled back on each other to deflect easy interpretation; and yet, despite this stylistic refraction of meaning, the critical force remains—interpreted differently by different people. As Swift himself famously put it in the preface to *The Battle of the Books*, "Satire is a sort of glass, wherein beholders do generally discover everybody's face but their own." Where Clarke saw Swift as a Deist, the Deists are in fact one of the main targets of *A Tale*.

Although not unlike the work of other satirists of this period in its exposure of abuses of religion, learning, and language, *A Tale* cuts much deeper in its philosophical anxiety and moral purpose. As Kenneth Craven asserts in his important contemporary study, "Swift's minority voice sees the modern world as having been constructed empirically of new sensibilities at the expense of immeasurable values and priceless standards." This "reductive process," in Swift's eyes, "had skewed scientific information to fit the optimistic parameters of its own myth, effectively burying other knowledge systems." Another contemporary critic, Frank Boyle, sees Swift's religious allegory of the three brothers and their coats, the narrative heart of *A Tale*, as a prop for exposing the "New Philosophy" as a methodological amalgam of historical heresies and emerging corruptions—combining gnosticism, alchemy, Roman Catholicism, and radical Protestant dissent. "This history culminates," Boyle says, "in the ridicule in *A Tale of A Tub* of the intellectual basis of the most formidable of all modern works, Newton's *Principia*." Closely related to the *Tale*, the finely drawn *Discourse Concerning the Mechanical Operation of the Spirit* satirizes the speculative and charismatic aspects of the new learning. For Swift, the new scientific "virtuosi" are part of a long history of "inspired" but misguided heretical movements, a worthy heir to the classic orthodox calumny linking religious dissent with sexual libertinism and "community of women."

A Tale's anti-modernism lies at the heart of Swift's satirical imagination, and he would return to these themes in *Gulliver's Travels*. But the interval between Swift's return to Ireland in 1714 and the spectacular success of *Travels* by the late 1720s was highlighted mainly by his remarkable patriotic pamphlet campaign against English commercial policies. Beginning in 1720, this campaign was Swift's greatest effort as a publicist and perhaps his most enduring political contribution.

In 1724, Swift wrote a series of letters under the name of "M. B. Drapier" (meaning "drape maker") in direct appeal to the Irish people. Drapier's Letters sought to arouse popular opposition to the Whig government's grant of a currency patent to English iron merchant William Wood, allowing him to introduce a specified volume of copper coins into Ireland. Swift and other patriotic leaders saw Wood's patent as a government attempt to, effectually, impose a debased currency on Ireland, with the goal of undermining its monetary system and national wealth.

Drapier's plain style and unadorned policy explanations could not be less Augustan, or for that matter less Swiftean, in their direct attempt to "conscientize" the Irish masses—to use Paolo Freire's term for a pedagogical process that aims to mobilize the poor by facilitating popular comprehension of oppressive structures. The letters' political appeal was modeled on a longstanding tradition of popular sovereignty Swift knew well from his classical studies. Indeed, the initials M. B. likely stood for Marcus Brutus, the Roman republican assassin. The letters provoked public demonstrations and petition campaigns, and a government reward for the author's identity went unclaimed—even though everyone knew the author was Swift. These rebellious events led the English Prime Minister, Robert Walpole, to finally withdraw the patent—a textbook example of the adage that the "pen is mightier than the sword."

Drapier's Letters also reveal a vein of deep human sympathy rarely seen in Swift's work. The opening of the fourth letter, addressed "To the Whole People of Ireland," cites the analogy of Esau, who "came fainting from the field at the point to die," causing him to sell his birthright for a mess of potage. Like Esau, the Irish have been weakened in claiming their liberty and rights by extreme hardship. There is hope, however, if the unvarnished truth, like "cordials . . . applied to their weak constitutions," is heard above the din of government rumors and lies, the "last howls of a dog dissected alive." Swift's sympathy for the Irish poor also galvanized his most famous short satire and arguably his darkest, *A Modest Proposal* (1729). Assuming the voice of a learned "projector"—what we would call a technocrat—Swift lays out, in painstaking methodical garb, a plan for introducing child cannibalism as the only feasible commercial policy left for Ireland, with its endemic hunger and poverty. The backdrop to this masterpiece of ironic tone was Swift's own 1720 *Proposal for the Universal Use of Irish Manufacture,* which urged a boycott of English imports and was condemned for sedition. Failing this kind of unified social effort, the only commercial policy finally left for Ireland, *A Modest Proposal* imperturbably argued a decade later, is to commodify her plentiful stock of children as gourmet food. Swift turns colonial economics on its head by dignifying that chief maxim of political economy—"people are the riches of a nation"—with its most literal application.

It is no wonder Swift was wary of his audience right from the beginning, dedicating *A Tale of a Tub* to "His Royal Highness, Prince Posterity." Among his last works, the poem *A Character, Panegyric, and Description of the Legion Club* (1736) —a bizarre prophetic indictment of the Dublin Parliament—is perhaps indicative of the degree of alienation he came to experience over the course of his diverse but always volatile career. Although he had defenders in his own time and has many enthusiasts besides Bloom in ours, few great writers have been subjected to the kind of critical abuse Swift suffered from his contemporaries on forward, well into the nineteenth century. In one of the first official blows after Swift's death, the Earl of Orrery set the tone by plainly calling Swift a misanthrope who "ridiculed human nature itself." The nineteenth-century Whig historian Thomas Macaulay wrote that Swift had "a heart burning with hatred against the whole human race," and the Victorian novelist Thackeray condemned his "gibbering shrieks and gnashing imprecations against mankind." Setting aside the moralistic tone of earlier criticism, the preeminent twentieth-century critic F. R. Leavis famously ascribed Swift's satirical genius to "the power of vanity," taking a strong cue from his contentious biography.

But Swift's satirical genius cannot be guilty of such moralistic and biographical indictments; otherwise, what would be the point of satire? The posterity Swift hoped would vindicate him has seen the point better than his contemporaries did, although not under circumstances Swift himself would have liked. A modernist and avant-garde progenitor above all the great Augustan stylists, it is notable that Swift's surest champions often celebrate those aspects of his work most despised by his fiercest enemies. His influence can be felt in the multivalent narratives and allegorical systems of later prose masters such as Herman Melville and James Joyce, in the existential absurdism of Samuel Beckett, and in the Surrealists' psychological attack on bourgeois culture. It is surely a very Swiftean irony that this Church of England man and doubter of all things new eventually became a leading icon of modernist counterculture. Swift was placed at the head of André Breton's seminal *Anthologie de l'Humour Noir,* leading the way, as the "*véritable intiateur,*" for the likes of Sade, Poe, Baudelaire, and Dali. He was also a formative influence on the psychedelic revolution's greatest prose innovator, William S. Burroughs, of *Naked Lunch* fame. Perhaps Swift would have agreed that such surprising influence shows the important truth that great satire knows no boundaries.

Lewis C. Daly is a senior research fellow of the Democracy Collaborative of the University of Maryland. He holds a Ph.D. in early modern English literature from the State University of New York at Buffalo.

A FULL AND TRUE ACCOUNT OF THE BATTEL FOUGHT LAST FRIDAY, BETWEEN THE ANTIENT AND THE MODERN BOOKS IN ST. JAMES' LIBRARY (1697)

THE BOOKSELLER TO THE READER

The following Discourse, as it is unquestionably of the same author, so it seems to have been written about the same time with the former; I mean the year 1697, when the famous dispute was on foot about ancient and modern learning. The controversy took its rise from an essay of Sir William Temple's upon that subject, which was answered by W. Wotton, B.D., with an Appendix by Dr. Bentley, endeavouring to destroy the credit of Æsop and Phalaris for authors, whom Sir William Temple had, in the essay before-mentioned, highly commended. In that appendix the doctor falls hard upon a new edition of Phalaris put out by the Honourable Charles Boyle, now Earl of Orrery, to which Mr. Boyle replied at large, with great learning and wit; and the doctor voluminously rejoined. In this dispute, the town highly resented to see a person of Sir William Temple's character and merits roughly used by the two reverend gentlemen aforesaid, and without any manner of provocation. At length, there appearing no end of the quarrel, our author tells us that the BOOKS in St. James' Library, looking upon themselves as parties principally concerned, took up the controversy and came to a decisive battle. But the manuscript by the injury of fortune or weather being in several places imperfect, we cannot learn to which side the victory fell.

I must warn the reader to beware of applying to persons what is here meant only of books, in the most literal sense. So, when Virgil is mentioned, we are not to understand the person of a famous poet called by that name, but only certain sheets of paper, bound up in leather, containing in print the works of the said poet; and so of the rest.

THE PREFACE OF THE AUTHOR

Satire is a sort of glass, wherein beholders do generally discover everybody's face but their own; which is the chief reason for that kind of reception it meets in the world, and that so very few are offended with it. But if it should happen otherwise, the danger is not great; and I have learned from long experience never to apprehend mischief from those understandings I have been able to provoke; for anger and fury, though they add strength to the sinews of the body, yet are found to relax those of the mind, and to render all its efforts feeble and impotent.

There is a brain that will endure but one scumming; let the owner gather it with discretion, and manage his little stock with husbandry; but of all things, let him beware of bringing it under the lash of his betters, because that will make it all bubble up into impertinence, and he will find no new supply. Wit, without knowledge, being a sort of cream, which gathers in a night to the top, and by a skilful hand may be soon whipped into froth; but once scummed away, what appears underneath will be fit for nothing but to be thrown to the hogs.

A FULL AND TRUE ACCOUNT OF THE BATTLE FOUGHT LAST FRIDAY, &C.

Whoever examines with due circumspection into the *Annual Records of Time*,[1] will find it remarked that War is the child of Pride, and Pride the daughter of Riches. The former of which assertions may be soon granted, but one cannot so easily subscribe to the latter; for Pride is nearly related to Beggary and Want, either by father or mother, and sometimes by both: and to speak naturally, it very seldom happens among men to fall out when all have enough, invasions usually travelling from north to south, that is to say, from poverty upon plenty. The most ancient and natural grounds of quarrels are lust and avarice; which, though we may allow to be brethren, or collateral branches of pride, are certainly the issues of want. For, to speak in the phrase of writers upon politics, we may observe in the Republic of Dogs (which, in its original, seems to be an institution of the Many) that the whole state is ever in the profoundest peace after a full meal; and that civil broils arise among them when it happens for one great bone to be seized on by some leading dog, who either divides it among the few and then it falls to an oligarchy, or keeps it to himself and then it runs up to a tyranny. The same reasoning also holds place among them in those dissensions we behold upon a turgescency in any of their females. For the right of possession lying in common (it being impossible to establish a property in so delicate a case) jealousies and suspicions do so abound that the whole commonwealth of that street is reduced to a manifest state of war, of every citizen against every citizen, till someone of more courage, conduct, or fortune than the rest, seizes and enjoys the prize; upon which naturally arises plenty of heart-burning, and envy, and snarling against the happy dog. Again, if we look upon any of these republics engaged in a foreign war either of invasion or defence, we shall find the same reasoning will serve as to the grounds and occasions of each, and that poverty or want in some degree or other (whether real or in opinion, which makes no alteration in the case) has a great share, as well as pride, on the part of the aggressor.

Now, whoever will please to take this scheme, and either reduce or adapt it to an intellectual state or commonwealth of learning, will soon discover the first ground of disagreement between the two great parties at this time in arms, and may form just conclusions upon the merits of either cause. But the issue or events of this war are not so easy to conjecture at; for the present quarrel is so inflamed by the warm heads of either faction, and the pretensions *somewhere or other* so exorbitant, as not to admit the least overtures of accommodation. This quarrel first began (as I have heard it affirmed by an old dweller in the neighbourhood) about a small spot of ground, lying and being upon one of the two tops of the hill Parnassus; the highest and largest of which had, it seems, been time out of mind in quiet possession of certain tenants called the Ancients, and the other was held by the Moderns. But these, disliking their present station, sent certain ambassadors to the Ancients, complaining of a great nuisance; how the height of that part of Parnassus quite spoiled the prospect of theirs, especially towards the *East*; and therefore, to avoid a war, offered them the choice of this alternative—either that the Ancients would please to remove themselves and their effects down to the lower summity, which the Moderns would graciously surrender to them, and advance in their place; or else that the said Ancients will give leave to the Moderns to come with shovels and mattocks, and level the said hill as low as they shall think it convenient. To which the Ancients made answer, how little they expected such a message as this from a colony whom they had admitted, out of their own free grace, to so near a neighbourhood. That, as to their own seat, they were aborigines of it, and therefore to talk with them of a removal or surrender, was a language they did not understand. That if the height of the hill on their side shortened the prospect of the Moderns, it was a disadvantage they could not help; but desired them to consider whether that injury (if it be any) were not largely recompensed by the shade and shelter it afforded them. That as to levelling or digging down, it was either folly or ignorance to propose it, if they did, or did not know, how that side of the hill was an entire rock, which would break their tools and hearts without any damage to itself. That they would therefore advise the Moderns rather to raise their own side of the hill than dream of pulling down that of the Ancients; to the former of which they would not only give licence, but also largely contribute. All this was rejected by the Moderns with much indignation, who still insisted upon one of the two expedients. And so this difference broke out into a long and obstinate war, maintained on the one part by resolution and by the courage of certain leaders and allies; but on the other by the greatness of their number, upon all defeats affording continual recruits. In this quarrel whole rivulets of ink have been exhausted, and the virulence of both parties enormously augmented. Now, it must here be understood that ink is the great missive weapon in all battles of the learned, which, conveyed through a sort of engine called a quill, infinite numbers of these are darted at the enemy by the valiant on each side, with equal skill and violence, as if it were an engagement of porcupines. This malignant liquor was compounded by the engineer who invented it, of two ingredients, which are gall and copperas; by its bitterness and venom to suit in some degree, as well as to foment, the genius of the combatants. And as the Grecians, after an engagement, when they could not agree about the victory, were wont to set up trophies on both sides, the beaten party being content to be at the same expense to keep itself in countenance (a laudable and ancient custom, happily revived of late in the art of war); so the learned, after a sharp and bloody dispute, do on both sides hang out their trophies too, whichever comes by the worst. These trophies have largely inscribed on them the merits of the cause, a full impartial account of such a battle, and how the victory fell clearly to the party that set them up. They are known to the world under several names, as *disputes, arguments, rejoinders, brief considerations, answers, replies, remarks, reflections, objections, confutations.* For a very few days they are fixed up in all public places either by themselves or their representatives,[2] for passengers to gaze at; from whence the chiefest and largest are removed to certain magazines they call libraries, there to remain in a quarter purposely assigned them, and from thenceforth begin to be called *Books of Controversy.*

In these books is wonderfully instilled and preserved the spirit of each warrior, while he is alive; and after his death his soul transmigrates there to inform them. This at least is the more common opinion; but I believe it is with libraries as with other cemeteries, where some philosophers affirm that a certain spirit, which they call *brutum hominis*, hovers over the monument till the body is corrupted and turns to dust or to worms, but then vanishes or dissolves. So, we may say, a restless spirit haunts over every book till dust or worms have seized upon it, which to some may happen in a few days, but to others, later; and therefore books of controversy, being of all others haunted by the most disorderly spirits, have always been confined in a separate lodge from the rest; and, for fear of mutual violence against each other, it was thought prudent by our ancestors to bind them to the peace with strong iron chains. Of which invention the original occasion was this. When the works of Scotus first came out, they were carried to a certain library and had lodgings appointed them; but this author was no sooner settled than he went to visit his master Aristotle; and there both concerted together to seize Plato by main force and turn him out from his ancient station among the divines, where he had peaceably dwelt near eight hundred years. The attempt succeeded, and the two usurpers have reigned ever since in his stead: but to maintain quiet for the future, it was decreed that all *polemics* of the larger size should be held fast with a chain.

By this expedient the public peace of libraries might certainly have been preserved, if a new species of controversial books had not arose of late years, instinct with a most malignant spirit, from the war above-mentioned between the learned, about the higher summity of Parnassus.

When these books were first admitted into the public libraries, I remember to have said upon occasion to several persons concerned, how I was sure they would create broils wherever they came, unless a world of care were taken; and therefore I advised that the champions of each side should be coupled together or otherwise mixed, that, like the blending of contrary poisons, their malignity might be employed among themselves. And it seems I was neither an ill prophet nor an ill counsellor; for it was nothing else but the neglect of this caution which gave occasion to the terrible fight that happened on Friday last, between the ancient and modern books in the King's Library. Now, because the talk of this battle is so fresh in everybody's mouth, and the expectation of the town so great to be informed in the particulars; I, being possessed of all qualifications requisite in an historian, and retained by neither party, have resolved to comply with the urgent *importunity of my friends* by writing down a full impartial account thereof.

The guardian of the regal library, a person of great valour but chiefly renowned for his *humanity*,[3] had been a fierce champion for the Moderns; and, in an engagement upon Parnassus, had vowed, with his own hands, to knock down two of the Ancient chiefs who guarded a small pass on the superior rock; but endeavouring to climb up was cruelly obstructed by his own unhappy weight and tendency towards his centre, a quality to which those of the Modern party are extreme subject; for, being light-headed, they have in speculation a wonderful agility, and conceive nothing too high for them to mount; but in reducing to practice, discover a mighty pressure about their posteriors and their heels. Having thus failed in his design, the disappointed champion bore a cruel rancour to the Ancients, which he resolved to gratify by showing all marks of his favour to the books of their adversaries, and lodging them in the fairest apartments; when at the same time, whatever book had the boldness to own itself for an advocate of the Ancients, was buried alive in some obscure corner, and threatened upon the least displeasure to be turned out of doors. Besides, it so happened that about this time there was a strange confusion of place among all the books in the library, for which several reasons were assigned. Some imputed it to a great heap of learned dust, which a perverse wind blew off from a shelf of Moderns into the keeper's eyes. Others affirmed he had a humour to pick the worms out of the schoolmen, and swallow them fresh and fasting; whereof some fell upon his spleen, and some climbed up into his head, to the great perturbation of both. And lastly, others maintained that by walking much in the dark about the library, he had quite lost the situation of it out of his head; and therefore, in replacing his books, he was apt to mistake and clap Des Cartes next to Aristotle; poor Plato had got between Hobbes and the *Seven Wise Masters*, and Virgil was hemmed in with Dryden on one side, and Withers on the other.

Meanwhile, those books that were advocates for the Moderns chose out one from among them to make a progress through the whole library, examine the number and strength of their party, and concert their affairs. This messenger performed all things very industriously, and brought back with him a list of their forces, in all fifty thousand, consisting chiefly of light-horse, heavy-armed foot, and mercenaries; whereof the foot were in general but sorrily armed, and worse clad; their horses large, but extremely out of case and heart; however, some few, by trading among the Ancients, had furnished themselves tolerably enough.

While things were in this ferment, discord grew extremely high; hot words passed on both sides, and ill blood was plentifully bred.

Here a solitary Ancient, squeezed up among a whole shelf of Moderns, offered fairly to dispute the case, and to prove by manifest reasons, that the priority was due to them, from long possession, and in regard of their prudence, antiquity, and, above all, their great merits towards the Moderns. But these denied the premisses, and seemed very much to wonder how the Ancients could pretend to insist upon their antiquity, when it was so plain (if they went to that) that the Moderns were much the more *ancient*[4] of the two. As for any obligations they owed to the Ancients, they renounced them all. "'Tis true," said they, "we are informed some few of our party have been so mean to borrow their subsistence from you; but the rest, infinitely the greater number (and especially we French and English), were so far from stooping to so base an example that there never passed, till this very hour, six words between us. For our horses are of our own breeding, our arms of our own forging, and our clothes of our own cutting out and sewing." Plato was by chance upon the next shelf, and observing those that spoke to be in the ragged plight mentioned a while ago; their jades lean and foundered, their weapons of rotten wood, their armour rusty, and nothing but rags underneath; he laughed loud, and in his pleasant way swore, by G—he believed them.

Now, the Moderns had not proceeded in their late negotiation with secrecy enough to escape the notice of the enemy. For those advocates who had begun the quarrel by setting first on foot the dispute of precedency, talked so loud of coming to a battle, that Temple happened to overhear them, and gave immediate intelligence to the Ancients, who thereupon drew up their scattered troops together, resolving to act upon the defensive; upon which several of the Moderns fled over to their party, and among the rest Temple himself. This Temple, having been educated and long conversed among the Ancients, was, of all the Moderns, their greatest favourite, and became their greatest champion.

Things were at this crisis, when a material accident fell out. For, upon the highest corner of a large window, there dwelt a certain spider, swollen up to the first magnitude by the destruction of infinite numbers of flies, whose spoils lay scattered before the gates of his palace, like human bones before the cave of some giant. The avenues to his castle were guarded with turnpikes and palisadoes, all after the modern way of fortification. After you had passed several courts, you came to the centre, wherein you might behold the constable himself in his own lodgings, which had windows fronting to each avenue, and ports to sally out upon all occasions of prey or defence. In this mansion he had for sometime dwelt in peace and plenty, without danger to his person by swallows from above, or to his palace by brooms from below; when it was the pleasure of fortune to conduct thither a wandering bee, to whose curiosity a broken pane in the glass had discovered itself, and in he went; where, expatiating a while, he at last happened to alight upon one of the outward walls of the spider's citadel, which, yielding to the unequal weight, sunk down to the very foundation. Thrice he endeavoured to force his passage, and thrice the centre shook. The spider within, feeling the terrible convulsion, supposed at first that nature was approaching to her final dissolution; or else that Beelzebub, with all his legions, was come to revenge the death of many thousands of his subjects, whom this enemy had slain and devoured. However, he at length valiantly resolved to issue forth, and meet his fate. Meanwhile the bee had acquitted himself of his toils, and, posted securely at some distance, was employed in cleansing his wings and disengaging them from the ragged remnants of the cobweb. By this time the spider was adventured out, when, beholding the chasms and ruins and dilapidations of his fortress, he was very near at his wit's end; he stormed and swore like a madman, and swelled till he was ready to burst. At length, casting his eye upon the bee, and wisely gathering causes from events (for they knew each other by sight), "A plague split you," said he, "for a giddy son of a whore. Is it you, with a vengeance, that have made this litter here? Could you not look before you, and be d—d? Do you think I have nothing else to do (in the devil's name) but to mend and repair after your arse?" "Good words, friend," said the bee (having now pruned himself and being disposed to droll). "I'll give you my hand and word to come near your kennel no more; I was never in such a confounded pickle since I was born." "Sirrah," replied the spider, "if it were not for breaking an old custom in our family never to stir abroad against an enemy, I should come and teach you better manners." "I pray have patience," said the bee, "or you will spend your substance, and for aught I see, you may stand in need of it all towards the repair of your house." "Rogue, rogue," replied the spider, "yet, methinks you should have more respect to a person whom all the world allows to be so much your betters." "By my troth," said the bee, "the comparison will amount to a very good jest, and you will do me a favour to let me know the reasons that all the world is pleased to use in so hopeful a dispute." At this the spider, having swelled himself into the size and posture of a disputant, began his argument in the true spirit of controversy with a resolution to be heartily scurrilous and angry, to urge *on* his own reasons without the least regard to the answers or objections of his opposite, and fully predetermined in his mind against all conviction.

"Not to disparage myself," said he, "by the comparison with such a rascal, what art thou but a vagabond without house or home, without stock or inheritance? Born to no possession of your own, but a pair of wings and a drone-pipe. Your livelihood is an universal plunder upon nature; a free-booter over fields and gardens; and for the sake of stealing, will rob a nettle as readily as a violet. Whereas I am a domestic animal, furnished with a native stock within myself. This large castle (to show my improvements in the mathematics) is all built with my own hands, and the materials extracted altogether out of my own person."

"I am glad," answered the bee, "to hear you grant at least that I am come honestly by my wings and my voice; for then, it seems, I am obliged to Heaven alone for my flights and my music; and Providence would never have bestowed me two such gifts, without designing them for the noblest ends. I visit indeed all the flowers and blossoms of the field and the garden; but whatever I collect from thence enriches myself without the least injury to their beauty, their smell, or their taste. Now, for you and your skill in architecture and other mathematics, I have little to say. In that building of yours there might, for aught I know, have been labour and method enough; but, by woeful experience for us both, 'tis too plain the materials are naught, and I hope you will henceforth take warning, and consider duration and matter as well as method and art. You boast, indeed, of being obliged to no other creature but of drawing and spinning out all from yourself; that is to say, if we may judge of the liquor in the vessel by what issues out, you possess a good plentiful store of dirt and poison in your breast; and though I would by no means lessen or disparage your genuine stock of either, yet I doubt you are somewhat obliged, for an increase of both, to a little foreign assistance. Your inherent portion of dirt does not fail of acquisitions by sweepings exhaled from below; and one insect furnishes you with a share of poison to destroy another. So that, in short, the question comes all to this—Whether is the nobler being of the two, that which, by a lazy contemplation of four inches round, by an overweening pride, which feeding and engendering on itself, turns all into excrement and venom, produc[es] nothing at last but flybane and a cobweb; or that which, by an universal range, with long search, much study, true judgment, and distinction of things, brings home honey and wax."

This dispute was managed with such eagerness, clamour, and warmth, that the two parties of books in arms below stood silent a while, waiting in suspense what would be the issue, which was not long undetermined. For the bee, grown impatient at so much loss of time, fled straight away to a bed of roses without looking for a reply, and left the spider like an orator, *collected* in himself, and just prepared to burst out.

It happened upon this emergency, that Æsop broke silence first. He had been of late most barbarously treated by a strange effect of the regent's *humanity,* who had tore off his title-page, sorely defaced one half of his leaves, and chained him fast among a shelf of Moderns. Where, soon discovering how high the quarrel was like to proceed, he tried all his arts, and turned himself to a thousand forms. At length, in the borrowed shape of an ass, the regent mistook him for a Modern, by which means he had time and opportunity to escape to the Ancients, just when the spider and the bee were entering into their contest, to which he gave his attention with a world of pleasure; and when it was ended, swore in the loudest key that in all his life he had never known two cases so parallel and adapt to each other, as that in the window, and this upon the shelves. "The disputants," said he, "have admirably managed the dispute between them, have taken in the full strength of all that is to be said on both sides, and exhausted the substance of every argument *pro* and *con*. It is but to adjust the reasonings of both to the present quarrel, then to compare and apply the labours and fruits of each, as the bee has learnedly deduced them, and we shall find the conclusions fall plain and close upon the Moderns and us. For pray, gentlemen, was ever anything so modern as the spider in his air, his turns, and his paradoxes? He argues in the behalf of you his brethren, and himself, with many boastings of his native stock and great genius; that he spins and spits wholly from himself, and scorns to own any obligation or assistance from without. Then he displays to you his great skill in architecture and improvement in the mathematics. To all this the bee, as an advocate retained by us the Ancients, thinks fit to answer—that if one may judge of the great genius or inventions of the Moderns by what they have produced, you will hardly have countenance to bear you out in boasting of either. Erect your schemes with as much method and skill as you please; yet if the materials be nothing but dirt, spun out of your own entrails (the guts of modern brains), the edifice will conclude at last in a cobweb, the duration of which, like that of other spiders' webs, may be imputed to their being forgotten, or neglected, or hid in a corner. For anything else of genuine that the Moderns may pretend to, I cannot recollect, unless it be a large vein of wrangling and satire, much of a nature and substance with the spider's poison; which, however they pretend to spit wholly out of themselves, is improved by the same arts, by feeding upon the insects and vermin of the age. As for us, the Ancients, we are content, with the bee, to pretend to nothing of our own beyond our wings and our voice, that is to say, our flights and our language. For the rest, whatever we have got has been by infinite labour, and search, and ranging through every corner of nature; the difference is that instead of dirt and poison, we have rather chose to fill our hives with honey and wax, thus furnishing mankind with the two noblest of things, which are sweetness and light."

'Tis wonderful to conceive the tumult arisen among the books, upon the close of this long descant of Æsop; both parties took the hint, and heightened their animosities so on a sudden that they resolved it should come to a battle. Immediately the two main bodies withdrew under their several ensigns to the further parts of the library, and there entered into cabals and consults upon the present emergency. The Moderns were in very warm debates upon the choice of their leaders; and nothing less than the fear impending from their enemies could have kept them from mutinies upon this occasion. The difference was greatest among the horse, where every private trooper pretended to the chief command, from Tasso and Milton to Dryden and Withers. The light-horse were commanded by Cowley and Despréaux. There came the bowmen under their valiant leaders, Des Cartes, Gassendi, and Hobbes, whose strength was such that they could shoot their arrows beyond the atmosphere, never to fall down again, but turn like that of Evander into meteors; or, like the cannon-ball, into stars. Paracelsus brought a squadron of stink-pot-flingers from the snowy mountains of Rhœtia. There came a vast body of dragoons, of different nations, under the leading of Harvey, their great aga: part armed with scythes, the weapons of death, part with lances and long knives, all steeped in poison; part shot bullets of a most malignant nature, and used white powder which infallibly killed without report. There came several bodies of heavy-armed foot, all mercenaries, under the ensigns of Guicciardine, Davila, Polydore Virgil, Buchanan, Mariana, Cambden, and others. The engineers were commanded by Regiomontanus and Wilkins. The rest were a confused multitude, led by Scotus, Aquinas, and Bellarmine; of mighty bulk and stature, but without either arms, courage, or discipline. In the last place came infinite swarms of *calones*,[5] a disorderly rout led by L'Estrange; rogues and ragamuffins that follow the camp for nothing but the plunder, all without coats to cover them.

The army of the Ancients was much fewer in number. Homer led the horse, and Pindar the light-horse; Euclid was chief engineer; Plato and Aristotle commanded the bowmen, Herodotus and Livy the foot, Hippocrates the dragoons. The allies, led by Vossius and Temple, brought up the rear.

All things violently tending to a decisive battle, Fame, who much frequented, and had a large apartment formerly assigned her in the regal library, fled up straight to Jupiter to whom she delivered a faithful account of all that had passed between the two parties below (for, among the gods, she always tells truth). Jove, in great concern, convokes a council in the Milky-Way. The senate assembled, he declares the occasion of convening them: a bloody battle just impendent between two mighty armies of Ancient and Modern creatures called books, wherein the celestial interest was but too deeply concerned. Momus, the patron of the Moderns, made an excellent speech in their favour, which was answered by Pallas, the protectress of the Ancients. The assembly was divided in their affections, when Jupiter commanded the book of fate to be laid before him. Immediately were brought by Mercury three large volumes in folio containing memoirs of all things, past, present, and to come. The clasps were of silver double gilt, the covers of celestial turkey leather, and the paper such as here on earth might pass almost for vellum. Jupiter, having silently read the decree, would communicate the import to none, but presently shut up the book.

Without the doors of this assembly, there attended a vast number of light, nimble gods, menial servants to Jupiter: these are his ministering instruments in all affairs below. They travel in a caravan, more or less together, and are fastened to each other like a link of galley-slaves, by a light chain which passes from them to Jupiter's great toe; and yet, in receiving or delivering a message they may never approach above the lowest step of his throne, where he and they whisper to each other through a long hollow trunk. These deities are called by mortal men *accidents* or *events*; but the gods call them second causes. Jupiter having delivered his message to a certain number of these divinities, they flew immediately down to the pinnacle of the regal library, and consulting a few minutes, entered unseen and disposed the parties according to their orders.

Meanwhile, Momus fearing the worst, and calling to mind an ancient prophecy which bore no very good face to his children the Moderns, bent his flight to the region of a malignant deity called Criticism. She dwelt on the top of a snowy mountain in Nova Zembla; there Momus found her extended in her den, upon the spoils of numberless volumes half devoured. At her right hand sat Ignorance, her father and husband, blind with age; at her left, Pride her mother, dressing her up in the scraps of paper herself had torn. There was Opinion her sister, light of foot, hoodwinked, and headstrong, yet giddy and perpetually turning. About her played her children, Noise and Impudence, Dulness and Vanity, Positiveness, Pedantry, and Ill-Manners. The goddess herself had claws like a cat; her head, and ears, and voice, resembled those of an ass; her teeth fallen out before, her eyes turned inward as if she looked only upon herself; her diet was the overflowing of her own gall; her spleen was so large as to stand prominent like a dug of the first rate, nor wanted excrescencies in form of teats, at which a crew of ugly monsters were greedily sucking; and what is wonderful to conceive, the bulk of spleen increased faster than the sucking could diminish it. "Goddess," said Momus, "can you sit idly here while our devout worshippers the Moderns are this minute entering into a cruel battle, and perhaps now lying under the swords of their enemies? Who then hereafter will ever sacrifice or build altars to our divinities? Haste, therefore, to the British Isle, and if possible prevent their destruction, while I make factions among the gods and gain them over to our party."

Momus, having thus delivered himself, stayed not for an answer, but left the goddess to her own resentments. Up she rose in a rage and, as it is the form upon such occasions, began a soliloquy. "'Tis I" (said she) "who give wisdom to infants and idiots; by me, children grow wiser than their parents; by me, beaux become politicians, and schoolboys judges of philosophy; by me, sophisters debate and conclude upon the depths of knowledge; and coffeehouse wits, instinct by me, can correct an author's style and display his minutest errors without understanding a syllable of his matter or his language. By me, striplings spend their judgment as they do their estate, before it comes into their hands. 'Tis I who have deposed wit and knowledge from their empire over poetry, and advanced myself in their stead. And shall a few upstart Ancients dare to oppose me? But come, my aged parents, and you my children dear, and thou my beauteous sister; let us ascend my chariot and haste to assist our devout Moderns, who are now sacrificing to us a hecatomb, as I perceive by that grateful smell which from thence reaches my nostrils."

The goddess and her train having mounted the chariot, which was drawn by tame geese, flew over infinite regions shedding her influence in due places, till at length she arrived at her beloved island of Britain; but in hovering over its metropolis, what blessings did she not let fall upon her seminaries of Gresham and Covent Garden! And now she reached the fatal plain of St. James' Library, at what time the two armies were upon the point to engage; where, entering with all her caravan unseen, and landing upon a case of shelves, now desert but once inhabited by a colony of virtuosos, she stayed a while to observe the posture of both armies.

But here the tender cares of a mother began to fill her thoughts and move in her breast. For, at the head of a troop of Modern bowmen, she cast her eyes upon her son Wotton, to whom the fates had assigned a very short thread; Wotton, a young hero, whom an unknown father of mortal race begot by stolen embraces with this goddess. He was the darling of his mother above all her children, and she resolved to go and comfort him. But first according to the good old custom of deities she cast about to change her shape, for fear the divinity of her countenance might dazzle his mortal sight and overcharge the rest of his senses. She therefore gathered up her person into an octavo compass: her body grew white and arid, and split in pieces with dryness; the thick turned into pasteboard, and the thin into paper, upon which her parents and children artfully strewed a black juice, or decoction of gall and soot, in form of letters; her head, and voice, and spleen, kept their primitive form, and that which before was a cover of skin did still continue so. In which guise she marched on towards the Moderns, undistinguishable in shape and dress from the divine Bentley, Wotton's dearest friend. "Brave Wotton," said the goddess, "why do our troops stand idle here, to spend their present vigour and opportunity of the day? Away, let us haste to the generals and advise to give the onset immediately." Having spoke thus, she took the ugliest of her monsters, full glutted from her spleen, and flung it invisibly into his mouth, which flying straight up into his head squeezed out his eyeballs, gave him a distorted look, and half overturned his brain. Then she privately ordered two of her beloved children, Dulness and Ill-Manners, closely to attend his person in all encounters. Having thus accoutred him she vanished in a mist, and the hero perceived it was the goddess his mother.

The destined hour of fate being now arrived, the fight began; whereof, before I dare adventure to make a particular description, I must, after the example of other authors, petition for a hundred tongues, and mouths, and hands, and pens, which would all be too little to perform so immense a work. Say, goddess, that presidest over History, who it was that first advanced in the field of battle! Paracelsus, at the head of his dragoons, observing Galen in the adverse wing, darted his javelin with a mighty force, which the brave Ancient received upon his shield, the point breaking in the second fold.

* * * * * * * *
* * * * * * *Hic pauca*
* * * * * * *desunt.*
* * * * * * * *

They bore the wounded aga on their shields to his chariot *

* * * * * * * *
Desunt * * * * * * *
nonnulla. * * * * * * *
* * * * * * * *

Then Aristotle, observing Bacon advance with a furious mien, drew his bow to the head and let fly his arrow, which missed the valiant Modern and went hizzing over his head. But Des Cartes it hit; the steel point quickly found a defect in his headpiece; it pierced the leather and the pasteboard and went in at his right eye. The torture of the pain whirled the valiant bowman round till death, like a star of superior influence, drew him into his own vortex.

* * * * * * * *
Ingens hiatus * * * * * *
hic in MS. * * * * * *
* * * * * * * *

* * * * when Homer appeared at the head of the cavalry, mounted on a furious horse with difficulty managed by the rider himself, but which no other mortal durst approach; he rode among the enemy's ranks, and bore down all before him. Say,

goddess, whom he slew first and whom he slew last! First, Gondibert advanced against him, clad in heavy armour and mounted on a staid, sober gelding, not so famed for his speed as his docility in kneeling whenever his rider would mount or alight. He had made a vow to Pallas, that he would never leave the field till he had spoiled Homer[6] of his armour; madman, who had never once seen the wearer nor understood his strength! Him Homer overthrew, horse and man, to the ground, there to be trampled and choked in the dirt. Then with a long spear he slew Denham,[7] a stout Modern who from his father's side derived his lineage from Apollo, but his mother was of mortal race. He fell, and bit the earth. The celestial part Apollo took and made it a star, but the terrestrial lay wallowing upon the ground. Then Homer slew Wesley with a kick of his horse's heel; he took Perrault by mighty force out of his saddle, then hurled him at Fontenelle, with the same blow dashing out both their brains.

On the left wing of the horse, Virgil appeared in shining armour, completely fitted to his body. He was mounted on a dapple grey steed, the slowness of whose pace was an effect of the highest mettle and vigour. He cast his eye on the adverse wing, with a desire to find an object worthy of his valour, when, behold, upon a sorrel gelding of a monstrous size appeared a foe issuing from among the thickest of the enemy's squadrons; but his speed was less than his noise, for his horse, old and lean, spent the dregs of his strength in a high trot, which though it made slow advances yet caused a loud clashing of his armour, terrible to hear. The two cavaliers had now approached within the throw of a lance, when the stranger desired a parley, and, lifting up the vizard of his helmet, a face hardly appeared from within, which after a pause was known for that of the renowned Dryden. The brave Ancient suddenly started, as one possessed with surprise and disappointment together; for the helmet was nine times too large for the head, which appeared situate far in the hinder part, even like the lady in a lobster, or like a mouse under a canopy of state, or like a shrivelled beau from within the penthouse of a modern periwig; and the voice was suited to the visage, sounding weak and remote. Dryden, in a long harangue, soothed up the good Ancient, called him "father" and by a large deduction of genealogies made it plainly appear that they were nearly related. Then he humbly proposed an exchange of armour, as a lasting mark of hospitality between them. Virgil consented (for the goddess Diffidence came unseen and cast a mist before his eyes), though his was of gold[8] and cost a hundred beeves, the other's but of rusty iron. However, this glittering armour became the Modern yet worse than his own. Then they agreed to exchange horses; but when it came to the trial, Dryden was afraid and utterly unable to mount. * * * * *

* * * * * * * *

* * * * * * *Alter hiatus*

* * * * * * *in MS.*

* * * * * * * *

Lucan appeared upon a fiery horse of admirable shape, but head-strong, bearing the rider where he list over the field; he made a mighty slaughter among the enemy's horse, which destruction to stop, Blackmore, a famous Modern (but one of the mercenaries) strenuously opposed himself and darted a javelin with a strong hand, which falling short of its mark, struck deep in the earth. Then Lucan threw a lance, but Æsculapius came unseen and turned off the point. "Brave Modern," said Lucan, "I perceive some god protects you, for never did my arm so deceive me before. But what mortal can contend with a god? Therefore let us fight no longer, but present gifts to each other." Lucan then bestowed the Modern a pair of spurs, and Blackmore gave Lucan a bridle. * * * * *

* * * * * * * *

Pauca de- * * * * * * *

sunt. * * * * * * *

* * * * * * * *

Creech; but the goddess Dulness took a cloud, formed into the shape of Horace, armed and mounted, and placed it in a flying posture before him. Glad was the cavalier to begin a combat with a flying foe, and pursued the image, threatening loud, till at last it lead him to the peaceful bower of his father Ogleby, by whom he was disarmed and assigned to his repose.

Then Pindar slew—and —Oldham, and—and Afra the Amazon, light of foot. Never advancing in a direct line but wheeling with

incredible agility and force, he made a terrible slaughter among the enemy's light horse. Him when Cowley observed, his generous heart burnt within him and he advanced against the fierce Ancient, imitating his address, and pace, and career, as well as the vigour of his horse and his own skill would allow. When the two cavaliers had approached within the length of three javelins, first Cowley threw a lance, which missed Pindar, and passing into the enemy's ranks, fell ineffectual to the ground. Then Pindar darted a javelin so large and weighty that scarce a dozen cavaliers, as cavaliers are in our degenerate days, could raise it from the ground; yet he threw it with ease, and it went by an unerring hand singing through the air; nor could the Modern have avoided present death, if he had not luckily opposed the shield that had been given him by Venus. And now both heroes drew their swords, but the Modern was so aghast and disordered that he knew not where he was; his shield dropped from his hands; thrice he fled, and thrice he could not escape. At last he turned, and lifting up his hand in the posture of a suppliant, "Godlike Pindar," said he, "spare my life, and possess my horse with these arms, besides the ransom which my friends will give when they hear I am alive and your prisoner." "Dog!" said Pindar, "let your ransom stay with your friends; but your carcass shall be left for the fowls of the air and the beasts of the field." With that he raised his sword, and with a mighty stroke cleft the wretched Modern in twain, the sword pursuing the blow; and one half lay panting on the ground, to be trod in pieces by the horses' feet; the other half was borne by the frighted steed through the field. This Venus[9] took, washed it seven times in ambrosia, then struck it thrice with a sprig of amaranth; upon which the leather grew round and soft, and the leaves turned into feathers, and being gilded before, continued gilded still; so it became a dove, and she harnessed it to her chariot. * * * * * *
* * * * * * *Hiatus valdè deflendus in* MS.
* * * * * *
* * * * * * * *

Day being far spent, and the numerous forces of the Moderns half inclining to a retreat, there issued forth from a squadron of their heavy-armed foot, a captain whose name was Bentley, in person the most deformed of all the Moderns; tall, but without shape or comeliness; large, but without strength or proportion. His armour was patched up of a thousand incoherent pieces, and the sound of it as he marched was loud and dry, like that made by the fall of a sheet of lead which an Etesian wind blows suddenly down from the roof of some steeple. His helmet was of old rusty iron, but the vizard was brass, which tainted by his breath corrupted into copperas, nor wanted gall from the same fountain; so that whenever provoked by anger or labour, an atramentous quality of most malignant nature was seen to distil from his lips. In his right[10] hand he grasped a flail; and (that he might never be unprovided of an *offensive* weapon) a vessel full of ordure in his left. Thus completely armed he advanced with a slow and heavy pace where the Modern chiefs were holding a consult upon the sum of things; who, as he came onwards, laughed to behold his crooked leg and hump shoulder, which his boot and armour vainly endeavouring to hide, were forced to comply with and expose. The generals made use of him for his talent of railing which, kept within government, proved frequently of great service to their cause, but at other times did more mischief than good; for at the least touch of offence, and often without any at all, he would like a wounded elephant convert it against his leaders. Such at this juncture was the disposition of Bentley: grieved to see the enemy prevail, and dissatisfied with everybody's conduct but his own. He humbly gave the Modern generals to understand that he conceived, with great submission, they were all a pack of *rogues,* and *fools,* and *sons of whores,* and *d-mned cowards,* and *confounded loggerheads,* and *illiterate whelps,* and *nonsensical scoundrels*; that if himself had been constituted general, those presumptuous dogs the Ancients would long before this have been beaten out of the field. "You,"[11] said he, "sit here idle; but when I or any other valiant Modern kill an enemy, you are sure to seize the spoil. But I will not march one foot against the foe till you all swear to me that whomever I take or kill, his arms I shall quietly possess." Bentley having spoke thus, Scaliger, bestowing him a sour look, "Miscreant prater!" said he, "eloquent only in thine own eyes, thou railest without wit, or truth, or discretion. The malignity of thy temper perverteth nature; thy learning makes thee more barbarous, thy study of humanity more inhuman; thy converse amongst poets more grovelling, miry, and dull. All arts of civilizing others render thee rude and untractable; courts have taught thee ill manners, and polite conversation has finished thee a pedant. Besides, a greater coward burdeneth not the army. But never despond; I pass my word, whatever spoil thou takest shall certainly be thy own, though I hope that vile carcass will first become a prey to kites and worms."

Bentley durst not reply, but half choked with spleen and rage withdrew, in full resolution of performing some great achievement. With him, for his aid and companion, he took his beloved Wotton; resolving by policy or surprise to attempt some neglected quarter of the Ancients' army. They began their march over carcasses of their slaughtered friends; then to the right of their own forces; then wheeled northward, till they came to Aldrovandus' tomb which they passed on the side of the declining sun. And now they arrived, with fear, towards the enemy's out-guards, looking about if haply they might spy the quarters of the wounded, or some straggling sleepers, unarmed and remote from the rest. As when two mongrel curs, whom native greediness and domestic want provoke and join in partnership, though fearful, nightly to invade the folds of some rich grazier, they with tails depressed, and lolling tongues, creep soft and slow; meanwhile, the conscious moon, now in her zenith, on their guilty heads darts perpendicular rays; nor dare they bark, though much provoked at her refulgent visage, whether seen in puddle by reflection, or in sphere direct; but one surveys the region round, while t'other scouts the plain, if haply to discover, at distance from the flock, some carcass half devoured, the refuse of gorged wolves or ominous ravens. So marched this lovely, loving pair of friends, nor with less fear and circumspection when, at distance, they might perceive two shining suits of armour hanging upon an oak, and the owners not far off in a profound sleep. The two friends drew lots, and the pursuing of this adventure fell to Bentley; on he went, and in his van Confusion and Amaze, while Horror and Affright brought up the rear. As he came near, behold two heroes of the Ancients' army, Phalaris and Æsop, lay fast asleep. Bentley would fain have dispatched them both, and stealing close, aimed his flail at Phalaris' breast. But then the goddess

Affright interposing caught the Modern in her icy arms, and dragged him from the danger she foresaw; for both the dormant heroes happened to turn at the same instant, though soundly sleeping and busy in a dream.[12] For Phalaris was just that minute dreaming how a most vile poetaster had lampooned him, and how he had got him roaring in his bull. And Æsop dreamed that as he and the Ancient chiefs were lying on the ground, a wild ass broke loose, ran about, trampling and kicking and dunging in their faces. Bentley, leaving the two heroes asleep, seized on both their armours and withdrew in quest of his darling Wotton.

He in the meantime had wandered long in search of some enterprize, till at length he arrived at a small rivulet that issued from a fountain hard by, called in the language of mortal men, Helicon. Here he stopped, and parched with thirst resolved to allay it in this limpid stream. Thrice with profane hands he essayed to raise the water to his lips, and thrice it slipped all through his fingers. Then he stooped prone on his breast, but ere his mouth had kissed the liquid crystal, Apollo came and in the channel held his shield betwixt the Modern and the fountain, so that he drew up nothing but mud. For, although no fountain on earth can compare with the clearness of Helicon, yet there lies at bottom a thick sediment of slime and mud; for so Apollo begged of Jupiter, as a punishment to those who durst attempt to taste it with unhallowed lips, and for a lesson to all not to *draw too deep* or *far from the spring.*

At the fountainhead Wotton discerned two heroes. The one he could not distinguish but the other was soon known for Temple, general of the allies to the Ancients. His back was turned, and he was employed in drinking large draughts in his helmet from the fountain, where he had withdrawn himself to rest from the toils of the war. Wotton, observing him, with quaking knees and trembling hands spoke thus to himself:[13] "O that I could kill this destroyer of our army, what renown should I purchase among the chiefs! But to issue out against him, man for man, shield against shield, and lance against lance, what Modern of us dare? For he fights like a god, and Pallas or Apollo are ever at his elbow. But, O mother! If what Fame reports be true, that I am the son of so great a goddess, grant me to hit Temple with this lance that the stroke may send him to hell, and that I may return in safety and triumph, laden with his spoils." The first part of his prayer, the gods granted at the intercession of his mother and of Momus; but the rest, by a perverse wind sent from Fate, was scattered in the air. Then Wotton grasped his lance, and brandishing it thrice over his head, darted it with all his might, the goddess, his mother, at the same time adding strength to his arm. Away the lance went hizzing, and reached even to the belt of the averted Ancient, upon which, lightly grazing, it fell to the ground. Temple neither felt the weapon touch him, nor heard it fall; and Wotton might have escaped to his army, with the honour of having remitted his lance against so great a leader, unrevenged; but Apollo, enraged that a javelin flung by the assistance of so foul a goddess should pollute his fountain, put on the shape of———, and softly came to young Boyle, who then accompanied Temple. He pointed first to the lance, then to the distant Modern that flung it, and commanded the young hero to take immediate revenge. Boyle, clad in a suit of armour which had *been given him by all the gods,* immediately advanced against the trembling foe, who now fled before him. As a young lion in the Libyan plains, or Araby desert, sent by his aged sire to hunt for prey, or health, or exercise, he scours along wishing to meet some tiger from the mountains or a furious boar; if chance a wild ass, with brayings importune, affronts his ear, the generous beast, though loathing to distain his claws with blood so vile, yet much provoked at the offensive noise which Echo, foolish nymph, like her ill-judging sex, repeats much louder and with more delight than Philomela's song, he vindicates the honour of the forest, and hunts the noisy long-eared animal. So Wotton fled, so Boyle pursued. But Wotton, heavy-armed and slow of foot, began to slack his course, when his lover Bentley appeared, returning laden with the spoils of the two sleeping Ancients. Boyle observed him well, and soon discovering the helmet and shield of Phalaris his friend, both which he had lately with his own hands new polished and gilded, rage sparkled in his eyes, and leaving his pursuit after Wotton, he furiously rushed on against this new approacher. Fain would he be revenged on both, but both now fled different ways. And, as a woman[14] in a little house, that gets a painful livelihood by spinning,[15] if chance her geese be scattered o'er the common, she courses round the plain from side to side, compelling here and there the stragglers to the flock; they cackle loud, and flutter o'er the champaign—so Boyle pursued, so fled this pair of friends. Finding at length their flight was vain, they bravely joined, and drew themselves in phalanx. First, Bentley threw a spear with all his force, hoping to pierce the enemy's breast; but Pallas came unseen, and in the air took off the point and clapped on one of lead, which, after a dead bang against the enemy's shield, fell blunted to the ground. Then Boyle, observing well his time, took a lance of wondrous length and sharpness; and as this pair of friends compacted stood close side to side, he wheeled him to the right, and with unusual force darted the weapon. Bentley saw his fate approach, and flanking down his arms close to his ribs, hoping to save his body, in went the point passing through arm and side, nor stopped or spent its force till it had also pierced the valiant Wotton, who, going to sustain his dying friend, shared his fate. As when a skilful cook has trussed a brace of woodcocks, he with iron skewer pierces the tender sides of both, their legs and wings close pinioned to the ribs; so was this pair of friends transfixed, till down they fell, joined in their lives, joined in their deaths; so closely joined that Charon will mistake them both for one and waft them over Styx for half his fare. Farewell, beloved loving pair! Few equals have you left behind. And happy and immortal shall you be, if all my wit and eloquence can make you.

And, now * * * * * *
* * * * * * * *
* * * * * * * *
* * *Desunt cætera.*

WHEN I COME TO BE OLD (1699)

NOT TO MARRY A YOUNG WOMAN.

Not to keep young company unless they really desire it.

Not to be peevish, or morose, or suspicious.

Not to scorn present ways, or wits, or fashions, or men, or war, &c.

Not to be fond of children, or let them come near me hardly.

Not to tell the same story over and over to the same people.

Not to be covetous.

Not to neglect decency, or cleanliness, for fear of falling into nastiness.

Not to be over severe with young people, but give allowances for their youthful follies and weaknesses.

Not to be influenced by, or give ear to knavish tattling servants, or others.

Not to be too free of advice, nor trouble any but those that desire it.

To conjure some good friends to inform me which of these resolutions I break, or neglect, and wherein; and reform accordingly.

Not to talk much, nor of myself.

Not to boast of my former beauty, or strength, or favour with ladies, &c.

Not to hearken to flatteries, nor conceive I can be beloved by a young woman. *Et eos qui hereditatem captant, odisse ac vitare.*

Not to be positive or opiniatre.

Not to set up for observing all these rules, for fear I should observe none.

A MEDITATION UPON A BROOMSTICK (1701)

ACCORDING TO THE STYLE AND MANNER OF THE HONOURABLE ROBERT BOYLE'S MEDITATIONS

This single stick, which you now behold ingloriously lying in that neglected corner, I once knew in a flourishing state in a forest; it was full of sap, full of leaves, and full of boughs; but now, in vain does the busy art of man pretend to vie with nature, by tying that withered bundle of twigs to its sapless trunk; 'tis now at best but the reverse of what it was, a tree turned upside down, the branches on the earth, and the root in the air; 'tis now handled by every dirty wench, condemned to do her drudgery, and, by a capricious kind of fate, destined to make other things clean, and be nasty itself: at length, worn to the stumps in the service of the maids, 'tis either thrown out of doors, or condemned to its last use, of kindling a fire. When I beheld this I sighed, and said within myself, Surely mortal man is a Broomstick! Nature sent him into the world strong and lusty, in a thriving condition, wearing his own hair on his head, the proper branches of this reasoning vegetable, till the axe of intemperance has lopped off his green boughs, and left him a withered trunk: he then flies to art, and puts on a periwig, valuing himself upon an unnatural bundle of hairs, all covered with powder, that never grew on his head; but now should this our broomstick pretend to enter the scene, proud of those birchen spoils it never bore, and all covered with dust, though the sweepings of the finest lady's chamber, we should be apt to ridicule and despise its vanity. Partial judges that we are of our own excellencies, and other men's defaults!

But a broomstick, perhaps you will say, is an emblem of a tree standing on its head; and pray what is man, but a topsyturvy creature, his animal faculties perpetually mounted on his rational, his head where his heels should be, grovelling on the earth! And yet with all his faults, he sets up to be an universal reformer and corrector of abuses, a remover of grievances, rakes into every slut's corner of Nature, bringing hidden corruptions to the light, and raises a mighty dust where there was none before; sharing deeply all the while in the very same pollutions he pretends to sweep away. His last days are spent in slavery to women, and generally the least deserving, till, worn out to the stumps, like his brother besom, he is either kicked out of doors, or made use of to kindle flames for others to warm themselves by.

A TALE OF A TUB (1704)

Written for the Universal Improvement of Mankind

Diu multumque desideratum

Basima eacabasa eanaa irraurista, diarba da caeotaba fobor camelanthi. Iren. Lib. 1. *C.* 18.

——*Juvatque novos decerpere flores,*
Insignemque meo capiti petere inde coronam,
Unde prius nulli velarunt tempora Musæ. Lucret.

TREATISES WRITTEN BY THE SAME AUTHOR, MOST OF THEM MENTIONED in the following Discourses; which will be speedily published.

A Character of the present set of Wits *in this Island.*
A panegyrical Essay upon the Number Three.
A Dissertation upon the principal Productions of Grub Street.
Lectures upon a Dissection of Human Nature.
A Panegyric upon the World.
An analytical Discourse upon Zeal, histori-theo-physi-logically *considered.*
A general History of Ears.
A modest Defence of the Proceedings of the Rabble *in all ages.*
A Description of the Kingdom of Absurdities.
A Voyage into England, *by a Person of Quality in* Terra Australis incognita, *translated from the Original.*
A critical Essay upon the Art of Canting, *philosophically, physically, and musically considered.*

AN APOLOGY
FOR THE [TALE OF A TUB]

If good and ill nature equally operated upon Mankind, I might have saved myself the trouble of this Apology; for it is manifest by the reception the following discourse hath met with, that those who approve it are a great majority among the men of taste; yet there have been two or three treatises written expressly against it besides many others that have flirted at it occasionally, without one syllable having been ever published in its defence, or even quotation to its advantage that I can remember, except by the polite author of a late discourse between a Deist and a Socinian.

Therefore, since the book seems calculated to live at least as long as our language and our taste admit no great alterations, I am content to convey some Apology along with it.

The greatest part of that book was finished above thirteen years since, 1696, which is eight years before it was published. The author was then young, his invention at the height, and his reading fresh in his head. By the assistance of some thinking, and much conversation, he had endeavour'd to strip himself of as many real prejudices as he could; I say real ones because, under the notion of prejudices, he knew to what dangerous heights some men have proceeded. Thus prepared, he thought the numerous and gross corruptions in Religion and Learning might furnish matter for a satire that would be useful and diverting. He resolved to proceed in a manner that should be altogether new, the world having been already too long nauseated with endless repetitions upon every subject. The abuses in Religion he proposed to set forth in the Allegory of the Coats and the three Brothers, which was to make up the body of the discourse. Those in Learning he chose to introduce by way of digressions. He was then a young gentleman much in the world, and wrote to the taste of those who were like himself; therefore in order to allure them, he gave a liberty to his pen, which might not suit with maturer years or graver characters, and which he could have easily corrected with a very few blots, had he been master of his papers for a year or two before their publication.

Not that he would have governed his judgment by the ill-placed cavils of the sour, the envious, the stupid, and the tasteless, which he mentions with disdain. He acknowledges there are several youthful sallies which, from the grave and the wise, may deserve a rebuke. But he desires to be answerable no farther than he is guilty, and that his faults may not be multiplied by the ignorant, the unnatural, and uncharitable applications of those who have neither candour to suppose good meanings, nor palate to distinguish true ones. After which he will forfeit his life if anyone opinion can be fairly deduced from that book which is contrary to Religion or Morality.

Why should any clergyman of our church be angry to see the follies of fanaticism and superstition exposed, though in the most ridiculous manner; since that is perhaps the most probable way to cure them, or at least to hinder them from farther spreading? Besides, though it was not intended for their perusal, it rallies nothing but what they preach against. It contains nothing to provoke them, by the least scurrility upon their persons or their functions. It celebrates the Church of England as the most perfect of all others in discipline and doctrine; it advances no opinion they reject, nor condemns any they receive. If the clergy's resentments lay upon their hands, in my humble opinion they might have found more proper objects to employ them on: nondum tibi defuit hostis; *I mean those heavy, illiterate scribblers, prostitute in their reputations, vicious in their lives, and ruined in their fortunes, who, to the shame of good sense as well as piety, are greedily read merely upon the strength of bold, false, impious assertions, mixed with unmannerly reflections upon the priesthood, and openly intended against all Religion; in short, full of such principles as are kindly received because they are levelled to remove those terrors that Religion tells men will be the consequence of immoral lives. Nothing like which is to be met with in this discourse, though some of them are pleased so freely to censure it. And I wish there were no other instance of what I have too frequently observed, that many of that reverend body are not always very nice in distinguishing between their enemies and their friends.*

Had the author's intentions met with a more candid interpretation from some whom out of respect he forbears to name, he might have been encouraged to an examination of books written by some of those authors above described, whose errors, ignorance, dulness and villainy, he thinks he could have detected and exposed in such a manner that the persons who are most conceived to be affected by them, would soon lay them aside and be ashamed. But he has now given over those thoughts; since the weightiest *men in the* weightiest *stations are pleased to think it a more dangerous point to laugh at those corruptions in Religion, which they themselves must disapprove, than to endeavour pulling up those very foundations wherein all Christians have agreed.*

He thinks it no fair proceeding that any person should offer determinately to fix a name upon the author of this discourse, who hath all along concealed himself from most of his nearest friends. Yet several have gone a farther step, and pronounced another book to have been the work of the same hand with this, which the author directly affirms to be a thorough mistake, he having as yet never so much as read that discourse; a plain instance how little truth there often is in general surmises, or in conjectures drawn from a similitude of style or way of thinking.

Letter of Enthusiasm.

Had the author written a book to expose the abuses in Law, or in Physic, he believes the learned professors in either faculty would have been so far from resenting it as to have given him thanks for his pains, especially if he had made an honourable reservation for the true practice of either science. But Religion, they tell us, ought not to be ridiculed, and they tell us truth. Yet surely the corruptions in it may; for we are taught by the tritest maxim in the world that Religion being the best of things, its corruptions are likely to be the worst.

There is one thing which the judicious reader cannot but have observed, that some of those passages in this discourse which appear most liable to objection, are what they call parodies, where the author personates the style and manner of other writers whom he has a mind to expose. I shall produce one instance, it is in the [93]*d page. Dryden, L'Estrange, and some others I shall not name, are here levelled at, who having spent their lives in faction and apostacies and all manner of vice, pretended to be sufferers for Loyalty and Religion. So Dryden tells us in one of his prefaces of his merits and suffering, and thanks God that he* possesses his soul in patience. *In other places he talks at the same rate, and L'Estrange often uses the like style; and I believe the reader may find more persons to give that passage an application. But this is enough to direct those who may have overlooked the author's intention.*

There are three or four other passages which prejudiced or ignorant readers have drawn by great force to hint at ill meanings, as if they glanced at some tenets in religion. In answer to all which, the author solemnly protests he is entirely innocent; and never had it once in his thoughts that anything he said would in the least be capable of such interpretations, which he will engage to deduce full as fairly from the most innocent book in the world. And it will be obvious to every reader that this was not any part of his scheme or design, the abuses he notes being such as all Church of England men agree in; nor was it proper for his subject to meddle with other points than such as have been perpetually controverted since the Reformation.

To instance only in that passage about the three wooden machines mentioned in the Introduction: in the original manuscript there was a description of a fourth, which those who had the papers in their power blotted out, as having something in it of satire that I suppose they thought was too particular; and therefore they were forced to change it to the number Three, from whence some have endeavoured to squeeze out a dangerous meaning that was never thought on. And indeed the conceit was half spoiled by changing the numbers, that of Four being much more cabalistic, and therefore better exposing the pretended virtue of Numbers, a superstition there intended to be ridiculed.

Another thing to be observed is, that there generally runs an irony through the thread of the whole book, which the men of taste will observe and distinguish, and which will render some objections that have been made, very weak and insignificant.

This Apology being chiefly intended for the satisfaction of future readers, it may be thought unnecessary to take any notice of such treatises as have been written against this ensuing discourse, which are already sunk into waste paper and oblivion after the usual fate of common answerers to books which are allowed to have any merit. They are indeed like annuals, that grow about a young tree and seem to vie with it for a summer, but fall and die with the leaves in autumn and are never heard of anymore. When Dr. Eachard writ his book about the Contempt of the Clergy, numbers of these answerers immediately started up, whose memory if he had not kept alive by his replies it would now be utterly unknown that he were ever answered at all. There is indeed an exception, when any great genius thinks it worth his while to expose a foolish piece; so we still read Marvell's Answer to Parker with pleasure, though the book it answers be sunk long ago: so the Earl of Orrery's Remarks will be read with delight when the Dissertation he exposes will neither be sought nor found: but these are no enterprizes for common hands, nor to be hoped for above once or twice in an age. Men would be more cautious of losing their time in such an undertaking, if they did but consider that to answer a book effectually requires more pains and skill, more wit, learning, and judgment than were employed in the writing it. And the author assures those gentlemen who have given themselves that trouble with him, that his discourse is the product of the study, the observation, and the invention of several years; that he often blotted out much more than he left, and if his papers had not been a long time out of his possession, they must have still undergone more severe corrections: and do they think such a building is to be battered with dirt-pellets, however envenomed the mouths may be that discharge them? He hath seen the productions but of two answerers, one of which at first appeared as from an unknown hand, but since avowed by a person who upon some occasions hath discovered no ill vein of humour. 'Tis a pity any *occasions should put him under a necessity of being so hasty in his productions, which otherwise might often be entertaining. But there were other reasons obvious enough for his miscarriage in this; he writ against the conviction of his talent, and entered upon one of the wrongest attempts in nature, to turn into ridicule by a week's labour a work which had cost so much time and met with so much success in ridiculing others: the manner how he has handled his* subject *I have now forgot, having just looked it over when it first came out, as others did, merely for the sake of the title.*

The other answer is from a person of a graver character, and is made up of half invective and half annotation, in the latter of which he hath generally succeeded well enough. And the project at that time was not amiss, to draw in readers to his pamphlet, several having appeared desirous that there might be some explication of the more difficult passages. Neither can he be altogether blamed for offering at the invective part, because it is agreed on all hands that the author had given him sufficient provocation. The great objection is against his manner of treating it, very unsuitable to one of his function. It was determined by a fair majority that this answerer had in a way not to be pardoned drawn his pen against a certain great man then alive and universally reverenced for every good quality that could possibly enter into the composition of the most accomplished person; it was observed how he was pleased, and affected to have that noble writer called his adversary; and it was a point of satire well directed, for I have been told Sir W[illiam] T[emple] was sufficiently mortified at the term. All the men of wit and politeness were immediately up in arms through indignation, which prevailed over their contempt, by the consequences they apprehended from such an example, and it grew Porsenna's case, idem trecenti juravimus. *In short, things were ripe for a general insurrection till my Lord Orrery had a little laid the spirit and settled the ferment. But his lordship being principally engaged with another antagonist, it was thought necessary in order to quiet the minds of men, that this opposer should receive a reprimand, which partly occasioned that discourse of the Battle of the Books;*

and the author was further at the pains to insert one or two remarks on him in the body of the book.

This answerer has been pleased to find fault with about a dozen passages, which the author will not be at the trouble of defending further than by assuring the reader that for the greater part the reflecter is entirely mistaken, and forces interpretations which never once entered into the writer's head, nor will he is sure into that of any reader of taste and candour; he allows two or three at most, there produced, to have been delivered unwarily: for which he desires to plead the excuse offered already, of his youth, and frankness of speech, and his papers being out of his power at the time they were published.

But this answerer insists, and says what he chiefly dislikes is the design: *what that was I have already told, and I believe there is not a person in England, who can understand that book, that ever imagined it to have been anything else but to expose the abuses and corruptions in Learning and Religion.*

But it would be good to know what design *this reflecter was serving when he concludes his pamphlet with a caution to readers to beware of thinking the author's wit was entirely his own: surely this must have had some allay of personal animosity at least mixed with the* design *of serving the public, by so useful a discovery; and it indeed touches the author in a tender point, who insists upon it that through the whole book he has not borrowed one single hint from any writer in the world; and he thought, of all criticisms, that would never have been one. He conceived it was never disputed to be an original, whatever faults it might have. However, this answerer produces three instances to prove* this author's wit is not his own in many places. *The first is, that the names of Peter, Martin and Jack, are borrowed from a Letter of the late Duke of Buckingham. Whatever wit is contained in those three names the author is content to give it up, and desires his readers will subtract as much as they placed upon that account; at the same time protesting solemnly that he never once heard of that letter except in this passage of the answerer: so that the names were not borrowed, as he affirms, though they should happen to be the same, which however is odd enough, and what he hardly believes, that of Jack being not quite so obvious as the other two. The second instance to show the author's wit is not his own, is Peter's banter (as he calls it in his Alsatia phrase) upon Transubstantiation, which is taken from the same Duke's conference with an Irish priest, where a cork is turned into a horse.*

This the author confesses to have seen about ten years after his book was writ, and a year or two after it was published. Nay, the answerer overthrows this himself, for he allows the Tale was written in 1697, *and I think that pamphlet was not printed in many years after. It was necessary that corruption should have some allegory as well as the rest, and the author invented the properest he could, without inquiring what other people had writ; and the commonest reader will find there is not the least resemblance between the two stories. The third instance is in these words: "I have been assured, that the Battle in St. James' Library is,* mutatis mutandis, *taken out of a French book entitled* Combat des Livres, *if I misremember not." In which passage there are two clauses observable, "I have been assured" and, "if I misremember not." I desire first to know whether, if that conjecture proves an utter falsehood, those two clauses will be a sufficient excuse for this worthy critic? The matter is a trifle; but would he venture to pronounce at this rate upon one of greater moment? I know nothing more contemptible in a writer than the character of a plagiary, which he here fixes at a venture; and this not for a passage but a whole discourse taken out from another book, only* mutatis mutandis. *The author is as much in the dark about this as the answerer, and will imitate him by an affirmation at random; that if there be a word of truth in this reflection, he is a paltry, imitating pedant and the answerer is a person of wit, manners and truth. He takes his boldness from never having seen any such treatise in his life nor heard of it before; and he is sure it is impossible for two writers of different times and countries to agree in their thoughts after such a manner that two continued discourses shall be the same, only* mutatis mutandis. *Neither will he insist upon the mistake of the title, but let the answerer and his friend produce any book they please, he defies them to show one single particular where the judicious reader will affirm he has been obliged for the smallest hint; giving only allowance for the accidental encountering of a single thought, which he knows may sometimes happen, though he has never yet found it in that discourse, nor has heard it objected by anybody else.*

So that if ever any design was unfortunately executed, it must be that of this answerer who, when he would have it observed that the author's wit is not his own, is able to produce but three instances, two of them mere trifles, and all three manifestly false. If this be the way these gentlemen deal with the world in those criticisms where we have not leisure to defeat them, their readers had need be cautious how they rely upon their credit; and whether this proceeding can be reconciled to humanity or truth, let those who think it worth their while determine.

It is agreed this answerer would have succeeded much better if he had stuck wholly to his business as a commentator upon the Tale of a Tub, *wherein it cannot be denied that he hath been of some service to the public, and has given very fair conjectures towards clearing up some difficult passages; but it is the frequent error of those men (otherwise very commendable for their labours) to make excursions beyond their talent and their office, by pretending to point out the beauties and the faults; which is no part of their trade, which they always fail in, which the world never expected from them, nor gave them any thanks for endeavouring at. The part of Minellius or Farnaby would have fallen in with his genius, and might have been serviceable to many readers who cannot enter into the abstruser parts of that discourse; but* optat ephippia bos piger: *the dull, unwieldy, ill-shaped ox, would needs put on the furniture of a horse, not considering he was born to labour, to plough the ground for the sake of superior beings, and that he has neither the shape, mettle nor speed of that nobler animal he would affect to personate.*

It is another pattern of this answerer's fair dealing to give us hints that the author is dead, and yet to lay the suspicion upon somebody, I know not who, in the country; to which can only be returned that he is absolutely mistaken in all his conjectures; and surely conjectures are at best too light a pretence to allow a man to assign a name in public. He condemns a book and consequently the author, of whom he is utterly ignorant, yet at the same time fixes, in print, what he thinks a disadvantageous character upon those who never deserved it. A man who receives a buffet in the dark may be allowed to be vexed, but it is an odd kind of revenge to go to cuffs in broad day with the first he meets with, and lay the last night's injury at his door. And thus much for this discreet, candid, pious, *and* ingenious *answerer.*

How the author came to be without his papers is a story not proper to be told and of very little use, being a private fact of which the reader would believe as little or as much as he thought good. He had, however, a blotted copy by him which he intended to have writ over with many alterations, and this the publishers were well aware of, having put it into the bookseller's preface, that they apprehended a surreptitious copy, which was to be altered, *&c. This though not regarded by readers, was a real truth, only the surreptitious copy was rather that which was printed; and they made all haste* *they could, which indeed was needless, the author not being at all prepared; but he has been told the bookseller was in much pain, having given a good sum of money for the copy.*

In the author's original copy there were not so many chasms as appear in the book, and why some of them were left, he knows not; had the publication been trusted to him, he would have made several corrections of passages against which nothing hath been ever objected. He would likewise have altered a few of those that seem with any reason to be excepted against; but to deal freely, the greatest number he should have left untouched as never suspecting it possible any wrong interpretations could be made of them.

The author observes at the end of the book there is a discourse called A Fragment, *which he more wondered to see in print than all the rest. Having been a most imperfect sketch, with the addition of a few loose hints, which he once lent a gentleman who had designed a discourse of somewhat the same subject, he never thought of it afterwards; and it was a sufficient surprise to see it pieced up together, wholly out of the method and scheme he had intended, for it was the ground work of a much larger discourse, and he was sorry to observe the materials so foolishly employed.*

There is one further objection made by those who have answered this book, as well as by some others, that Peter is frequently made to repeat oaths and curses. Every reader observes it was necessary to know that Peter did swear and curse. The oaths are not printed out, but only supposed; and the idea of an oath is not immoral like the idea of a profane or immodest speech. A man may laugh at the Popish folly of cursing people to hell, and imagine them swearing, without any crime; but lewd words or dangerous opinions though printed by halves, fill the reader's mind with ill ideas; and of these the author cannot be accused. For the judicious reader will find that the severest strokes of satire in his book are levelled against the modern custom of employing wit upon those topics, of which there is a remarkable instance in the [132] *d page as well as in several others, though perhaps once or twice expressed in too free a manner, excusable only for the reasons already alleged. Some overtures have been made by a third hand to the bookseller, for the author's altering those passages which he thought might require it; but it seems the bookseller will not hear of any such thing, being apprehensive it might spoil the sale of the book.*

The author cannot conclude this Apology without making this one reflection; that, as wit is the noblest and most useful gift of human nature, so humour is the most agreeable; and where these two enter far into the composition of any work they will render it always acceptable to the world. Now, the great part of those who have no share or taste of either, but by their pride, pedantry, and ill manners, lay themselves bare to the lashes of both, think the blow is weak because they are insensible; and where wit hath any mixture of raillery, 'tis but calling it banter and the work is done. This polite word of theirs was first borrowed from the bullies in White-Friars, then fell among the footmen, and at last retired to the pedants, by whom it is applied as properly to the production of wit as if I should apply it to Sir Isaac Newton's mathematics. But, if this bantering as they call it be so despisable a thing, whence comes it to pass they have such a perpetual itch towards it themselves? To instance only in the answerer already mentioned, it is grievous to see him in some of his writings at every turn going out of his way to be waggish, to tell us of a cow that pricked up her tail *and in his answer to this discourse he says,* it is all a farce and a ladle; *with other passages equally shining. One may say of these* impedimenta literarum, *that wit owes them a shame, and they cannot take wiser counsel than to keep out of harm's way, or at least, not to come till they are sure they are called.*

To conclude: with those allowances above required this book should be read; after which the author conceives few things will remain which may not be excused in a young writer. He wrote only to the men of wit and taste, and he thinks he is not mistaken in his accounts when he says they have been all of his side, enough to give him the vanity of telling his name, wherein the world, with all its wise conjectures, is yet very much in the dark; which circumstance is no disagreeable amusement either to the public or himself.

The author is informed, that the bookseller has prevailed on several gentlemen to write some explanatory notes, for the goodness of which he is not to answer, having never seen any of them, nor intends it, till they appear in print, when it is not unlikely he may have the pleasure to find twenty meanings which never entered into his imagination.

June 3, 1709

POSTSCRIPT

Since the writing of this, which was about a year ago, a prostitute bookseller hath published a foolish paper under the name of Notes on the Tale of a Tub, *with some account of the author, and with an insolence which I suppose is punishable by law, hath presumed to assign certain names. It will be enough for the author to assure the world that the writer of that paper is utterly wrong in all his conjectures upon that affair. The author further asserts that the whole work is entirely of one hand, which every reader of judgment will easily discover. The gentleman who gave the copy to the bookseller being a friend of the author, and using no other liberties besides that of expunging certain passages where now the chasms appear under the name of* desiderata. *But if any person will prove his claim to three lines in the whole book, let him step forth and tell his name and titles; upon which the bookseller shall have orders to prefix them to the next edition, and the claimant shall from henceforward be acknowledged the undisputed author.*

TO THE RIGHT HONOURABLE
JOHN LORD SOMERS

My Lord,

Tho' the author has written a large Dedication, yet that being addressed to a prince whom I am never likely to have the honour of being known to (a person besides, as far as I can observe, not at all regarded, or thought on by any of our present writers) and I being wholly free from that slavery which booksellers usually lie under to the caprices of authors, I think it a wise piece of presumption to inscribe these papers to your Lordship and to implore your Lordship's protection of them. God and your Lordship know their faults and their merits; for as to my own particular, I am altogether a stranger to the matter, and though everybody else should be equally ignorant, I do not fear the sale of the book at all the worse, upon that score. Your Lordship's name on the front in capital letters will at anytime get off one edition, neither would I desire any other help to grow an alderman than a patent for the sole privilege of dedicating to your Lordship.

I should now, in right of a dedicator, give your Lordship a list of your own virtues and at the same time be very unwilling to offend your modesty; but chiefly I should celebrate your liberality towards men of great parts and small fortunes, and give you broad hints that I mean myself. And I was just going on in the usual method, to peruse a hundred or two of dedications, and transcribe an abstract to be applied to your Lordship; but I was diverted by a certain accident. For, upon the covers of these papers, I casually observed written in large letters the two following words, DETUR DIGNISSIMO; *which, for aught I knew, might contain some important meaning. But it unluckily fell out that none of the authors I employ understood Latin (though I have them often in pay to translate out of that language); I was therefore compelled to have recourse to the curate of our parish, who Englished it thus,* Let it be given to the worthiest: *and his comment was, that the author meant his work should be dedicated to the sublimest genius of the age for wit, learning, judgment, eloquence, and wisdom. I called at a poet's chamber (who works for my shop) in an alley hard by, showed him the translation and desired his opinion who it was that the author could mean. He told me after some consideration, that vanity was a thing he abhorred, but by the description, he thought himself to be the person aimed at; and at the same time he very kindly offered his own assistance* gratis *towards penning a Dedication to himself. I desired him, however, to give a second guess. Why, then, said he, it must be I, or my Lord Somers. From thence I went to several other wits of my acquaintance, with no small hazard and weariness to my person, from a prodigious number of dark, winding stairs; but found them all in the same story, both of your Lordship and themselves. Now, your Lordship is to understand that this proceeding was not of my own invention; for I have somewhere heard it is a maxim that those to whom everybody allows the second place, have an undoubted title to the first.*

This infallibly convinced me that your Lordship was the person intended by the author. But being very unacquainted in the style and form of dedications, I employed those wits aforesaid to furnish me with hints and materials towards a panegyric upon your Lordship's virtues.

In two days they brought me ten sheets of paper, filled up on every side. They swore to me that they had ransacked whatever could be found in the characters of Socrates, Aristides, Epaminondas, Cato, Tully, Atticus, *and other hard names which I cannot now recollect. However, I have reason to believe they imposed upon my ignorance, because when I came to read over their collections, there was not a syllable there but what I and everybody else knew as well as themselves. Therefore I grievously suspect a cheat, and that these authors of mine stole and transcribed every word from the universal report of mankind. So that I look upon myself as fifty shillings out of pocket to no manner of purpose.*

If by altering the title I could make the same materials serve for another Dedication (as my betters have done) it would help to make up my loss; but I have made several persons dip here and there in those papers, and before they read three lines they have all assured me plainly that they cannot possibly be applied to any person besides your Lordship.

I expected, indeed, to have heard of your Lordship's bravery at the head of an army; of your undaunted courage in mounting a breach, or scaling a wall; or to have had your pedigree traced in a lineal descent from the House of Austria; or of your wonderful talent at dress and dancing; or your profound knowledge in algebra, metaphysics, and the oriental tongues. But to ply the world with an old beaten story of your wit, and eloquence, and learning, and wisdom, and justice, and politeness, and candour, and evenness of temper in all scenes of life; of that great discernment in discovering, and readiness in favouring deserving men; with forty other common topics; I confess I have neither conscience nor countenance to do it. Because there is no virtue, either of a public or private life, which some circumstances of your own have not often produced upon the stage of the world; and those few which, for want of occasions to exert them, might otherwise have passed unseen, or unobserved by your friends, *your* enemies *have at length brought to light.*

'Tis true, I should be very loth the bright example of your Lordship's virtues should be lost to after-ages, both for their sake and your own; but chiefly because they will be so very necessary to adorn the history of a late reign. *And that is another reason why I would forbear to make a recital of them here, because I have been told by wise men that as Dedications have run for some years past, a good historian will not be apt to have recourse thither in search of characters.*

There is one point, wherein I think we dedicators would do well to change our measures; I mean, instead of running on so far upon the praise of our patrons' liberality, *to spend a word or two in admiring their* patience. *I can put no greater compliment on your Lordship's than by giving you so ample an occasion to exercise it at present; though perhaps I shall not be apt to reckon much merit to your Lordship upon that score, who having been formerly used to tedious harangues, and sometimes to as little purpose, will be the readier to pardon this, especially when it is offered by one who is with all respect and veneration,*

My Lord,
Your Lordship's most obedient
and most faithful servant,
The Bookseller

THE BOOKSELLER TO THE READER

It is now six years since these papers came first to my hands, which seems to have been about a twelvemonth after they were writ; for the author tells us in his preface to the first treatise, that he has calculated it for the year 1697, and in *several passages of that Discourse, as well as the second, it appears they were written about that time.*

As to the author, I can give no manner of satisfaction. However, I am credibly informed that this publication is without his knowledge, for he concludes the copy is lost, having lent it to a person since dead, and being never in possession of it after. So that whether the work received his last hand, or whether he intended to fill up the defective places, is like to remain a secret.

If I should go about to tell the reader by what accident I became master of these papers, it would in this unbelieving age pass for little more than the cant or jargon of the trade. I therefore gladly spare both him and myself so unnecessary a trouble. There yet remains a difficult question, why I published them no sooner. I forbore upon two accounts. First, because I thought I had better work upon my hands; and secondly, because I was not without some hope of hearing from the author, and receiving his directions. But I have been lately alarmed with intelligence of a surreptitious copy which a certain great wit had new polished and refined, or as our present writers express themselves, fitted to the humour of the age, *as they have already done with great felicity to* Don Quixote, Boccalini, la Bruyere, *and other authors. However, I thought it fairer dealing to offer the whole work in its naturals. If any gentleman will please to furnish me with a key in order to explain the more difficult parts, I shall very gratefully acknowledge the favour, and print it by itself.*

THE EPISTLE DEDICATORY,
TO HIS ROYAL HIGHNESS
PRINCE POSTERITY[1]

Sir,

I here present Your Highness with the fruits of a very few leisure hours, stolen from the short intervals of a world of business and of an employment quite alien from such amusements as this; the poor production of that refuse of time, which has lain heavy upon my hands during a long prorogation of parliament, a great dearth of foreign news, and a tedious fit of rainy weather; for which and other reasons, it cannot choose extremely to deserve such a patronage as that of Your Highness, whose numberless virtues, in so few years, make the world look upon you as the future example to all princes; for although Your Highness is hardly got clear of infancy, yet has the universal learned world already resolved upon appealing to your future dictates with the lowest and most resigned submission; fate having decreed you sole arbiter of the productions of human wit, in this polite and most accomplished age. Methinks, the number of appellants were enough to shock and startle any judge, of a genius less unlimited than yours: but in order to prevent such glorious trials, the person *(it seems) to whose care the education of Your Highness is committed, has resolved (as I am told) to keep you in almost an universal ignorance of our studies, which it is your inherent birthright to inspect.*

It is amazing to me that this person *should have assurance, in the face of the sun, to go about persuading Your Highness that our age is almost wholly illiterate, and has hardly produced one writer upon any subject. I know very well that when Your Highness shall come to riper years, and have gone through the learning of antiquity, you will be too curious to neglect inquiring into the authors of the very age before you: and to think that this* insolent, *in the account he is preparing for your view, designs to reduce them to a number so insignificant as I am ashamed to mention, it moves my zeal and my spleen for the honour and interest of our vast flourishing body, as well as of myself, for whom, I know by long experience, he has professed and still continues a peculiar malice.*

'Tis not unlikely that when Your Highness will one day peruse what I am now writing, you may be ready to expostulate with your governor upon the credit of what I here affirm, and command him to shew you some of our productions. To which he will answer (for I am well informed of his designs) by asking Your Highness, where they are? And what is become of them? And pretend it a demonstration that there never were any, because they are not then to be found. Not to be found! Who has mislaid them? Are they sunk in the abyss of things? 'Tis certain that in their own nature they were light *enough to swim upon the surface for all eternity. Therefore the fault is in him who tied weights so heavy to their heels as to depress them to the centre. Is their very essence destroyed? Who has annihilated them? Were they drowned by* purges, *or martyred by* pipes? *Who administered them to the posteriors of——? But that it may no longer be a doubt with Your Highness who is to be the author of this universal ruin, I beseech you to observe that large and terrible* scythe *which your governor affects to bear continually about him. Be pleased to remark the length and strength, the sharpness and hardness, of his* nails *and* teeth: *consider his baneful, abominable* breath, *enemy to life and matter, infectious and corrupting. And then reflect whether it be possible for any mortal ink and paper of this generation to make a suitable resistance. O! That Your Highness would one day resolve to disarm this usurping* maitre de palais[2] *of his furious engines, and bring your empire* hors du page.[3]

It were endless to recount the several methods of tyranny and destruction which your governor is pleased to practise upon this occasion. His inveterate malice is such to the writings of our age that of several thousands produced yearly from this renowned city, before the next revolution of the sun there is not one to be heard of. Unhappy infants, many of them barbarously destroyed before they have so much as learnt their mother tongue *to beg for pity. Some he stifles in their cradles; others he frights into convulsions, whereof they suddenly die; some he flays alive; others he tears limb from limb. Great numbers are offered to Moloch, and the rest, tainted by his breath, die of a languishing consumption.*

But the concern I have most at heart, is for our corporation of poets, *from whom I am preparing a petition to Your Highness, to be subscribed with the names of one hundred thirty six of the first rate, but whose immortal productions are never likely to reach your eyes, though each of them is now an humble and an earnest appellant for the laurel, and has large comely volumes ready to show for a support to his pretensions. The* never-dying *works of these illustrious persons, your governor, sir, has devoted to unavoidable death, and Your Highness is to be made believe that our age has never arrived at the honour to produce one single poet.*

We confess Immortality *to be a great and powerful goddess, but in vain we offer up to her our devotions and our sacrifices if Your Highness' governor, who has usurped the* priesthood, *must by an unparallelled ambition and avarice, wholly intercept and devour them.*

To affirm that our age is altogether unlearned, and devoid of writers in any kind, seems to be an assertion so bold and so false that I have been sometime thinking the contrary may almost be proved by uncontrollable demonstration. 'Tis true indeed, that although their numbers be vast, and their productions numerous in proportion, yet are they hurried so hastily off the scene, that they escape our memory, and delude our sight. When I first thought of this address, I had prepared a copious list of titles *to present Your Highness as an undisputed argument for what I affirm. The originals were posted fresh upon all gates and corners of streets but, returning in a very few hours to take a review, they were all torn down, and fresh ones in their places. I inquired after them among readers and booksellers, but I inquired in vain; the* memorial of them was lost among men, their place was no more to be found; *and I was laughed to scorn for a clown and a pedant, without all taste and refinement, little versed in the course of present affairs, and that knew nothing of what had passed in the best companies of court and town. So that I can only avow in general to Your Highness, that we* do *abound in learning and wit; but to fix upon particulars, is a task too slippery for my slender abilities. If I should venture in a windy day to affirm to Your Highness that there is a large cloud near the* horizon *in the form of a* bear, *another in the* zenith *with the head of an* ass, *a third to the westward with claws like a* dragon, *and Your Highness should in a few minutes think fit to examine the truth, 'tis certain they would all be changed in figure and* position: new ones would arise, and all we could agree upon would be that clouds there were, but that I was grossly mistaken in the zoography and topography of them.

But your governor perhaps may still insist, and put the question, What is then become of those immense bales of paper which must needs have been employed in such numbers of books? Can these also be wholly annihilate, and so of a sudden as I pretend? What shall I say in return of so invidious an objection? It ill befits the distance between Your Highness and me to send you for ocular conviction to a jakes, or an oven, to the windows of a bawdy-house, or to a sordid lantern. Books, like men their authors, have no more than one way of coming into the world, but there are ten thousand to go out of it and return no more.

I profess to Your Highness, in the integrity of my heart, that what I am going to say is literally true this minute I am writing. What revolutions may happen before it shall be ready for your perusal, I can by no means warrant. However, I beg you to accept it as a specimen of our learning, our politeness, and our wit. I do therefore affirm, upon the word of a sincere man, that there is now actually in being a certain poet called John Dryden, whose translation of Virgil was lately printed in a large folio, well bound, and if diligent search were made, for aught I know is yet to be seen. There is another called Nahum Tate, who is ready to make oath that he has caused many reams of verse to be published, whereof both himself and his bookseller (if lawfully required) can still produce authentic copies, and therefore wonders why the world is pleased to make such a secret of it. There is a third, known by the name of Tom Durfey, a poet of a vast comprehension, an universal genius, and most profound learning. There are also one Mr. Rymer, and one Mr. Dennis, most profound critics. There is a person styled Dr. B[en]tl[e]y, who has written near a thousand pages of immense erudition, giving a full and true account of a certain squabble, of wonderful importance, between himself and a bookseller. He is a writer of infinite wit and humour; no man rallies with a better grace, and in more sprightly turns. Further, I avow to Your Highness that with these eyes I have beheld the person of William W[o]tt[o]n, B.D., who has written a good sizeable volume against a friend of your governor (from whom, alas! He must therefore look for little favour) in a most *gentlemanly style, adorned with utmost politeness and civility, replete with discoveries equally valuable for their novelty and use, and embellished with* traits *of wit so poignant and so apposite, that he is a worthy yokemate to his forementioned* friend.

Why should I go upon further particulars which might fill a volume with the just eulogies of my contemporary brethren? I shall bequeath this piece of justice to a larger work, wherein I intend to write a character of the present set of wits *in our nation. Their persons I shall describe particularly and at length, their genius and understandings in* miniature.

In the meantime I do here make bold to present Your Highness with a faithful abstract, drawn from the universal body of all arts and sciences, intended wholly for your service and instruction. Nor do I doubt in the least but Your Highness will peruse it as carefully, and make as considerable improvements, as other *young* princes *have already done by the many volumes of late years written for a help to their studies.*

That Your Highness may advance in wisdom and virtue, as well as years, and at last outshine all your royal ancestors, shall be the daily prayer of,

Sir,
Your Highness'
Most devoted, &c.
December 1697

THE PREFACE

The wits of the present age being so very numerous and penetrating, it seems the grandees of Church and State begin to fall under horrible apprehensions lest these gentlemen, during the intervals of a long peace, should find leisure to pick holes in the weak sides of Religion and Government. To prevent which there has been much thought employed of late upon certain projects for taking off the force and edge of those formidable enquirers from canvassing and reasoning upon such delicate points. They have at length fixed upon one which will require sometime as well as cost to perfect. Meanwhile, the danger hourly increasing by new levies of wits, all appointed (as there is reason to fear) with pen, ink, and paper, which may at an hour's warning be drawn out into pamphlets and other offensive weapons ready for immediate execution, it was judged of absolute necessity that some present expedient be thought on, till the main design can be brought to maturity. To this end, at a Grand Committee some days ago, this important discovery was made by a certain curious and refined observer: that seamen have a custom when they meet a *whale,* to fling him out an empty *tub* by way of amusement, to divert him from laying violent hands upon the ship. This parable was immediately mythologised; the whale was interpreted to be Hobbes' *Leviathan,* which tosses and plays with all schemes of Religion and Government, whereof a great many are hollow, and dry, and empty, and noisy, and wooden, and given to rotation. This is the *Leviathan* whence the terrible wits of our age are said to borrow their weapons. The *ship* in danger is easily understood to be its old antitype, the Commonwealth. But how to analyze the tub was a matter of difficulty; when, after long enquiry and debate, the literal meaning was preserved, and it was decreed that in order to prevent these *Leviathans* from tossing and sporting with the Commonwealth (which of itself is too apt to *fluctuate)* they should be diverted from that game by *a Tale of a Tub.* And my genius being conceived to lie not unhappily that way, I had the honour done me to be engaged in the performance.

This is the sole design in publishing the following treatise, which I hope will serve for an *interim* of some months to employ those unquiet spirits till the perfecting of that great work; into the secret of which it is reasonable the courteous reader should have some little light.

It is intended that a large Academy be erected, capable of containing nine thousand seven hundred forty and three persons, which by modest computation is reckoned to be pretty near the current number of *wits* in this island. These are to be disposed into the several schools of this academy, and there pursue those studies to which their genius most inclines them. The undertaker himself will publish his proposals with all convenient speed, to which I shall refer the curious reader for a more particular account, mentioning at present only a few of the principal schools. There is first a large *Pederastic* School, with French and Italian masters. There is also the *Spelling* School, *a very spacious building*: the School of *Looking-glasses*: the School of

Swearing: the School of *Critics*: the School of *Salivation*: the School of *Hobby-horses*: the School of *Poetry*: the School of *Tops*:[4] the School of *Spleen*: the School of *Gaming*: with many others too tedious to recount. No person to be admitted member into any of these schools without an attestation under two sufficient persons' hands, certifying him to be a *wit*.

But, to return. I am sufficiently instructed in the principal duty of a preface, if my genius were capable of arriving at it. Thrice have I forced my imagination to make the *tour* of my invention, and thrice it has returned empty, the latter having been wholly drained by the following treatise. Not so, my more successful brethren the *moderns*, who will by no means let slip a preface or dedication without some notable distinguishing stroke to surprise the reader at the entry, and kindle a wonderful expectation of what is to ensue. Such was that of a most ingenious poet who, soliciting his brain for something new, compared himself to the *hangman*, and his patron to the *patient*. This was *insigne, recens, indictum ore alio*.[5] When I went through that necessary and noble course of study[6] I had the happiness to observe many such egregious touches, which I shall not injure the authors by transplanting; because I have remarked that nothing is so very tender as a *modern* piece of wit, and which is apt to suffer so much in the carriage. Some things are extremely witty *today*, or *fasting*, or *in this place*, or *at eight o'clock*, or *over a bottle*, or *spoke by* Mr. What d'y'call'm, or *in a summer's morning*: any of the which, by the smallest transposal or misapplication, is utterly annihilate. Thus, *wit* has its walks and purlieus, out of which it may not stray the breadth of a hair, upon peril of being lost. The *moderns* have artfully fixed this *mercury*, and reduced it to the circumstances of time, place, and person. Such a jest there is that will not pass out of Covent Garden, and such a one that is nowhere intelligible but at Hyde Park corner. Now, though it sometimes tenderly affects me to consider that all the towardly passages I shall deliver in the following treatise will grow quite out of date and relish with the first shifting of the present scene, yet I must need subscribe to the justice of this proceeding; because I cannot imagine why we should be at expense to furnish wit for succeeding ages, when the former have made no sort of provision for ours; wherein I speak the sentiment of the very newest, and consequently the most orthodox refiners, as well as my own. However, being extremely solicitous that every accomplished person who has got into the taste of wit calculated for this present month of August 1697, should descend to the very *bottom* of all the *sublime* throughout this treatise, I hold fit to lay down this general maxim. Whatever reader desires to have a thorough comprehension of an author's thoughts cannot take a better method than by putting himself into the circumstances and posture of life that the writer was in upon every important passage as it flowed from his pen. For this will introduce a parity and strict correspondence of ideas between the reader and the author. Now, to assist the diligent reader in so delicate an affair as far as brevity will permit, I have recollected that the shrewdest pieces of this treatise were conceived in bed in a garret; at other times (for a reason best known to myself) I thought fit to sharpen my invention with hunger; and in general the whole work was begun, continued, and ended, under a long course of physic, and a great want of money. Now, I do affirm it will be absolutely impossible for the candid peruser to go along with me in a great many bright passages unless, upon the several difficulties emergent, he will please to capacitate and prepare himself by these directions. And this I lay down as my principal *postulatum*.

Because I have professed to be a most devoted servant of all *modern* forms, I apprehend some curious *wit* may object against me for proceeding thus far in a preface, without declaiming according to the custom against the multitude of writers, whereof the whole multitude of writers most reasonably complains. I am just come from perusing some hundreds of prefaces, wherein the authors do at the very beginning address the gentle reader concerning this enormous grievance. Of these I have preserved a few examples and shall set them down as near as my memory has been able to retain them.

One begins thus:

For a man to set up for a writer, when the press swarms with, &c.

Another:

The tax upon paper does not lessen the number of scribblers, who daily pester, &c.

Another:

When every little would-be wit takes pen in hand, 'tis in vain to enter the lists, &c.

Another:

To observe what trash the press swarms with, &c.

Another:

Sir, It is merely in obedience to your commands that I venture into the public; for who upon a less consideration would be of a party with such a rabble of scribblers, &c.

Now, I have two words in my own defence against this objection. First, I am far from granting the number of writers a nuisance to our nation, having strenuously maintained the contrary in several parts of the following Discourse. Secondly, I do not well understand the justice of this proceeding, because I observe many of these polite prefaces to be not only from the same hand, but from those who are most voluminous in their several productions. Upon which, I shall tell the reader a short tale.

A mountebank in Leicester-Fields *had drawn a huge assembly about him. Among the rest, a fat unwieldy fellow, half stifled in the press, would be every fit crying out, Lord! What a filthy crowd is here! Pray, good people, give way a little. Bless me! What a devil has raked this rabble together! Z—ds, what squeezing is this! Honest friend, remove your elbow. At last a weaver that stood next him could hold no longer. A plague confound you* (said he) *for an overgrown sloven; and who (in the devil's name) I wonder, helps to make up the crowd half so much as yourself? Don't you consider (with a pox) that you take up more room with that carcase than any five here? Is not the place as free for us as for you? Bring your own guts to a reasonable compass (and be d—n'd) and then I'll engage we shall have room enough for us all.*

There are certain common privileges of a writer, the benefit whereof I hope there will be no reason to doubt; particularly, that where I am not understood it shall be concluded that something very useful and profound is couched underneath; and again, that whatever word or sentence is printed in a different character shall be judged to contain something extraordinary either of *wit* or *sublime.*

As for the liberty I have thought fit to take of praising myself upon some occasions or none, I am sure it will need no excuse if a multitude of great examples be allowed sufficient authority. For it is here to be noted that *praise* was originally a pension paid by the world; but the *moderns,* finding the trouble and charge too great in collecting it, have lately bought out the *fee-simple,* since which time the right of presentation is wholly in ourselves. For this reason it is that when an author makes his own elogy, he uses a certain form to declare and insist upon his title which is commonly in these or the like words, "I speak without vanity"; which I think plainly shows it to be a matter of right and justice. Now, I do here once for all declare that in every encounter of this nature through the following treatise, the form aforesaid is implied; which I mention to save the trouble of repeating it on so many occasions.

'Tis a great ease to my conscience that I have written so elaborate and useful a discourse without one grain of satire intermixed; which is the sole point wherein I have taken leave to dissent from the famous originals of our age and country. I have observed some satirists to use the public much at the rate that pedants do a naughty boy ready horsed for discipline: first expostulate the case, then plead the necessity of the rod from great provocations, and conclude every period with a lash. Now if I know anything of mankind, these gentlemen might very well spare their reproof and correction, for there is not through all nature another so callous and insensible a member as the *world's posteriors,* whether you apply to it the *toe* or the *birch.* Besides, most of our late satirists seem to lie under a sort of mistake, that because *nettles* have the prerogative to sting, therefore all *other weeds* must do so too. I make not this comparison out of the least design to detract from these worthy writers; for it is well known among *mythologists* that *weeds* have the preeminence over all other vegetables; and therefore the first *monarch* of this island, whose taste and judgment were so acute and refined, did very wisely root out the *roses* from the collar of the *Order,* and plant the *thistles* in their stead as the nobler flower of the two. For which reason it is conjectured by profounder antiquaries that the satirical itch, so prevalent in this part of our island, was first brought among us from beyond the Tweed. Here may it long flourish and abound. May it survive and neglect the scorn of the world with as much ease and contempt as the world is insensible to the lashes of it. May their own dulness, or that of their party, be no discouragement for the authors to proceed, but let them remember it is with *wits* as with *razors,* which are never so apt to *cut* those they are employed on as when they have *lost their edge.* Besides, those whose teeth are too rotten to bite, are best of all others, qualified to revenge that defect with their breath.

I am not like other men to envy or undervalue the talents I cannot reach; for which reason I must needs bear a true honour to this large eminent sect of our British writers. And I hope this little panegyric will not be offensive to their ears since it has the advantage of being only designed for themselves. Indeed, nature herself has taken order that fame and honour should be purchased at a better pennyworth by satire than by any other productions of the brain, the world being soonest provoked to *praise* by *lashes,* as men are to *love.* There is a problem in an ancient author, why Dedications and other bundles of flattery run all upon stale musty topics, without the smallest tincture of anything new; not only to the torment and nauseating of the Christian reader, but (if not suddenly prevented) to the universal spreading of that pestilent disease the lethargy, in this island: whereas there is very little satire which has not something in it untouched before. The defects of the former are usually imputed to the want of invention among those who are dealers in that kind, but I think with a great deal of injustice, the solution being easy and natural; for the materials of panegyric, being very few in number, have been long since exhausted. For, as health is but one thing and has been always the same, whereas diseases are by thousands, besides new and daily additions; so, all the virtues that have been ever in mankind are to be counted upon a few fingers; but his follies and vices are innumerable and time adds hourly to the heap. Now the utmost a poor poet can do is to get by heart a list of the cardinal virtues, and deal them with his utmost liberality to his hero or his patron: he may ring the changes as far as it will go, and vary his phrase till he has talked round, but the reader quickly finds it is all *pork*[7] with a little variety of sauce. For there is no inventing terms of art beyond our ideas, and when our ideas are exhausted, terms of art must be so too.

But though the matter for panegyric were as fruitful as the topics of satire, yet would it not be hard to find out a sufficient reason why the latter will be always better received than the first. For, this being bestowed only upon one or a few persons at a time, is sure to raise envy, and consequently ill words from the rest who have no share in the blessing. But satire being levelled at all is never resented for an offence by any, since every individual person makes bold to understand it of others, and very wisely removes his particular part of the burden upon the shoulders of the world, which are broad enough and able to bear it. To this purpose I have sometimes reflected upon the difference between Athens and England, with respect to the point before us. In the Attic commonwealth[8] it was the privilege and birthright of every citizen and poet to rail aloud and in public, or to expose upon the stage by name, any person they pleased, though of the greatest figure, whether a C[l]eon, an Hyperbolus, an Alcibiades, or a Demosthenes. But on the other side, the least reflecting word let fall against the *people* in general was immediately caught up and revenged upon the authors, however considerable for their quality or their merits. Whereas in England, it is just the reverse of all this. Here you may securely display your utmost *rhetoric* against mankind, in the face of the world; tell them, "That all are gone astray, that there is none that doth good, no not one; that we live in the very dregs of time; that knavery and atheism are epidemic as the pox; that honesty is fled with Astræa"; with any other commonplaces, *equally* new and eloquent, which are furnished by the *splendida bilis.*[9] And when you have done, the whole audience, far from being offended, shall return you thanks as a deliverer of precious and useful truths. Nay, further, it is but to venture your lungs, and you may preach in Covent Garden against foppery and fornication, and *something else*: against pride, and dissimulation, and bribery, at White-Hall: you may expose rapine and injustice in the Inns of Court Chapel: and in a city pulpit be as fierce as you please against avarice, hypocrisy, and extortion. 'Tis but a *ball* bandied to and fro, and every man carries a *racket* about him to strike it from himself among the rest of the company. But on the other side, whoever should mistake the nature of things so far as to drop but a single hint in public, how *such a one* starved half the fleet and half poisoned the rest: how *such a one,* from a true principle of *love* and *honour,* pays no debts but for *wenches* and *play*: how *such a one* has got a clap, and runs out of his estate: how Paris bribed by Juno and Venus,[10] loth to offend either party, slept out the whole cause on the bench: or, how *such an orator* makes long speeches in the senate, with much thought, little sense, and to no purpose; whoever, I say, should venture to be thus particular must expect to be imprisoned for *scandalum magnatum,* to have *challenges* sent him, to be sued for *defamation,* and to be *brought before the bar of the house.*

But I forget that I am expatiating on a subject wherein I have no concern, having neither a talent nor an inclination for satire. On the other side I am so entirely satisfied with the whole present procedure of human things that I have been for some years preparing materials towards *A Panegyric upon the World,* to which I intended to add a second part entitled *A Modest Defence of the Proceedings of the Rabble in all Ages.* Both these I had thoughts to publish by way of appendix to the following treatise; but finding my commonplace book fill much slower than I had reason to expect, I have chosen to defer them to another occasion. Besides, I have been unhappily prevented in that design by a certain domestic misfortune, in the particulars whereof, though it would be very seasonable and much in the *modern* way to inform the *gentle reader,* and would also be of great assistance towards extending this preface into the size now in vogue, which by rule ought to be *large* in proportion as the subsequent volume is *small*; yet I shall now dismiss our impatient reader from any further attendance at the *porch,* and having duly prepared his mind by a preliminary discourse, shall gladly introduce him to the sublime mysteries that ensue.

A TALE OF A TUB, &C.

SECT. I

THE INTRODUCTION

Whoever hath an ambition to be heard in a crowd must press, and squeeze, and thrust, and climb, with indefatigable pains, till he has exalted himself to a certain degree of altitude above them. Now, in all assemblies though you wedge them ever so close, we may observe this peculiar property that over their heads there is room enough, but how to reach it is the difficult point, it being as hard to get quit of *number* as of *hell*;

[11]——*Evadere ad auras,*
Hoc opus, hic labour est.

To this end, the philosopher's way in all ages has been by erecting certain *edifices in the air.* But whatever practice and reputation these kind of structures have formerly possessed, or may still continue in, not excepting even that of Socrates when he was suspended in a basket to help contemplation, I think with due submission they seem to labour under two inconveniences. First, that the foundations being laid too high, they have been often out of *sight,* and ever out of *hearing.* Secondly, that the materials being very transitory have suffered much from inclemencies of air, especially in these northwest regions.

Therefore, towards the just performance of this great work there remain but three methods that I can think on; whereof the wisdom of our ancestors being highly sensible, has, to encourage all aspiring adventurers, thought fit to erect three wooden machines for the use of those orators who desire to talk much without interruption. These are the *pulpit,* the *ladder,* and the *stage itinerant.* For, as to the *Bar,* though it be compounded of the same matter and designed for the same use, it cannot however be well allowed the honour of a fourth, by reason of its level or inferior situation exposing it to perpetual interruption from collaterals. Neither can the *Bench* itself, though raised to a proper eminency, put in a better claim whatever its advocates insist on. For, if they please to look into the original design of its erection and the circumstances or adjuncts subservient to that design, they will soon acknowledge the present practice exactly correspondent to the primitive institution, and both to answer the etymology of the name, which in the Phœnician tongue is a word of great signification, importing if literally interpreted, *the place of sleep*; but in common acceptation, *a seat well bolstered and cushioned for the repose of old and gouty limbs*: *senes ut in otia tuta recedant.* Fortune being indebted to them this part of retaliation that, as formerly they have long *talked* whilst others *slept,* so now they may *sleep* as long, whilst others *talk.*

But if no other argument could occur to exclude the Bench and the Bar from the list of oratorial machines, it were sufficient that the admission of them would overthrow a number which I was resolved to establish whatever argument it might cost me; in imitation of that prudent method observed by many other philosophers and great clerks, whose chief art in division has been to grow fond of some proper mystical number which their imaginations have rendered sacred, to a degree that they force common reason to find room for it in every part of nature; reducing, including, and adjusting every *genus* and *species* within that compass, by coupling some against their wills, and banishing others at any rate. Now, among all the rest the profound number *THREE* is that which hath most employed my sublimest speculations, nor ever without wonderful delight. There is now in the press (and will be published next Term) a panegyrical essay of mine upon this number, wherein I have by most convincing proofs not only reduced the *senses* and the *elements* under its banner, but brought over several deserters from its two great rivals, *SEVEN* and *NINE*.

Now, the first of these oratorial machines, in place as well as dignity, is the *pulpit*. Of pulpits there are in this island several sorts, but I esteem only that made of timber from the *sylva Caledonia*, which agrees very well with our climate. If it be upon its decay, 'tis the better both for conveyance of sound and for other reasons to be mentioned by and by. The degree of perfection in shape and size, I take to consist in being extremely narrow with little ornament, and, best of all, without a cover (for by ancient rule it ought to be the only uncovered *vessel* in every assembly where it is rightfully used) by which means, from its near resemblance to a pillory, it will ever have a mighty influence on human ears.

Of *ladders* I need say nothing. 'Tis observed by foreigners themselves, to the honour of our country, that we excel all nations in our practice and understanding of this machine. The ascending orators do not only oblige their audience in the agreeable delivery, but the whole world in their *early* publication of these speeches which I look upon as the choicest treasury of our British eloquence, and whereof, I am informed, that worthy citizen and bookseller, Mr. John Dunton, hath made a faithful and a painful collection which he shortly designs to publish in twelve volumes in folio, illustrated with copperplates. A work highly useful and curious, and altogether worthy of such a hand.

The last engine of orators is the *stage itinerant*,[12] erected with much sagacity *sub Jove pluvio, in triviis et quadriviis.*[13] It is the great seminary of the two former, and its orators are sometimes preferred to the one and sometimes to the other, in proportion to their deservings, there being a strict and perpetual intercourse between all three.

From this accurate deduction it is manifest that for obtaining attention in public, there is of necessity required a *superior position of place.* But although this point be generally granted, yet the cause is little agreed in; and it seems to me that very few philosophers have fallen into a true, natural solution of this phenomenon. The deepest account, and the most fairly digested of any I have yet met with, is this, that air being a heavy body, and therefore (according to the system of Epicurus[14]) continually descending, must needs be more so when loaden and pressed down by words, which are also bodies of much weight and gravity, as it is manifest from those deep *impressions* they make and leave upon us; and therefore must be delivered from a due altitude, or else they will neither carry a good aim nor fall down with a sufficient force.

> *Corpoream quoque enim vocem constare fatendum est,*
> *Et sonitum, quoniam possunt impellere sensus.*[15]
>
> LUCR. Lib. 4

And I am the readier to favour this conjecture, from a common observation that in the several assemblies of these orators, nature itself has instructed the hearers to stand with their mouths open and erected parallel to the horizon, so as they may be intersected by a perpendicular line from the zenith to the centre of the earth. In which position, if the audience be well compact, everyone carries home a share and little or nothing is lost.

I confess there is something yet more refined in the contrivance and structure of our modern theatres. For, first, the pit is sunk below the stage, with due regard to the institution above deduced; that whatever *weighty* matter shall be delivered thence (whether it be *lead* or *gold*) may fall plumb into the jaws of certain *critics* (as I think they are called) which stand ready open to devour them. Then the boxes are built round and raised to a level with the scene, in deference to the ladies, because that large portion of wit laid out in raising pruriences and protuberancies, is observed to run much upon a line and ever in a circle. The whining passions and little starved conceits are gently wafted up by their own extreme levity to the middle region, and there fix and are frozen by the frigid understandings of the inhabitants. Bombast and buffoonery, by nature lofty and light, soar highest of all and would be lost in the roof, if the prudent architect had not with much foresight contrived for them a fourth place called *the twelve-penny gallery*, and there planted a suitable colony who greedily intercept them in their passage.

Now this physico-logical scheme of oratorial receptacles or machines contains a great mystery, being a type, a sign, an emblem, a shadow, a symbol, bearing analogy to the spacious commonwealth of writers, and to those methods by which they must exalt themselves to a certain eminency above the inferior world. By the *pulpit* are adumbrated the writings of our *modern saints* in Great Britain, as they have spiritualized and refined them from the dross and grossness of *sense* and *human reason*. The matter, as we have said, is of rotten wood, and that upon two considerations; because it is the quality of rotten wood to give *light* in the dark, and secondly, because its cavities are full of worms; which is a type with a pair of handles,[16] having a respect to the two principal qualifications of the orator and the two different fates attending upon his work.

The *ladder* is an adequate symbol of *faction* and of *poetry*, to both of which so noble a number of authors are indebted for their fame. Of *faction* because[17] * * * * *
* * * * * * * *
Hiatus in MS * * * * * *
* * * * Of *poetry*, because its orators do *perorare* with a song and because climbing up by slow degrees, fate is sure to turn them off before they can reach within many steps of the top, and because it is a preferment attained by transferring of propriety, and a confounding of *meum* and *tuum*.

Under the *stage itinerant* are couched those productions designed for the pleasure and delight of mortal man, such as Sixpenny-worth of Wit, Westminster Drolleries, Delightful Tales, Compleat Jesters, and the like, by which the writers of and for *GRUB-STREET* have in these latter ages so nobly triumphed over Time; have clipped his wings, pared his nails, filed his teeth, turned back his hourglass, blunted his scythe, and drawn the hobnails out of his shoes. It is under this classis I have presumed to list my present treatise, being just come from having the honour conferred upon me to be adopted a member of that illustrious fraternity.

Now, I am not unaware how the productions of the Grub Street brotherhood have of late years fallen under many prejudices, nor how it has been the perpetual employment of two *junior* start-up societies to ridicule them and their authors as unworthy their established post in the commonwealth of wit and learning. Their own consciences will easily inform them whom I mean, nor has the world been so negligent a looker-on, as not to observe the continual efforts made by the societies of *Gresham* and of *Will's*[18] to edify a name and reputation upon the ruin of OURS. And this is yet a more feeling grief to us upon the regards of tenderness as well as of justice, when we reflect on their proceedings not only as unjust, but as ungrateful, undutiful, and unnatural. For how can it be forgot by the world or themselves (to say nothing of our own records, which are full and clear in the point) that they both are seminaries not only of our *planting*, but our *watering* too? I am informed our two *rivals* have lately made an offer to enter into the lists with united forces, and challenge us to a comparison of books both as to *weight* and *number*. In return to which (with licence from our president) I humbly offer two answers. First, we say the proposal is like that which Archimedes made upon a *smaller* affair,[19] including an impossibility in the practice, for, where can they find scales of *capacity* enough for the first, or an arithmetician of *capacity* enough for the second? Secondly, we are ready to accept the challenge, but with this condition, that a third indifferent person be assigned, to whose impartial judgment it should be left to decide which society each book, treatise, or pamphlet, do most properly belong to. This point, God knows, is very far from being fixed at present, for we are ready to produce a catalogue of some thousands which in all common justice ought to be entitled to our fraternity, but by the revolted and newfangled writers most perfidiously ascribed to the others. Upon all which we think it very unbecoming our prudence that the determination should be remitted to the authors themselves, when our adversaries, by briguing and caballing, have caused so universal a defection from us that the greatest part of our society hath already deserted to them, and our nearest friends begin to stand aloof as if they were half ashamed to own us.

This is the utmost I am authorized to say upon so ungrateful and melancholy a subject, because we are extreme unwilling to inflame a controversy whose continuance may be so fatal to the interests of us all, desiring much rather that things be amicably composed. And we shall so far advance on our side as to be ready to receive the two *prodigals* with open arms, whenever they shall think fit to return from their *husks* and their *harlots* (which, I think from the present course of their studies,[20] they most properly may be said to be engaged in) and, like an indulgent parent, continue to them our affection and our blessing.

But the greatest maim given to that general reception which the writings of our society have formerly received (next to the transitory state of all sublunary things) hath been a superficial vein among many readers of the present age, who will by no means be persuaded to inspect beyond the surface and the rind of things. Whereas, *Wisdom* is a *fox* who after long hunting will at last cost you the pains to dig out. 'Tis a *cheese* which, by how much the richer, has the thicker, the homelier, and the coarser coat, and whereof, to a judicious palate, the *maggots* are the best. 'Tis a *sack-posset,* wherein the deeper you go you will find it the sweeter. *Wisdom* is a *hen* whose *cackling* we must value and consider because it is attended with an *egg.* But then lastly 'tis a *nut,* which unless you choose with judgment may cost you a tooth, and pay you with nothing but a *worm.* In consequence of these momentous truths, the Grubæan Sages have always chosen to convey their precepts and their arts shut up within the vehicles of types and fables; which having been perhaps more careful and curious in adorning than was altogether necessary, it has fared with these vehicles after the usual fate of coaches over-finely painted and gilt, that the transitory gazers have so dazzled their eyes and filled their imaginations with the outward lustre, as neither to regard nor consider the person or the parts of the owner within. A misfortune we undergo with somewhat less reluctancy because it has been common to us with Pythagoras, Æsop, Socrates, and other of our predecessors.

However, that neither the world nor ourselves may any longer suffer by such misunderstandings, I have been prevailed on, after much importunity from my friends, to travail in a complete and laborious dissertation upon the prime productions of our society, which besides their beautiful externals for the gratification of superficial readers, have darkly and deeply couched under them the most finished and refined systems of all sciences and arts; as I do not doubt to lay open by untwisting or unwinding, and either to draw up by exantlation or display by incision.

This great work was entered upon some years ago by one of our most eminent members. He began with the History of Reynard the Fox[21] but neither lived to publish his essay nor to proceed further in so useful an attempt; which is very much to be lamented because the discovery he made and communicated with his friends is now universally received; nor do I think any of the learned will dispute that famous treatise to be a complete body of civil knowledge and the *revelation,* or rather the *apocalypse,* of all State *Arcana.* But the progress I have made is much greater, having already finished my annotations upon several dozens, from some of which I shall impart a few hints to the candid reader, as far as will be necessary to the conclusion at which I aim.

The first piece I have handled is that of *Tom Thumb,* whose author was a Pythagorean philosopher. This dark treatise contains the whole scheme of the Metempsychosis, deducing the progress of the soul through all her stages.

The next is *Dr. Faustus,* penned by Artephius, an author *bonæ notæ* and an *adeptus.* He published it in the nine-hundred-eighty-fourth year[22] of his age; this writer proceeds wholly by *reincrudation,* or in the *via humida;* and the marriage between Faustus and Helen does most conspicuously dilucidate the fermenting of the *male and female dragon.*

Whittington and his Cat is the work of that mysterious rabbi Jehuda Hannasi, containing a defence of the Gemara of the Jerusalem Mishna and its just preference to that of Babylon, contrary to the vulgar opinion.

The Hind and Panther. This is the masterpiece of a famous writer now living,[23] intended for a complete abstract of sixteen thousand schoolmen from Scotus to Bellarmin.

Tommy Potts. Another piece supposed by the same hand, by way of supplement to the former.

The *Wise Men of Gotham, cum appendice.* This is a treatise of immense erudition, being the great original and fountain of those arguments bandied about both in France and England, for a just defence of the modern learning and wit, against the presumption, the pride, and ignorance of the ancients. This unknown author hath so exhausted the subject that a penetrating reader will easily discover whatever hath been written since upon that dispute, to be little more than repetition. An abstract of this treatise hath been lately published by a *worthy member* of our society.[24]

These notices may serve to give the learned reader an idea as well as a taste of what the whole work is likely to produce; wherein I have now altogether circumscribed my thoughts and my studies, and if I can bring it to a perfection before I die, shall reckon I have well employed the poor remains of an unfortunate life.[25] This, indeed, is more than I can justly expect from a quill worn to the pith in the service of the State, in *pros* and *cons* upon *Popish plots,* and *meal-tubs,*[26] and *exclusion bills,* and *passive obedience,* and *addresses of lives and fortunes,* and *prerogative,* and *property,* and *liberty of conscience,* and *Letters to a Friend:* from an understanding and a conscience threadbare and ragged with perpetual turning; from a head broken in a hundred places by the malignants of the opposite factions; and from a body spent with poxes ill cured by trusting to bawds and surgeons who (as it afterwards appeared) were professed enemies to me and the government, and revenged their party's quarrel upon my nose and shins. Fourscore and eleven pamphlets have I writ under three reigns, and for the service of six and thirty factions. But finding the state has no further occasion for me and my ink, I retire willingly to draw it out into speculations more becoming a philospher, having, to my unspeakable comfort, passed a long life with a conscience void of offence [towards God and towards Men].

But to return. I am assured from the reader's candour that the brief specimen I have given will easily clear all the rest of our society's productions from an aspersion grown, as it is manifest, out of envy and ignorance: that they are of little farther use or value to mankind beyond the common entertainments of their wit and their style. For these I am sure have never yet been disputed by our keenest adversaries, in both which, as well as the more profound and mystical part, I have throughout this treatise closely followed the most applauded originals. And to render all complete I have, with much thought and application of mind, so ordered that the chief title prefixed to it (I mean, that under which I design it shall pass in the common conversations of court and town) is modelled exactly after the manner peculiar to *our* society.

I confess to have been somewhat liberal in the business of titles,[27] having observed the humour of multiplying them to bear great vogue among certain writers whom I exceedingly reverence. And indeed it seems not unreasonable, that books, the children of the brain, should have the honour to be christened with variety of names as well as other infants of quality. Our famous Dryden has ventured to proceed a point farther, endeavouring to introduce also a multiplicity of *godfathers*[28] which is an improvement of much more advantage, upon a very obvious account. 'Tis a pity this admirable invention has not been better cultivated so as to grow by this time into general imitation, when such an authority serves it for a precedent. Nor have my endeavours been wanting to second so useful an example. But it seems there is an unhappy expense usually annexed to the calling of a godfather which was clearly out of my head, as it is very reasonable to believe. Where the pinch lay, I cannot certainly affirm; but having employed a world of thoughts and pains to split my treatise into forty sections, and having entreated forty lords of my acquaintance that they would do me the honour to stand, they all made it a matter of conscience and sent me their excuses.

SECT. II

Once upon a time, there was a man who had three sons by one wife,[29] and all at a birth, neither could the midwife tell certainly which was the eldest. Their father died while they were young, and upon his deathbed, calling the lads to him, spoke thus:

"Sons, because I have purchased no estate, nor was born to any, I have long considered of some good legacies to bequeath you; and at last, with much care as well as expense, have provided each of you (here they are) a new coat.[30] Now, you are to understand that these coats have two virtues contained in them: one is, that with good wearing they will last you fresh and sound as long as you live: the other is that they will grow in the same proportion with your bodies, lengthening and widening of themselves so as to be always fit. Here; let me see them on you before I die. So; very well; pray, children, wear them clean and brush them often. You will find in my will[31] (here it is) full instructions in every particular concerning the wearing and management of your coats, wherein you must be very exact to avoid the penalties I have appointed for every transgression or neglect, upon which your future fortunes will entirely depend. I have also commanded in my will that you should live together in one house like brethren and friends, for then you will be sure to thrive and not otherwise."

Here the story says this good father died, and the three sons went all together to seek their fortunes.

I shall not trouble you with recounting what adventures they met for the first seven years, any further than by taking notice that they carefully observed their father's will, and kept their coats in very good order, that they travelled through several countries, encountered a reasonable quantity of giants, and slew certain dragons.

Being now arrived at the proper age for producing themselves, they came up to town and fell in love with the ladies, but especially three who about that time were in chief reputation, the Duchess d'Argent, Madame de Grands Titres, and the Countess d'Orgueil.[32] On their first appearance our three adventurers met with a very bad reception, and soon with great sagacity guessing out the reason, they quickly began to improve in the good qualities of the town:

they writ, and rallied, and rhymed, and sung, and said, and said nothing; they drank, and fought, and whored, and slept, and swore, and took snuff; they went to new plays on the first night, haunted the *chocolate*-houses, beat the watch, lay on bulks, and got claps; they bilked hackney-coachmen, ran in debt with shopkeepers, and lay with their wives; they killed bailiffs, kicked fiddlers down stairs, eat at Locket's, loitered at Will's; they talked of the drawing room and never came there; dined with lords they never saw; whispered a duchess, and spoke never a word; exposed the scrawls of their laundress for billets-doux of quality; came ever just from court and were never seen in it; attended the Levee *sub dio;* got a list of the peers by heart in one company, and with great familiarity retailed them in another. Above all, they constantly attended those Committees of Senators who are silent in the *House,* and loud in the *Coffeehouse,* where they nightly adjourn to chew the cud of politics, and are encompassed with a ring of disciples who lie in wait to catch up their droppings. The three brothers had acquired forty other qualifications of the like stamp too tedious to recount, and by consequence were justly reckoned the most accomplished persons in town. But all would not suffice and the ladies aforesaid continued still inflexible. To clear up which difficulty I must, with the reader's good leave and patience, have recourse to some points of weight which the authors of that age have not sufficiently illustrated.

For about this time it happened a sect arose[33] whose tenets obtained and spread very far, especially in the *grande monde* and among everybody of good fashion. They worshipped a sort of *idol*[34] who, as their doctrine delivered, did daily create men by a kind of manufactory operation. This idol they placed in the highest parts of the house, on an altar erected about three foot. He was shewn in the posture of a Persian emperor, sitting on a *superficies* with his legs interwoven under him. This god had a *goose* for his ensign, whence it is that some learned men pretend to deduce his original from Jupiter Capitolinus. At his left hand beneath the altar, *Hell* seemed to open and catch at the animals the idol was creating; to prevent which, certain of his priests hourly flung in pieces of the uninformed mass or substance, and sometimes whole limbs already enlivened, which that horrid gulf insatiably swallowed, terrible to behold. The goose was also held a subaltern divinity or *deus minorum gentium,* before whose shrine was sacrificed that creature whose hourly food is human gore, and who is in so great renown abroad for being the delight and favourite of the Ægyptian Cercopithecus.[35] Millions of these animals were cruelly slaughtered everyday to appease the hunger of that consuming deity. The chief idol was also worshipped as the inventor of the *yard* and *needle,* whether as the god of seamen or on account of certain other mystical attributes, hath not been sufficiently cleared.

The worshippers of this deity had also a system of their belief which seemed to turn upon the following fundamentals. They held the universe to be a large *suit of clothes,* which *invests* everything: that the earth is invested by the air; the air is invested by the stars; and the stars are invested by the *primum mobile.* Look on this globe of earth, you will find it to be a very complete and fashionable *dress.* What is that which some call *land,* but a fine coat faced with green? Or the sea, but a waistcoat of water-tabby? Proceed to the particular works of the creation, you will find how curious *Journeyman* Nature hath been, to trim up the *vegetable* beaux; observe how sparkish a periwig adorns the head of a *beech,* and what a fine doublet of white satin is worn by the *birch.* To conclude from all, what is man himself but a *micro-coat,*[36] or rather a complete suit of clothes with all its trimmings? As to his body, there can be no dispute; but examine even the acquirements of his mind, you will find them all contribute in their order towards furnishing out an exact dress. To instance no more: is not religion a *cloak,* honesty a *pair of shoes* worn out in the dirt, self-love a *surtout,* vanity a *shirt,* and conscience a *pair of breeches* which, though a cover for lewdness as well as nastiness, is easily slipped down for the service of both?

These *postulata* being admitted, it will follow in due course of reasoning that those beings which the world calls improperly *suits of clothes* are in reality the most refined species of animals; or to proceed higher, that they are rational creatures, or men. For is it not manifest that they live, and move, and talk, and perform all other offices of human life? Are not beauty, and wit, and mien, and breeding, their inseparable proprieties? In short, we see nothing but them, hear nothing but them. Is it not they who walk the streets, fill *up parliament—coffee—play—bawdy-houses?* 'Tis true indeed, that these animals which are vulgarly called *suits of clothes,* or *dresses,* do, according to certain compositions, receive different appellations. If one of them be trimmed up with a gold chain, and a red gown, and a white rod, and a great horse, it is called a *Lord Mayor;* if certain ermines and furs be placed in a certain position we style them a *Judge;* and so an apt conjunction of lawn and black satin we entitle a *Bishop.*

Others of these professors, though agreeing in the main system, were yet more refined upon certain branches of it, and held that man was an animal compounded of two *dresses,* the *natural* and the *celestial suit,* which were the body and the soul; that the soul was the outward, and the body the inward clothing; that the latter was *ex traduce* but the former of daily creation and circumfusion. This last they proved by scripture, because *in them me live, and move, and have our being*; as likewise by philosophy because they are *all in all, and all in every part.* Besides, said they, separate these two, and you will find the body to be only a senseless unsavoury carcase. By all which it is manifest that the outward dress must needs be the soul.

To this system of religion were tagged several subaltern doctrines which were entertained with great vogue; as particularly, the faculties of the mind were deduced by the learned among them in this manner: *embroidery* was *sheer wit; gold fringe* was *agreeable conversation; gold lace* was *repartee;* a huge long *periwig* was *humour,* and a *coat full of powder was* very good *raillery;* all which required abundance *of finesse* and *delicatesse* to manage with advantage, as well as a strict observance after times and fashions.

I have with much pains and reading collected out of ancient authors this short summary of a body of philosophy and divinity, which seems to have been composed by a vein and race of thinking very different from any other systems either *ancient* or *modern.* And it was not merely to entertain or satisfy the reader's curiosity but rather to give him light into several circumstances of the following story; that knowing the state of dispositions and opinions in an age so remote, he may better comprehend those great events which were the issue of them. I advise therefore the courteous reader to peruse with a world of application, again and again, whatever I have written upon this matter. And so leaving these broken ends, I carefully gather up the chief thread of my story, and proceed.

These opinions therefore were so universal, as well as the practices of them, among the refined part of court and town, that our three brother-adventurers as their circumstances then stood were strangely at a loss.[37] For, on the one side, the three ladies they addressed themselves to (whom we have named already) were ever at the very top of the fashion, and abhorred all that were below it but the breadth of a hair. On the other side, their father's will was very precise, and it was the main precept in it with the greatest penalties annexed, not to add to, or diminish from their coats one thread without a positive command in the will. Now the coats[38] their father had left them were, 'tis true, of very good cloth and, besides, so neatly sewn you would swear they were all of a piece, but at the same time very plain, and with little or no ornament. And it happened that before they were a month in town, great *shoulder-knots*[39] came up. Straight, all the world was *shoulder-knots;* no approaching the ladies' *ruelles* without the *quota* of shoulder-knots. "That fellow," cries one, "has no soul; where is his shoulder-knot?" Our three brethren soon discovered their want by sad experience, meeting in their walks with forty mortifications and indignities. If they went to the playhouse, the doorkeeper showed them into the twelve-penny gallery. If they called a boat, says a waterman, "I am first sculler." If they stepped to the Rose to take a bottle, the drawer would cry, "Friend, we sell no ale." If they went to visit a lady, a footman met them at the door with, "Pray send up your message." In this unhappy case they went immediately to consult their father's Will, read it over and over, but not a word of the *shoulder-knot.* What should they do? What temper should they find? Obedience was absolutely necessary, and yet *shoulder-knots* appeared extremely requisite. After much thought one of the brothers who happened to be more book-learned than the other two, said he had found an expedient. "'Tis true," said he, "there is nothing here in this Will, *totidem verbis,*[40] making mention of *shoulder-knots,* but I dare conjecture we may find them *inclusivè,* or *totidem syllabis.*" This distinction was immediately approved by all, and so they fell again to examine the will. But their evil star had so directed the matter that the first syllable was not to be found in the whole writing. Upon which disappointment, he who found the former evasion took heart and said, "Brothers, there is yet hopes; for though we cannot find them *totidem verbis,* nor *totidem syllabis,* I dare engage we shall make them out *tertio modo,* or *totidem literis.*" This discovery was also highly commended, upon which they fell once more to the scrutiny, and soon picked out *S,H,O,U,L,D,E,R,* when the same planet, enemy to their repose, had wonderfully contrived that a *K* was not to be found. Here was a weighty difficulty! But the distinguishing brother (for whom we shall hereafter find a name) now his hand was in, proved by a very good argument that *K* was a modern, illegitimate letter, unknown to the learned ages nor anywhere to be found in ancient manuscripts. "'Tis true," said he, "the word Calendæ hath in *Q.V.C.*[41] been sometimes writ with a *K,* but erroneously, for in the best copies, it is ever spelt with a C. And by consequence it was a gross mistake in our language to spell 'knot' with a *K";* but that from henceforward he would take care it should be writ with a *C.* Upon this all further difficulty vanished; *shoulder-knots* were made clearly out to be *jure paterno,* and our three gentlemen swaggered with as large and as flaunting ones as the best.

But as human happiness is of a very short duration, so in those days were human fashions upon which it entirely depends. Shoulder-knots had their time, and we must now imagine them in their decline; for a certain lord came just from Paris with fifty yards of *gold lace* upon his coat, exactly trimmed after the court fashion of that *month.* In two days all mankind appeared closed up in bars of gold lace:[42] whoever durst peep abroad without his complement of gold lace, was as scandalous as a [eunuch], and as ill received among the women. What should our three knights do in this momentous affair? They had sufficiently strained a point already in the affair of shoulder-knots. Upon recourse to the Will nothing appeared there but *altum silentium.* That of the shoulder-knots was a loose, flying, circumstantial point; but this of gold lace seemed too considerable an alteration without better warrant. It did *aliquo modo essentiæ adhærere,* and therefore required a positive precept.

But about this time it fell out that the learned brother aforesaid had read *Aristotelis Dialectica,* and especially that wonderful piece *de Interpretatione* which has the faculty of teaching its readers to find out a meaning in everything but itself, like commentators on the Revelations who proceed prophets without understanding a syllable of the text. "Brothers," said he, "you are to be informed,[43] that of wills *duo sunt genera,* nuncupatory[44] and scriptory; that in the scriptory will here before us, there is no precept or mention about gold lace, *conceditur:* but, *si idem affirmetur de nuncupatorio, negatur.* For brothers, if you remember, we heard a fellow say when we were boys, that he heard my father's man say, that he heard my father say, that he would advise his sons to get *gold lace* on their coats, as soon as ever they could procure money to buy it." "By G! That is very true," cries the other. "I remember it perfectly well," said the third. And so without more ado they got the largest gold lace in the parish, and walked about as fine as lords.

A while after there came up *all in fashion* a pretty sort of *flame-coloured satin*[45] for linings, and the mercer brought a pattern of it immediately to our three gentlemen. "An please your worships," said he,[46] "my Lord C[lifford] and Sir J[ohn] W[alters] had linings out of this very piece last night; it takes wonderfully, and I shall not have a remnant left enough to make my wife a pincushion, by tomorrow morning at ten o'clock." Upon this, they fell again to rummage the Will, because the present case also required a positive precept, the lining being held by orthodox writers to be of the essence of the coat. After long search they could fix upon nothing to the matter in hand except a short advice of their father's in the Will to take care of *fire* and put out their *candles* before they went to sleep.[47] This, though a good deal for the purpose and helping very far towards self-conviction, yet not seeming wholly of force to establish a command; and being resolved to avoid farther scruple, as well as future occasion for scandal, says he that was the scholar, "I remember to have read in wills of a codicil annexed, which is indeed a part of the will, and what it contains hath equal authority with the rest. Now, I have been considering of this same will here before us, and I cannot reckon it to be complete, for want of such a codicil. I will therefore fasten one in its proper place very dexterously. I have had it by me sometime; it was written by a dog-keeper of my grandfather's,[48] and talks a great deal (as goodluck would have it) of this very flame-coloured satin." The project was immediately approved by the other two; an old parchment scroll was tagged on according to art, in the form of a *codicil annexed,* and the *satin* bought and worn.

Next winter a *player,* hired for the purpose by the corporation of *fringe-makers,* acted his part in a new comedy all covered with silver fringe,[49] and according to the laudable custom, gave rise to that fashion. Upon which the brothers consulting their father's Will, to their great astonishment found these words, "*Item,* I charge and command my said three sons to wear no sort of *silver fringe* upon or about their said coats," etc., with a penalty in case of disobedience, too long here to insert. However, after some pause, the brother so often mentioned for his erudition, who was well skilled in criticisms, had found in a certain author which he said should be nameless, that the same word which in the will is called *fringe,* does also signify a *broomstick,* and doubtless ought to have the same interpretation in this paragraph. This, another of the brothers disliked because of that epithet *silver,* which could not, he humbly conceived, in propriety of speech be reasonably applied to a *broomstick;* but it was replied upon him that this epithet was understood in a *mythological* and *allegorical* sense. However, he objected again why their father should forbid them to wear a *broomstick* on their coats, a caution that seemed unnatural and impertinent; upon which he was taken up short, as one who spoke irreverently of a *mystery* which doubtless was very useful and significant, but ought not to be over-curiously pried into or nicely reasoned upon. And in short, their father's authority being now considerably sunk, this expedient was allowed to serve as a lawful dispensation for wearing their full proportion of silver fringe.

A while after was revived an old fashion, long antiquated, of *embroidery* with *Indian figures* of men, women, and children.[50] Here they had no occasion to examine the Will. They remembered but too well how their father had always abhorred this fashion; that he made several paragraphs on purpose importing his utter detestation of it, and bestowing his everlasting curse to his sons, whenever they should wear it. For all this, in a few days they appeared higher in the fashion than anybody else in town. But they solved the matter by saying that these figures were not at all the *same* with those that were formerly worn and were meant in the will. Besides, they did not wear them in that sense as forbidden by their father, but as they were a commendable custom, and of great use to the public. That these rigorous clauses in the will did therefore require some *allowance,* and a favourable intepretation, and ought to be understood *cum grano salis.*

But fashions perpetually altering in that age, the scholastic brother grew weary of searching further evasions and solving everlasting contradictions. Resolved, therefore, at all hazards to comply with the modes of the world, they concerted matters together and agreed unanimously to lock up their father's Will in a *strong box,*[51] brought out of Greece or Italy (I have forgot which) and trouble themselves no further to examine it, but only refer to its authority whenever they thought fit. In consequence whereof, a while after it grew a general mode to wear an infinite number of *points,* most of them tagged with silver: upon which, the scholar pronounced *ex cathedra*[52] that *points* were absolutely *jure paterno,* as they might very well remember. 'Tis true indeed, the fashion prescribed somewhat more than were directly named in the Will; however, that they as heirs general of their father had power to make and add certain clauses for public emolument, though not deducible *totidem verbis* from the letter of the Will, or else, *multa absurda sequerentur.* This was understood for *canonical,* and therefore on the following Sunday they came to church all covered with *points.*

The learned brother, so often mentioned, was reckoned the best scholar in all that or the next street to it; insomuch as, having run something behind-hand with the world, he obtained the favour from a *certain lord,*[53] to receive him into his house and to teach his children. A while after the lord died, and he, by long practice upon his father's Will, found the way of contriving a *deed of conveyance* of that house to himself and his heirs; upon which he took possession, turned the young squires out, and received his brothers in their stead.[54]

SECT. III

A DIGRESSION CONCERNING CRITICS

Though I have been hitherto as cautious as I could, upon all occasions most nicely to follow the rules and methods of writing laid down by the example of our illustrious *moderns;* yet has the unhappy shortness of my memory led me into an error from which I must immediately extricate myself, before I can decently pursue my principal subject. I confess with shame it was an unpardonable omission to proceed so far as I have already done, before I had performed the due discourses expostulatory, supplicatory, or deprecatory, with my *good lords* the *critics.* Towards some atonement for this grievous neglect, I do here make humbly bold to present them with a short account of themselves and their *art,* by looking into the original and pedigree of the word as it is generally understood among us, and very briefly considering the ancient and present state thereof.

By the word *critic,* at this day so frequent in all conversations, there have sometimes been distinguished three very different species of mortal men, according as I have read in *ancient books and pamphlets.* For first, by this term was understood such persons as invented or drew up rules for themselves and the world, by observing which a careful reader might be able to pronounce upon the productions of the *learned,* from his taste to a true relish of the *sublime* and the *admirable,* and divide every beauty of matter or of style from the corruption that apes it: in their common perusal of books singling out the errors and defects, the nauseous, the fulsome, the dull, and the impertinent, with the caution of a man that walks through Edinburgh streets in a morning, who is indeed as careful as he can to watch diligently and spy out the filth in his way; not that he is curious to observe the colour and complexion of the ordure, or take its dimensions, much less to be paddling in or tasting it, but only with a design to come out as cleanly as he may. These men seem, though very erroneously, to have understood the appellation of *critic* in a literal sense; that one principal part of his office was to praise and acquit; and that a *critic* who sets up to read only for an occasion of censure and reproof, is a creature as barbarous as a *judge* who should take up a resolution to hang all men that came before him upon a trial.

Again, by the word *critic* have been meant the restorers of ancient learning from the worms, and graves, and dust of manuscripts.

Now the races of those two have been for some ages utterly extinct; and besides, to discourse any further of them would not be at all to my purpose.

The third, and noblest sort, is that of the *TRUE CRITIC,* whose original is the most ancient of all. Every *true critic* is a hero born, descending in a direct line from a celestial stem by Momus and Hybris, who begat Zoilus, who begat Tigellius, who begat Etcætera the elder; who begat B[e]ntly, and Rym[e]r, and W[o]tton, and Perrault, and Dennis, who begat Etcætera the younger.

And these are the *critics* from whom the commonwealth of learning has in all ages received such immense benefits that the gratitude of their admirers placed their origin in Heaven, among those of Hercules, Theseus, Perseus, and other great deservers of mankind. But heroic virtue itself, hath not been exempt from the obloquy of evil tongues. For it hath been objected that those ancient heroes, famous for their combating so many giants, and dragons, and robbers, were in their own persons a greater nuisance to mankind than any of those monsters they subdued; and therefore to render their obligations more complete, when all *other* vermin were destroyed should, in conscience, have concluded with the same justice upon themselves; as Hercules most generously did, and hath upon that score procured to himself more temples and votaries than the best of his fellows. For these reasons I suppose it is, why some have conceived it would be very expedient for the public good of learning that every *true critic,* as soon as he had finished his task assigned, should immediately deliver himself up to ratsbane, or hemp, or from some convenient altitude; and that no man's pretensions to so illustrious a character should by any means be received before that operation were performed.

Now, from this heavenly descent of *criticism,* and the close analogy it bears to *heroic virtue,* 'tis easy to assign the proper employment of a *true ancient genuine critic;* which is to travell through this vast world of writings; to pursue and hunt those monstrous faults bred within them; to drag out the lurking errors, like Cacus from his den; to multiply them like Hydra's heads; and rake them together like Augeas' dung; or else to drive away a sort of *dangerous fowl* who have a perverse inclination to plunder the best branches of the *tree of knowledge,* like those Stymphalian birds that eat up the fruit.

These reasonings will furnish us with an adequate definition of a *true critic:* that he is *a discoverer and collector of writers' faults,* which may be further put beyond dispute by the following demonstration: That whoever will examine the writings in all kinds wherewith this ancient sect has honoured the world, shall immediately find, from the whole thread and tenor of them, that the ideas of the authors have been altogether conversant and taken up with the faults, and blemishes, and oversights, and mistakes of other writers; and let the subject treated on be whatever it will, their imaginations are so entirely possessed and replete with the defects of other pens that the very quintessence of what is bad, does of necessity distil into their own; by which means the whole appears to be nothing else but an *abstract* of the *criticisms* themselves have made.

Having thus briefly considered the original and office of a *critic,* as the word is understood in its most noble and universal acceptation, I proceed to refute the objections of those who argue from the silence and pretermission of authors; by which they pretend to prove that the very art *of criticism* as now exercised, and by me explained, is wholly *modern;* and consequently that the *critics* of Great Britain and France have no title to an original so ancient and illustrious as I have deduced. Now, if I can clearly make out on the contrary, that the most ancient writers have particularly described both the person and the office of a *true critic,* agreeable to the definition laid down by me, their grand objection from the silence of authors will fall to the ground.

I confess to have for a long time borne a part in this general error, from which I should never have acquitted myself but through the assistance of our noble *moderns* whose most edifying volumes I turn indefatigably over night and day, for the improvement of my mind and the good of my country. These have with unwearied pains made many useful searches into the weak side of the *ancients,* and given us a comprehensive list of them.[55] Besides, they have proved beyond contradiction that the very finest things delivered of old, have been long since invented and brought to light by much later pens; and that the noblest discoveries those *ancients* ever made, of art or of nature, have all been produced by the transcending genius of the present age. Which clearly shows how little merit those *ancients* can justly pretend to, and takes off that blind admiration paid them by men in a corner, who have the unhappiness of conversing too little with *present things.* Reflecting maturely upon all this, and taking in the whole compass of human nature, I easily concluded that these *ancients,* highly sensible of their many imperfections, must needs have endeavoured from some passages in their works, to obviate, soften, or divert the censorious reader by *satire,* or *panegyric* upon the *true critics,* in imitation of their *masters,* the *moderns.* Now, in the *commonplaces* of both these[56] I was plentifully instructed by a long course of useful study in *prefaces* and *prologues;* and therefore immediately resolved to try what I could discover of either, by a diligent perusal of the most ancient writers, and especially those who treated of the earliest times. Here I found to my great surprise that although they all entered, upon occasion, into particular descriptions of the *true critic,* according as they were governed by their fears or their hopes; yet whatever they touched of that kind was with abundance of caution, adventuring no farther than *mythology* and *hieroglyphic.* This, I suppose, gave ground to superficial readers for urging the silence of authors against the antiquity of the *true critic,* though the *types* are so apposite, and the applications so necessary and natural, that it is not easy to conceive how any reader of a *modern eye* and *taste* could overlook them. I shall venture from a great number to produce a few, which I am very confident will put this question beyond dispute.

It well deserves considering that these *ancient writers,* in treating enigmatically upon this subject, have generally fixed upon the very *same hieroglyph,* varying only the story according to their affections, or their wit. For first; Pausanias is of opinion that the perfection of writing correct was entirely owing to the institution of *critics;* and, that he can possibly mean no other than the *true critic,* is I think manifest enough from the following description. He says, *they were a race of men who delighted to nibble at the superfluities and excrescencies of books; which the learned at length observing, took warning of their own accord, to lop the luxuriant, the rotten, the dead, the sapless, and the overgrown branches from their works.* But now, all this he cunningly shades under the following allegory; *that the Nauplians in Argia learned the art of pruning their vines by observing, that when an* ASS *had browsed upon one of them, it thrived the better and bore fairer fruit.* But Herodotus,[57] holding the very same *hieroglyph,* speaks much plainer and almost *in terminis.* He hath been so bold as to tax the *true critics* of ignorance and malice, telling us openly, for I think nothing can be plainer, that *in the western part of Libya, there were* ASSES *with* HORNS. Upon which relation Ctesias[58] yet refines, mentioning the very same animal about India, adding, *that whereas all other* ASSES *wanted a gall, these horned ones were so redundant in that part that their flesh was not to be eaten because of its extreme bitterness.*

Now, the reason why those ancient writers treated this subject only by types and figures was, because they durst not make open attacks against a party so potent and terrible as the *critics* of those ages were, whose very voice was so dreadful, that a legion of authors would tremble and drop their pens at the sound; for so Herodotus[59] tells us expressly in another place, how *a vast army of Scythians was put to flight in a panic terror, by the braying of an* ASS. From hence it is conjectured by certain profound *philologers,* that the great awe and reverence paid to a *true critic* by the writers of Britain have been derived to us from those our Scythian ancestors. In short, this dread was so universal that in process of time those authors who had a mind to publish their sentiments more freely, in describing the *true critics* of their several ages were forced to leave off the use of the former *hieroglyph,* as too nearly approaching the *prototype,* and invented other terms instead thereof that were more cautious and mystical. So Diodorus, speaking to the same purpose, ventures no farther than to say that in the mountains of Helicon there grows a certain *weed,* which bears a flower of so damned a scent as to poison those who offer to smell it. Lucretius gives exactly the same relation:

Est etiam in magnis Heliconis montibus arbos,
Floris odore hominem retro consueta necare.[60]
Lib. 6

But Ctesias, whom we lately quoted, hath been a great deal bolder; he had been used with much severity by the *true critics* of his own age, and therefore could not forbear to leave behind him at least one deep mark of his vengeance against the whole tribe. His meaning is so near the surface that I wonder how it possibly came to be overlooked by those who deny the antiquity of the *true critics*. For, pretending to make a description of many strange animals about India, he hath set down these remarkable words: "Among the rest," says he, "there is a *serpent* that wants *teeth,* and consequently cannot bite; but if its *vomit* (to which it is much addicted) happens to fall upon anything, a certain rottenness or corruption ensues. These *serpents* are generally found among the mountains where *jewels* grow, and they frequently emit a *poisonous juice,* whereof whoever drinks, that person's brains fly out of his nostrils."

There was also among the *ancients* a sort of critic not distinguished in *specie* from the former but in growth or degree, who seem to have been only the *tyros* or *junior* scholars; yet, because of their differing employments, they are frequently mentioned as a sect by themselves. The usual exercise of these younger students was to attend constantly at theatres, and learn to spy out the *worst parts* of the play, whereof they were obliged carefully to take note and render a rational account to their tutors. Fleshed at these smaller sports, like young wolves, they grew up in time to be nimble and strong enough for hunting down large game. For it hath been observed both among ancients and moderns, that a *true critic* hath one quality in common with a *whore* and an *alderman,* never to change his title or his nature; that a *grey critic* has been certainly a *green* one, the perfections and acquirements of his age being only the improved talents of his youth; like *hemp,* which some naturalists inform us is bad for *suffocations* though taken but in the seed. I esteem the invention or at least the refinement of *prologues,* to have been owing to these younger proficients, of whom Terence makes frequent and honourable mention under the name of *malevoli.*

Now, 'tis certain, the institution of the *true critics* was of absolute necessity to the commonwealth of learning. For all human actions seem to be divided like Themistocles and his company: one man can *fiddle,* and another can make *a small town a great city;* and he that cannot do either one or the other deserves to be kicked out of the creation. The avoiding of which penalty has doubtless given the first birth to the nation *of critics,* and withal, an occasion for their secret detractors to report that a *true critic* is a sort of mechanic, set up with a stock and tools for his trade at as little expense as a tailor; and that there is much analogy between the utensils and abilities of both: that the tailor's *hell* is the type of a critic's *commonplace book,* and his wit and learning held forth by the *goose;* that it requires at least as many of these to the making up of one scholar, as of the others to the composition of a man; that the valour of both is equal, and their *weapons* near of a size. Much may be said in answer to those invidious reflections, and I can positively affirm the first to be a falsehood. For on the contrary, nothing is more certain than that it requires greater layings out to be free of the *critic's* company, than of any other you can name. For, as to be a *true beggar* it will cost the richest candidate every groat he is worth; so, before one can commence a *true critic* it will cost a man all the good qualities of his mind; which, perhaps for a less purchase, would be thought but an indifferent bargain.

Having thus amply proved the antiquity of *criticism* and described the primitive state of it, I shall now examine the present condition of this empire and show how well it agrees with its ancient self. A certain author[61] whose works have many ages since been entirely lost, does, in his fifth book and eighth chapter, say of *critics,* that "their writings are the mirrors of learning." This I understand in a literal sense, and suppose our author must mean that whoever designs to be a perfect writer must inspect into the books of *critics,* and correct his invention there as in a mirror. Now, whoever considers that the *mirrors* of the ancients were made of brass and *sine mercurio,* may presently apply the two principal qualifications of a *true modern critic,* and consequently must needs conclude that these have always been and must be forever the same. For *brass* is an emblem of duration, and when it is skilfully burnished will cast *reflections* from its own *superficies,* without any assistance of *mercury* from behind. All the other talents of a *critic* will not require a particular mention, being included or easily deducible to these. However, I shall conclude with three maxims which may serve both as characteristics to distinguish a *true modern critic* from a pretender, and will be also of admirable use to those worthy spirits who engage in so useful and honourable an art.

The first is that *criticism,* contrary to all other faculties of the intellect, is ever held the truest and best when it is the very *first* result of the *critic's* mind; as fowlers reckon the first aim for the surest, and seldom fail of missing the mark if they stay for a second.

Secondly, the *true critics* are known by their talent of swarming about the noblest writers, to which they are carried merely by instinct, as a rat to the best cheese, or a wasp to the fairest fruit. So when the king is a horseback, he is sure to be the *dirtiest* person of the company, and they that make their court best, are such as *bespatter* him most.

Lastly, a *true critic* in the perusal of a book is like a *dog* at a feast, whose thoughts and stomach are wholly set upon what the guests *fling away,* and consequently is apt to *snarl* most when there are the fewest *bones.*

Thus much, I think, is sufficient to serve by way of address to my patrons, the *true modern critics,* and may very well atone for my past silence as well as that which I am like to observe for the future. I hope I have deserved so well of their whole *body* as to meet with generous and tender usage from their *hands.* Supported by which expectation, I go on boldly to pursue those adventures already so happily begun.

SECT. IV

A TALE OF A TUB

I have now, with much pains and study, conducted the reader to a period where he must expect to hear of great revolutions. For no sooner had our *learned brother,* so often mentioned, got a warm house of his own over his head than he began to look big, and to take mightily upon him; insomuch that unless the gentle reader, out of his great candour, will please a little to exalt his idea, I am afraid he will henceforth hardly know the *hero* of the play when he happens to meet him, his part, his dress, and his mien being so much altered.

He told his brothers he would have them to know that he was their elder, and consequently his father's sole heir; nay, a while after he would not allow them to call him *brother,* but *Mr. PETER;* and then he must be styled *Father PETER;* and sometimes, *My Lord PETER.*

To support this grandeur, which he soon began to consider could not be maintained without a better *fonde* than what he was born to, after much thought he cast about at last to turn *projector* and *virtuoso,* wherein he so well succeeded that many famous discoveries, projects, and machines, which bear great vogue and practice at present in the world, are owing entirely to Lord Peter's invention. I will deduce the best account I have been able to collect of the chief amongst them, without considering much the order they came out in, because I think authors are not well agreed as to that point.

I hope, when this treatise of mine shall be translated into foreign languages (as I may without vanity affirm that the labour of collecting, the faithfulness in recounting, and the great usefulness of the matter to the public, will amply deserve that justice) that the worthy members of the several *academies* abroad, especially those of France and Italy, will favourably accept these humble offers for the advancement of universal knowledge. I do also advertise the most reverend Fathers the Eastern Missionaries, that I have, purely for their sakes, made use of such words and phrases as will best admit an easy turn into any of the oriental languages, especially the Chinese. And so I proceed with great content of mind, upon reflecting how much emolument this whole globe of the earth is likely to reap by my labours.

The first undertaking of Lord Peter was to purchase a large continent,[62] lately said to have been discovered in *Terra Australis Incognita.* This tract of land he bought at a very great pennyworth from the discoverers themselves (though some pretended to doubt whether they had ever been there), and then retailed it into several cantons to certain dealers, who carried over colonies but were all shipwrecked in the voyage. Upon which Lord Peter sold the said continent to other customers *again,* and *again,* and *again,* and *again,* with the same success.

The second project I shall mention was his sovereign remedy for the *worms,*[63] especially those in the *spleen.* The patient was to eat nothing after supper for three nights:[64] as soon as he went to bed he was carefully to lie on one side, and when he grew weary, to turn upon the other. He must also duly confine his two eyes to the same object, and by no means break wind at both ends together without manifest occasion. These prescriptions diligently observed, the *worms* would void insensibly by perspiration, ascending through the *brain*.

A third invention was the erecting of a *whispering-office*,[65] for the public good and ease of all such as are hypochondriacal, or troubled with the colic; likewise of all eavesdroppers, physicians, midwives, small politicians, friends fallen out, repeating poets, lovers happy or in despair, bawds, privy-councillors, pages, parasites, and buffoons: in short, of all such as are in danger of bursting with too much *wind*. An *ass'* head was placed so conveniently that the party affected might easily with his mouth accost either of the animal's ears; which he was to apply close for a certain space, and by a fugitive faculty, peculiar to the ears of that animal, receive immediate benefit either by eructation, or expiration, or evomition.

Another very beneficial project of Lord Peter's was, an *office of insurance* for tobacco-pipes,[66] martyrs of the modern zeal, volumes of poetry, shadows, —— and rivers: that these, nor any of these, shall receive damage by *fire*. From whence our *friendly societies* may plainly find themselves to be only transcribers from this original, though the one and the other have been of *great* benefit to the undertakers, as well as of *equal* to the public.

Lord Peter was also held the original author of *puppets* and *raree-shows*[67] the great usefulness whereof being so generally known, I shall not enlarge further upon this particular.

But another discovery for which he was much renowned was his famous universal *pickle*.[68] For, having remarked how your common *pickle*,[69] in use among housewives, was of no further benefit than to preserve dead flesh and certain kinds of vegetables, Peter, with great cost as well as art, had contrived a *pickle* proper for houses, gardens, towns, men, women, children, and cattle, wherein he could preserve them as sound as insects in amber. Now, this *pickle* to the taste, the smell, and the sight, appeared exactly the same with what is in common service for beef and butter and herrings (and has been often that way applied with great success); but for its many sovereign virtues, was quite a different thing. For Peter would put in a certain quantity of his *powder pimperlim-pimp*,[70] after which it never failed of success. The operation was performed by *spargefaction* in a proper time of the moon. The patient who was to be *pickled,* if it were a house, would infallibly be preserved from all spiders, rats, and weasels. If the party affected were a dog, he should be exempt from mange, and madness, and hunger. It also infallibly took away all scabs and lice, and scalled heads from children, never hindering the patient from any duty either at bed or board.

But of all Peter's rarities he most valued a certain set of *bulls,*[71] whose race was by great fortune preserved in a lineal descent from those that guarded the *golden fleece.* Though some who pretended to observe them curiously, doubted the breed had not been kept entirely chaste, because they had degenerated from their ancestors in some qualities, and had acquired others very extraordinary, but a foreign mixture. The bulls of Colchos are recorded to have *brazen feet;* but whether it happened by ill pasture and running, by an allay from intervention of other parents, from stolen intrigues; whether a weakness in their progenitors had impaired the seminal virtue, or by a decline necessary through a long course of time, the originals of nature being depraved in these latter sinful ages of the world; whatever was the cause, it is certain that Lord Peter's *bulls* were extremely vitiated by the rust of time in the metal of their feet, which was now sunk into common *lead.* However, the terrible *roaring* peculiar to their lineage, was preserved, as likewise that faculty of breathing out *fire* from their nostrils; which, notwithstanding, many of their detractors took to be a feat of art, and to be nothing so terrible as it appeared, proceeding only from their usual course of diet, which was *of squibs* and *crackers*[72] However, they had two peculiar marks which extremely distinguished them from the bulls of Jason, and which I have not met together in the description of any other monster beside that in Horace—

> *Varias inducere plumas;*
> and
> *Atrum desinit in piscem.*

For these had *fishes' tails,* yet upon occasion could *outfly* any bird in the air. Peter put these *bulls* upon several employs. Sometimes he would set them *a-roaring* to fright *naughty boys*[73] and make them quiet. Sometimes he would send them out upon errands of great importance; where, it is wonderful to recount, and perhaps the cautious reader may think much to believe it, an *appetitus sensibilis* deriving itself through the whole family from their noble ancestors, guardians of *the golden fleece,* they continued so extremely fond of *gold,* that if Peter sent them abroad though it were only upon a compliment, they would *roar,* and *spit,* and *belch, and piss,* and *fart,* and snivel out *fire,* and keep a perpetual coil, till you flung them a bit *of gold;* but then, *pulveris exigui jactu,* they would grow calm and quiet as lambs. In short, whether by secret connivance or encouragement from their master, or out of their own liquorish affection to gold, or both; it is certain they were no better than a sort of sturdy, swaggering beggars; and where they could not prevail to get an alms, would make women miscarry and children fall into fits, who to this day usually call sprites and hobgoblins by the name of *bull-beggars.* They grew at last so very troublesome to the neighbourhood that some gentlemen of the *north-west* got a parcel of right English *bulldogs,* and baited them so terribly that they felt it ever after.

I must needs mention one more of Lord Peter's projects, which was very extraordinary and discovered him to be a master of a high reach and profound invention. Whenever it happened that any rogue of Newgate was condemned to be hanged, Peter would offer him a pardon for a certain sum of money, which when the poor caitiff had made all shifts to scrape up and send, his lordship would return a piece of paper in this form.[74]

To all mayors, sheriffs, jailors, constables, bailiffs, hangmen, &c. Whereas we are informed that A. B. remains in the hands of you, or any of you, under the sentence of death. We will and command you upon sight hereof, to let the said prisoner depart to his own habitation, whether he stands condemned for murder, sodomy, rape, sacrilege, incest, treason, blasphemy, &c., for which this shall be your sufficient warrant. And if you fail hereof, G—d d—mn you and yours to all eternity. And so we bid you heartily farewell.

Your most humble
man's man,
Emperor Peter

The wretches trusting to this, lost their lives and money too.

I desire of those whom the *learned* among posterity will appoint for commentators upon this elaborate treatise, that they will proceed with great caution upon certain dark points wherein all who are not *verè adepti* may be in danger to form rash and hasty conclusions, especially in some mysterious paragraphs where certain *arcana* are joined for brevity sake, which in the operation must be divided. And I am certain that future sons of art will return large thanks to my memory, for so grateful, so useful an *innuendo*.

It will be no difficult part to persuade the reader that so many worthy discoveries met with great success in the world, though I may justly assure him that I have related much the smallest number, my design having been only to single out such as will be of most benefit for public imitation, or which best served to give some idea of the reach and wit of the inventor. And therefore it need not be wondered, if by this time, Lord Peter was become exceeding rich. But alas, he had kept his brain so long and so violently upon the rack, that at last it *shook* itself and began to *turn round* for a little ease. In short, what with pride, projects, and knavery, poor Peter was grown distracted, and conceived the strangest imaginations in the world. In the height of his fits (as it is usual with those who run mad out of pride) he would call himself *God Almighty*,[75] and sometimes *monarch of the universe*. I have seen him (says my author) take three old *high-crowned hats*[76] and clap them all on his head three storey high, with a huge bunch of *keys* at his girdle,[77] and an *angling-rod* in his hand. In which guise, whoever went to take him by the hand in the way of salutation, Peter with much grace, like a well-educated spaniel, would present them with his *foot*;[78] and if they refused his civility then he would raise it as high as their chops, and give them a damned kick on the mouth, which hath ever since been called a *salute*. Whoever walked by without paying him their compliments, having a wonderful strong breath he would blow their hats off into the dirt. Meantime his affairs at home went upside down, and his two brothers had a wretched time; where his first *boutade*[79] was to kick both their *wives* one morning out of doors, and his own too;[80] and in their stead, gave orders to pick up the first three strollers could be met with in the streets. A while after, he nailed up the cellar-door, and would not allow his brothers a drop of *drink* to their victuals.[81] Dining one day at an alderman's in the city, Peter observed him expatiating after the manner of his brethren, in the praises of his sirloin of beef. "Beef," said the sage magistrate, "is the king of meat; beef comprehends in it the quintessence of partridge, and quail, and venison, and pheasant, and plum-pudding, and custard." When Peter came home, he would needs take the fancy of cooking up this doctrine into use and apply the precept, in default of a sirloin, to his brown loaf. "Bread," says he, "dear brothers, is the staff of life; in which bread is contained, *inclusivè,* the quintessence of beef, mutton, veal, venison, partridge, plum-pudding, and custard. And to render all complete, there is intermingled a due quantity of water whose crudities are also corrected by yeast or barm, through which means it becomes a wholesome fermented liquor, diffused through the mass of the bread." Upon the strength of these conclusions, next day at dinner was the brown loaf served up in all the formality of a city feast. "Come, brothers," said Peter, "fall to, and spare not; here is excellent good mutton;[82] or hold, now my hand is in, I'll help you." At which word, in much ceremony, with fork and knife, he carves out two good slices of the loaf and presents each on a plate to his brothers. The elder of the two, not suddenly entering into Lord Peter's conceit, began with very civil language to examine the mystery. "My lord," said he, "I doubt, with great submission, there may be some mistake." "What," says Peter, "you are pleasant; come then, let us hear this jest your head is so big with." "None in the world, my lord, but unless I am very much deceived, your lordship was pleased a while ago to let fall a word about mutton, and I would be glad to see it with all my heart." "How," said Peter, appearing in great surprise, "I do not comprehend this at all." Upon which, the younger interposing to set the business aright, "My lord," said he, "my brother, I suppose, is hungry, and longs for the mutton your lordship hath promised us to dinner." "Pray," said Peter, "take me along with you: either you are both mad, or disposed to be merrier than I approve of. If *you* there do not like your piece I will carve you another, though I should take that to be the choice bit of the whole shoulder." "What then, my lord," replied the first "it seems this is a shoulder of mutton all this while?" "Pray, sir," says Peter, "eat your victuals and leave off your impertinence if you please, for I am not disposed to relish it at present." But the other could not forbear, being over provoked at the affected seriousness of Peter's countenance. "By G—my lord," said he, "I can only say that to my eyes, and fingers, and teeth, and nose, it seems to be nothing but a crust of bread." Upon which the second put in his word, "I never saw a piece of mutton in my life so nearly resembling a slice from a twelve-penny loaf." "Look ye, gentlemen," cries Peter in a rage, "to convince you what a couple of blind, positive, ignorant, willful puppies you are, I will use but this plain argument: By G—it is true, good, natural mutton as any in Leadenhall market, and G— confound you both eternally if you offer to believe otherwise." Such a thundering proof as this left no further room for objection. The two unbelievers began to gather and pocket up their mistake as hastily as they could. "Why, truly," said the first, "upon more mature consideration" — "Ay," says the other, interrupting him, "now I have thought better on the thing, your lordship seems to have a great deal of reason." "Very well," said Peter, "here boy, fill me a beer-glass of claret. Here's to you both, with all my heart." The two brethren, much delighted to see him so readily appeased, returned their most humble thanks and said they would be glad to pledge his lordship. "That you shall," said Peter, "I am not a person to refuse you anything that is reasonable: wine, moderately taken, is a cordial; here is a glass apiece for you; 'tis true natural juice from the grape, none of your damned *vintners'* brewings." Having spoke thus, he presented to each of them another large dry crust, bidding them drink it off and not be bashful, for it would do them no hurt. The two brothers after having performed the usual office in such delicate conjunctures, of staring a sufficient period at Lord Peter and each other, and finding how matters were like to go, resolved not to enter on a new dispute but let him carry the point as he pleased; for he was now got into one of his mad fits, and to argue or expostulate further would only serve to render him a hundred times more untractable.

I have chosen to relate this worthy matter in all its circumstances, because it gave a principal occasion to that great and famous *rupture*[83] which happened about the same time among these brethren, and was never afterwards made up. But of that, I shall treat at large in another section.

However, it is certain that Lord Peter, even in his lucid intervals, was very lewdly given in his common conversation, extreme wilful and positive, and would at anytime rather argue to the death than allow himself once to be in an error. Besides, he had an abominable faculty of telling huge palpable *lies* upon all occasions; and swearing not only to the truth, but cursing the whole company to Hell if they pretended to make the least scruple of believing him. One time he swore he had a *cow*[84] at home, which gave as much milk at a meal as would fill three thousand churches, and what was yet more extraordinary, would never turn sour. Another time he was telling of an old *signpost*[85] that belonged to his *father,* with nails and timber enough on it to build sixteen large men-of-war. Talking one day of Chinese waggons, which were made so light as to sail over mountains: "Z — ds," said Peter, "where's the wonder of that? By G — I saw a large house of lime and stone[86] travell over sea and land (granting that it stopped sometimes to bait) above two thousand German leagues." And that which was the good of it, he would swear desperately all the while that he never told a lie in his life, and at every word, "By G — gentlemen, I tell you nothing but the truth, and the D — l broil them eternally that will not believe me."

In short, Peter grew so scandalous that all the neighbourhood began in plain words to say, he was no better than a knave. And his two brothers, long weary of his ill usage, resolved at last to leave him; but first they humbly desired a copy of their father's *Will,* which had now lain by neglected time out of mind. Instead of granting this request he called them *damned sons of whores, rogues, traitors,* and the rest of the vile names he could muster up. However, while he was abroad one day upon his projects, the two youngsters watched their opportunity, made a shift to come at the *Will*[87] and took a *copia vera,* by which they presently saw how grossly they had been abused; their father having left them equal heirs, and strictly commanded that whatever they got should lie in common among them all. Pursuant to which their next enterprise was to break open the cellar-door, and get a little good *drink*[88] to spirit and comfort their hearts. In copying the *Will* they had met another precept against whoring, divorce, and separate maintenance; upon which their next work[89] was to discard their concubines and send for their wives. While all this was in agitation there enters a solicitor from Newgate, desiring Lord Peter would please procure a *pardon* for a *thief* that was to be *hanged* tomorrow. But the two brothers told him he was a coxcomb to seek pardons from a fellow who deserved to be hanged much better than his client, and discovered all the method of that imposture, in the same form I delivered it a while ago, advising the solicitor to put his friend upon obtaining *a pardon from the king*.[90] In the midst of all this clutter and revolution, in comes Peter with a file of dragoons at his heels,[91] and gathering from all hands what was in the wind, he and his gang, after several millions of scurrilities and curses, not very important here to repeat, by main force very fairly kicks them both out of doors,[92] and would never let them come under his roof from that day to this.

SECT. V

A DIGRESSION IN THE MODERN KIND

We whom the world is pleased to honour with the title of *modern authors* should never have been able to compass our great design of an everlasting remembrance, and never-dying fame, if our endeavours had not been so highly serviceable to the general good of mankind. This, *O Universe*, is the adventurous attempt of me thy secretary;

——*Quemvis perferre laborem*
Suadet, et inducit noctes vigilare serenas.

To this end I have sometime since, with a world of pains and art, dissected the carcass of *human nature* and read many useful lectures upon the several parts, both *containing* and *contained,* till at last it *smelt* so strong I could preserve it no longer. Upon which, I have been at a great expense to fit up all the bones with exact contexture and in due symmetry, so that I am ready to show a complete anatomy thereof to all curious *gentlemen and others.* But not to digress further in the midst of a digression, as I have known some authors enclose digressions in one another, like a nest of boxes, I do affirm that having carefully cut up *human nature,* I have found a very strange, new, and important discovery, that the public good of mankind is performed by two ways, *instruction* and *diversion.* And I have further proved in my said several readings (which perhaps the world may one day see, if I can prevail on any friend to steal a copy, or on certain gentlemen of my admirers to be very importunate) that as mankind is now disposed, he receives much greater advantage by being *diverted* than *instructed;* his epidemical diseases being *fastidiosity, amorphy,* and *oscitation;* whereas, in the present universal empire of wit and learning, there seems but little matter left for *instruction.* However, in compliance with a lesson of great age and authority I have attempted carrying the point in all its heights, and accordingly, throughout this divine treatise, have skilfully kneaded up both together with a layer of *utile* and a layer of *dulce.*

When I consider how exceedingly our illustrious *moderns* have eclipsed the weak glimmering lights of the *ancients* and turned them out of the road of all fashionable commerce, to a degree that our choice town wits,[93] of most refined accomplishments, are in grave dispute whether there have been ever any *ancients* or no (in which point we are like to receive wonderful satisfaction from the most useful labours and lucubrations of that worthy *modern,* Dr. B[e]ntly); I say, when I consider all this I cannot but bewail that no famous *modern* hath ever yet attempted an universal system, in a small portable volume, of all things that are to be known, or believed, or imagined, or practised in life. I am, however, forced to acknowledge that such an enterprize was thought on sometime ago by a great philosopher of *O. Brazile.*[94] The method he proposed was by a certain curious *receipt,* a *nostrum,* which after his untimely death I found among his papers, and do here, out of my great affection to the *modern learned,* present them with it, not doubting it may one day encourage some worthy undertaker.

You take fair correct copies, well bound in calfskin, and lettered at the back, of all modern bodies of arts and sciences whatsoever, and in what language you please. These you distil in balneo Mariæ, *infusing* quintessence of poppy Q.S., *together with three pints of* Lethe, *to be had from the apothecaries. You cleanse away carefully the* sordes *and* caput mortuum, *letting all that is volatile evaporate. You preserve only the first running, which is again to be distilled seventeen times, till what remains will amount to about two drams. This you keep in a glass vial,* hermetically *sealed, for one and twenty days. Then you begin your Catholic treatise, taking every morning fasting (first shaking the vial) three drops of this* elixir, *snuffing it strongly up your nose. It will dilate itself about the brain (where there is any) in fourteen minutes, and you immediately perceive in your head an infinite number of* abstracts, summaries, compendiums, extracts, collections, medullas, excerpta quædams, florilegias, *and the like, all disposed into great order, and reducible upon paper.*

I must needs own it was by the assistance of this *arcanum* that I, though otherwise *impar,* have adventured upon so daring an attempt, never achieved or undertaken before but by a certain author called Homer, in whom, though otherwise a person not without some abilities and, *for an ancient,* of a tolerable genius, I have discovered many gross errors which are not to be forgiven his very ashes, if by chance any of them are left. For whereas we are assured he designed his work for a complete body of all knowledge,[95] human, divine, political, and mechanic, it is manifest he hath wholly neglected some, and been very imperfect in the rest. For first of all, as eminent a *cabalist* as his disciples would represent him, his account of the *opus magnum* is extremely poor and deficient; he seems to have read but very superficially either Sendivogius, Behmen, or *Anthroposophia Theomagica.*[96] He is also quite mistaken about the *sphæra pyroplastica,* a neglect not to be atoned for, and (if the reader will admit so severe a censure) *vix crederem autorem hunc, unquam audivisse ignis vocem.* His failings are not less prominent in several parts of the *mechanics.* For, having read his writings with the utmost application usual among *modern wits,* I could never yet discover the least direction about the structure of that useful instrument, a *save-all.* For want of which, if the *moderns* had not lent their assistance, we might yet have wandered *in the dark.* But I have still behind a fault far more notorious to tax the author with; I mean, his gross ignorance[97] in the *common laws of this realm,* and in the doctrine as well as discipline of the Church of England. A defect, indeed, for which both he and all the ancients stand most justly censured by my worthy and ingenious friend Mr. W[o]tt[o]n, Bachelor of Divinity, in his incomparable treatise of *Ancient and Modern Learning:*

a book never to be sufficiently valued, whether we consider the happy turns and flowings of the author's wit, the great usefulness of his sublime discoveries upon the subject of *flies* and *spittle,* or the laborious eloquence of his style. And I cannot forbear doing that author the justice of my public acknowledgments for the great *helps* and *liftings* I had out of his incomparable piece while I was penning this treatise.

But, besides these omissions in Homer already mentioned, the curious reader will also observe several defects in that author's writings for which he is not altogether so accountable. For whereas every branch of knowledge has received such wonderful acquirements since his age, especially within these last three years or thereabouts, it is almost impossible he could be so very perfect in modern discoveries as his advocates pretend. We freely acknowledge him to be the inventor of the *compass, of gunpowder,* and the *circulation of the blood*: but I challenge any of his admirers to show me in all his writings, a complete account of the *spleen.* Does he not also leave us wholly to seek in the art *of political wagering?* What can be more defective and unsatisfactory than his long dissertation upon *tea?* And as to his method of *salivation without mercury,* so much celebrated of late, it is to my own knowledge and experience a thing very little to be relied on.

It was to supply such momentous defects that I have been prevailed on, after long solicitation, to take pen in hand; and I dare venture to promise the judicious reader shall find nothing neglected here that can be of use upon any emergency of life. I am confident to have included and exhausted all that human imagination can *rise or fall* to. Particularly, I recommend to the perusal of the learned, certain discoveries that are wholly untouched by others, whereof I shall only mention among a great many more, my *New Help* [*for*] *Smatterers,* or the *Art of being Deep-learned and Shallow-read; A Curious Invention about Mouse-Traps; An Universal Rule of Reason, or every Man his own Carver;* together with a most useful engine for *catching of owls.* All which, the judicious reader will find largely treated on, in the several parts of this discourse.

I hold myself obliged to give as much light as is possible into the beauties and excellencies of what I am writing, because it is become the fashion and humour most applauded among the first authors of this polite and learned age, when they would correct the ill nature of critical, or inform the ignorance of courteous readers. Besides, there have been several famous pieces lately published both in verse and prose, wherein if the writers had not been pleased, out of their great humanity and affection to the public, to give us a nice detail of the *sublime* and the *admirable* they contain, it is a thousand to one whether we should ever have discovered one grain of either. For my own particular, I cannot deny that whatever I have said upon this occasion had been more proper in a preface, and more agreeable to the mode which usually directs it there. But I here think fit to lay hold on that great and honourable privilege, of being the *last writer.* I claim an absolute authority in right, as the *freshest modern,* which gives me a despotic power over all authors before me. In the strength of which title I do utterly disapprove and declare against that pernicious custom of making the preface a bill of fare to the book. For I have always looked upon it as a high point of indiscretion in *monster-mongers* and other *retailers of strange sights,* to hang out a fair large picture over the door, drawn after the life with a most eloquent description underneath. This hath saved me many a threepence, for my curiosity was fully satisfied and I never offered to go in, though often invited by the urging and attending orator with his last *moving* and *standing* piece of rhetoric, "Sir, upon my word, we are just going to begin." Such is exactly the fate at this time of Prefaces, Epistles, Advertisements, Introductions, Prolegomenas, Apparatuses, To the Reader's. This expedient was admirable at first. Our great Dryden has long carried it as far as it would go, and with incredible success. He has often said to me in confidence that the world would have never suspected him to be so great a poet, if he had not assured them so frequently in his Prefaces that it was impossible they could either doubt or forget it. Perhaps it may be so. However, I much fear his instructions have edified out of their place, and taught men to grow wiser in certain points where he never intended they should; for it is lamentable to behold with what a lazy scorn many of the yawning readers in our age do nowadays twirl over forty or fifty pages *of preface* and *dedication* (which is the usual *modern* stint) as if it were so much Latin. Though it must be also allowed on the other hand, that a very considerable number is known to proceed *critics* and *wits* by reading nothing else. Into which two factions, I think, all present readers may justly be divided. Now, for myself, I profess to be of the former sort; and therefore, having the *modern* inclination to expatiate upon the beauty of my own productions and display the bright parts of my discourse, I thought best to do it in the body of the work, where, as it now lies, it makes a very considerable addition to the bulk of the volume, *a circumstance by no means to be neglected by a skilful writer.*

Having thus paid my due deference and acknowledgment to an established custom of our newest authors, by *a long digression unsought for,* and *an universal censure unprovoked,* by forcing into the light, with much pains and and dexterity, my own excellencies and other men's defaults, with great justice to myself and candour to them, I now happily resume my subject, to the infinite satisfaction both of the reader and the author.

SECT. VI

A TALE OF A TUB

We left Lord Peter in open rupture with his two brethren, both forever discarded from his house and resigned to the wide world, with little or nothing to trust to; which are circumstances that render them proper subjects for the charity of a writer's pen to work on, scenes of misery ever affording the fairest harvest for great adventures. And in this, the world may perceive the difference between the integrity of a generous author and that of a common friend. The latter is observed to adhere close in prosperity but on the decline of fortune, to drop suddenly off. Whereas the generous author, just on the contrary, finds his hero on the dunghill, from thence by gradual steps raises him to a throne, and then immediately withdraws, expecting not so much as thanks for his pains. In imitation of which example I have placed Lord Peter in a noble house, given him a title to wear, and money to spend. There I shall leave him for sometime, returning where common charity directs me, to the assistance of his two brothers at their lowest ebb. However, I shall by no means forget my character of an historian to follow the truth step by step, whatever happens or wherever it may lead me.

The two exiles, so nearly united in fortune and interest, took a lodging together, where, at their first leisure, they began to reflect on the numberless misfortunes and vexations of their life past, and could not tell on the sudden to what failure in their conduct they ought to impute them, when, after some recollection, they called to mind the copy of their father's Will which they had so happily recovered. This was immediately produced, and a firm resolution taken between them to alter whatever was already amiss, and reduce all their future measures to the strictest obedience prescribed therein. The main body of the Will (as the reader cannot easily have forgot) consisted in certain admirable rules about the wearing of their coats, in the perusal whereof the two brothers, at every period, duly comparing the doctrine with the practice, there was never seen a wider difference between two things, horrible downright transgressions of every point. Upon which they both resolved, without further delay, to fall immediately upon reducing the whole, exactly after their father's model.

But here it is good to stop the hasty reader, ever impatient to see the end of an adventure before we writers can duly prepare him for it. I am to record that these two brothers began to be distinguished at this time by certain names. One of them desired to be called *MARTIN*,[98] and the other took the appellation of *JACK*.[99] These two had lived in much friendship and agreement under the tyranny of their brother Peter, as it is the talent of fellow-sufferers to do; men in misfortune being like men in the dark, to whom all colours are the same. But when they came forward into the world and began to display themselves to each other and to the light, their complexions appeared extremely different, which the present posture of their affairs gave them sudden opportunity to discover.

But, here the severe reader may justly tax me as a writer of short memory, a deficiency to which a true *modern* cannot but, of necessity, be a little subject. Because, *memory* being an employment of the mind upon things past, is a faculty for which the learned in our illustrious age have no manner of occasion, who deal entirely with *invention*, and strike all things out of themselves, or at least by collision from each other; upon which account, we think it highly reasonable to produce our great forgetfulness as an argument unanswerable for our great wit. I ought in method to have informed the reader, about fifty pages ago, of a fancy Lord Peter took, and infused into his brothers, to wear on their coats whatever trimmings came up in fashion; never pulling off any, as they went out of the mode, but keeping on all together, which amounted in time to a medley the most antic you can possibly conceive, and this to a degree that upon the time of their falling out there was hardly a thread of the original coat to be seen, but an infinite quantity of *lace* and *ribbons,* and *fringe,* and *embroidery,* and *points* (I mean only those *tagged with silver,*[100] for the rest fell off). Now this material circumstance having been forgot in due place, as good fortune hath ordered, comes in very properly here, when the two brothers are just going to reform their vestures into the primitive state, prescribed by their father's Will.

They both unanimously entered upon this great work, looking sometimes on their coats and sometimes on the Will. Martin laid the first hand; at one twitch brought off a large handful of *points;* and with a second pull, stripped away ten dozen yards *of fringe.* But when he had gone thus far he demurred a while. He knew very well there yet remained a great deal more to be done; however, the first heat being over, his violence began to cool, and he resolved to proceed more moderately in the rest of the work; having already narrowly scaped a swingeing rent in pulling off the *points,* which being *tagged with silver* (as we have observed before) the judicious workman had, with much sagacity, double sewn to preserve them from *falling.* Resolving therefore to rid his coat of a great quantity of *gold lace,* he picked up the stitches with much caution, and diligently gleaned out all the loose threads as he went, which proved to be a work of time. Then he fell about the embroidered Indian figures of men, women, and children, against which, as you have heard in its due place, their father's testament was extremely exact and severe: these, with much dexterity and application, were after a while quite eradicated, or utterly defaced. For the rest, where he observed the embroidery to be worked so close as not to be got away without damaging the cloth, or where it served to hide or strengthen any flaw in the body of the coat contracted by the perpetual tampering of workmen upon it, he concluded the wisest course was to let it remain, resolving in no case whatsoever that the substance of the stuff should suffer injury; which he thought the best method for serving the true intent and meaning of his father's Will. And this is the nearest account I have been able to collect of Martin's proceedings upon this great revolution.

But his brother Jack, whose adventures will be so extraordinary as to furnish a great part in the remainder of this discourse, entered upon the matter with other thoughts and a quite different spirit. For the memory of Lord Peter's injuries produced a degree of hatred and spite which had a much greater share of inciting him, than any regards after his father's commands, since these appeared at best only secondary and subservient to the other. However, for this medley of humour he made a shift to find a very plausible name, honouring it with the title *of zeal;* which is perhaps the most significant word that hath been ever yet produced in any language, as I think I have fully proved in my excellent *analytical* discourse upon that subject, wherein I have deduced a *histori-theo-physilogical* account *of zeal,* showing how it first proceeded from a *notion* into a *word,* and thence, in a hot summer, ripened into a *tangible substance.* This work, containing three large volumes in folio, I design very shortly to publish by the *modern* way of *subscription,* not doubting but the nobility and gentry of the land will give me all possible encouragement, having already had such a taste of what I am able to perform.

I record, therefore, that brother Jack, brimful of this miraculous compound, reflecting with indignation upon Peter's tyranny, and further provoked by the despondency of Martin, prefaced his resolutions to this purpose. "What!" said he, "a rogue that locked up his drink, turned away our wives, cheated us of our fortunes; palmed his damned crusts upon us for mutton; and, at last, kicked us out of doors; must we be in his fashions, with a pox? A rascal, besides, that all the street cries out against." Having thus kindled and inflamed himself as high as possible, and by consequence in a delicate temper for beginning a reformation, he set about the work immediately, and in three minutes made more dispatch than Martin had done in as many hours. For (courteous reader) you are given to understand, that *zeal* is never so highly obliged as when you set it a-*tearing*; and Jack, who doated on that quality in himself, allowed it at this time its full swinge. Thus it happened that, stripping down a parcel of *gold lace* a little too hastily, he rent the *main body* of his *coat* from top to bottom; and whereas his talent was not of the happiest in *taking up a stitch,* he knew no better way than to darn it again with *packthread* and a *skewer.* But the matter was yet infinitely worse (I record it with tears) when he proceeded to the *embroidery:* for being clumsy by nature, and of temper impatient; withal, beholding millions of stitches that required the nicest hand, and sedatest constitution, to extricate; in a great rage he tore off the whole piece, cloth and all, and flung them into the kennel, and furiously thus continuing his career: "Ah, good brother Martin," said he, "do as I do, for the love of God; strip, tear, pull, rend, flay off all, that we may appear as unlike the rogue Peter as it is possible. I would not for a hundred pounds carry the least mark about me, that might give occasion to the neighbours of suspecting that I was related to such a rascal." But Martin, who at this time happened to be extremely phlegmatic and sedate, begged his brother, of all love, not to damage his coat by any means; for he never would get such another: desired him to consider that it was not their business to form their actions by any reflection upon Peter's, but by observing the rules prescribed in their father's Will. That he should remember Peter was still their brother, whatever faults or injuries he had committed, and therefore they should, by all means, avoid such a thought as that of taking measures for good and evil, from no other rule than of opposition to him. That it was true, the testament of their good father was very exact in what related to the wearing of their *coats;* yet it was no less penal, and strict, in prescribing agreement and friendship and affection between them. And therefore, if straining a point were at all dispensible, it would certainly be so rather to the advance of unity, than increase of contradiction.

Martin had still proceeded as gravely as he began, and doubtless would have delivered an admirable lecture of morality, which might have exceedingly contributed to my reader's *repose both of body and mind* (the true ultimate end of *ethics);* but Jack was already gone a flight-shot beyond his patience. And as in scholastic disputes nothing serves to rouse the spleen of him that *opposes,* so much as a kind of pedantic affected calmness in the *respondent;* disputants being for the most part like unequal scales, where the *gravity* of one side advances the *lightness* of the other, and causes it to fly up and kick the beam; so it happened here that the *weight* of Martin's argument exalted Jack's *levity,* and made him fly out and spurn against his brother's moderation. In short, Martin's *patience* put Jack in a *rage;* but that which most afflicted him was to observe his brother's coat so well reduced into the state of innocence, while his own was either wholly rent to his shirt, or those places which had scaped his cruel clutches were still in Peter's livery. So that he looked like a drunken *beau,* half rifled by bullies; or like a fresh tenant of Newgate when he has refused the payment of *garnish*; or like a discovered *shoplifter,* left to the mercy of *Exchange-women*; or like a *bawd* in her old velvet petticoat, resigned into the secular hands of the *mobile.* Like any or like all of these, a medley of *rags,* and *lace,* and *rents,* and *fringes,* unfortunate Jack did now appear: he would have been extremely glad to see his coat in the condition of Martin's, but infinitely gladder to find that of Martin in the same predicament with his. However, since neither of these was likely to come to pass he thought fit to lend the whole business another turn, and to dress up necessity into a virtue. Therefore, after as many of the *fox's* arguments as he could muster up for bringing Martin to *reason,* as he called it; or as he meant it, into his own ragged, bobtailed condition; and observing he said all to little purpose; what, alas! Was left for the forlorn Jack to do, but after a million of scurrilities against his brother, to run mad with spleen, and spite, and contradiction. To be short, here began a mortal breach between these two. Jack went immediately to *new lodgings,* and in a few days it was for certain reported that he had run out of his wits. In a short time after, he appeared abroad and confirmed the report by falling into the oddest whimseys that ever a sick brain conceived.

And now the little boys in the streets began to salute him with several names. Sometimes they would call him Jack the Bald;[101] sometimes, Jack with a Lantern;[102] sometimes, Dutch Jack;[103] sometimes, French Hugh;[104] sometimes, Tom the Beggar;[105] and sometimes, Knocking Jack of the North.[106] And it was under one, or some, or all of these appellations (which I leave the learned reader to determine) that he hath given rise to the most illustrious and epidemic sect of

Æolists, who, with honourable commemoration, do still acknowledge the renowned *JACK* for their author and founder. Of whose original, as well as principles, I am now advancing to gratify the world with a very particular account.

—*Mellæo contingens cuncta Lepore.*

SECT. VII

A DIGRESSION IN PRAISE OF DIGRESSIONS

I have sometimes *heard* of an Iliad in a *nutshell,* but it hath been my fortune to have much oftener *seen* a *nutshell* in an Iliad. There is no doubt that human life has received most wonderful advantages from both; but to which of the two the world is chiefly indebted, I shall leave among the curious as a problem worthy of their utmost inquiry. For the invention of the latter, I think the commonwealth of learning is chiefly obliged to the great *modern* improvement of *digressions:* the late refinements in knowledge running parallel to those of diet in our nation, which among men of a judicious taste are dressed up in various compounds, consisting in *soups* and *olios, fricassees,* and *ragouts.*

'Tis true there is a sort of morose, detracting, ill-bred people, who pretend utterly to disrelish these polite innovations; and as to the similitude from diet, they allow the parallel but are so bold to pronounce the example itself a corruption and degeneracy of taste. They tell us that the fashion of jumbling fifty things together in a dish was at first introduced in compliance to a depraved and *debauched appetite,* as well as to a *crazy constitution:* and to see a man hunting through an *olio* after the *head* and *brains* of a *goose,* a *widgeon,* or a *woodcock,* is a sign he wants a stomach and digestion for more substantial victuals. Further, they affirm that *digressions* in a book are like *foreign troops* in a *state,* which argue the nation to want a *heart* and *hands* of its own, and often either *subdue* the *natives* or drive them into the most *unfruitful corners.*

But, after all that can be objected by these supercilious censors, 'tis manifest the society of writers would quickly be reduced to a very inconsiderable number, if men were put upon making books with the fatal confinement of delivering nothing beyond what is to the purpose.

'Tis acknowledged that were the case the same among us as with the Greeks and Romans, when learning was in its *cradle,* to be reared and fed and clothed by *invention,* it would be an easy task to fill up volumes upon particular occasions, without further expatiating from the subject than by moderate excursions, helping to advance or clear the main design. But with *knowledge* it has fared as with a numerous army encamped in a fruitful country, which for a few days maintains itself by the product of the soil it is on; till provisions being spent, they are sent to forage many a mile, among friends or enemies it matters not. Meanwhile the neighbouring fields, trampled and beaten down, become barren and dry, affording no sustenance but clouds of dust.

The whole course of things being thus entirely changed between *us* and the *ancients,* and the *moderns* wisely sensible of it, we of this age have discovered a shorter and more prudent method to become *scholars* and *wits,* without the fatigue of *reading* or of *thinking.* The most accomplished way of using books at present is two-fold; either first, to serve them as some men do *lords,* learn their *titles* exactly and then brag of their acquaintance. Or secondly, which is indeed the choicer, the profounder, and politer method, to get a thorough insight into the *index,* by which the whole book is governed and turned, like *fishes* by the *tail.* For, to enter the palace of learning at the *great gate* requires an expense of time and forms; therefore men of much haste and little ceremony are content to get in by the *back door.* For the arts are all in a *flying* march, and therefore more easily subdued by attacking them in the *rear.* Thus physicians discover the state of the whole body by consulting only what comes from *behind.* Thus men catch knowledge by throwing their *wit* on the *posteriors* of a book, as boys do sparrows with flinging *salt* upon their *tails.* Thus human life is best understood by the wise man's rule, of *regarding the end.* Thus are the sciences found like Hercules' oxen, by *tracing them backwards.* Thus are *old sciences* unravelled like *old stockings,* by beginning at the *foot.*

Besides all this, the army of the sciences hath been of late, with a world of martial discipline, drawn into its *close order,* so that a view or a muster may be taken of it with abundance of expedition. For this great blessing we are wholly indebted to *systems* and *abstracts,* in which the *modern* fathers of learning, like prudent usurers, spent their sweat for the ease of us their children. For *labour* is the seed of *idleness,* and it is the peculiar happiness of our noble age to gather the *fruit.*

Now, the method of growing wise, learned, and *sublime,* having become so regular an affair, and so established in all its forms, the number of writers must needs have increased accordingly, and to a pitch that has made it of absolute necessity for them to interfere continually with each other. Besides, it is reckoned that there is not at this present a sufficient quantity of new matter left in nature to furnish and adorn anyone particular subject to the extent of a volume. This I am told by a very skilful *computer,* who hath given a full demonstration of it from rules of *arithmetic.*

This, perhaps, may be objected against by those who maintain the infinity of matter, and therefore will not allow that any *species* of it can be exhausted. For answer to which, let us examine the noblest branch of *modern* wit or invention planted and cultivated by the present age, and which of all others hath borne the most and the fairest fruit. For though some remains of it were left us by the *ancients,* yet have not any of those, as I remember, been translated or compiled into systems for *modern* use. Therefore we may affirm to our own honour, that it has, in some sort, been both invented and brought to perfection by the same hands. What I mean is that highly celebrated talent among the *modern* wits, of deducing similitudes, allusions, and applications, very surprising, agreeable, and apposite, from the *pudenda* of either sex, together with *their proper uses.* And truly, having observed how little invention bears any vogue besides what is derived into these *channels,* I have sometimes had a thought that the happy genius of our age and country was prophetically held forth by that ancient typical description of the Indian pigmies,[107] *whose stature did not exceed above two foot; sed quorum pudenda crassa, et ad talos usque pertingentia.* Now, I have been very curious to inspect the late productions wherein the beauties of this kind have most prominently appeared. And although this *vein* hath bled so freely, and all endeavours have been used in the power of human breath to dilate, extend, and keep it open; like the Scythians,[108] *who had a custom, and an instrument, to blow up the privities of their mares, that they might yield the more milk*; yet I am under an apprehension it is near growing dry, and past all recovery, and that either some new *fonde* of wit should if possible be provided, or else that we must even be content with repetition here, as well as upon all other occasions.

This will stand as an uncontestable argument that our *modern* wits are not to reckon upon the infinity of matter for a constant supply. What remains therefore but that our last recourse must be had to large *indexes,* and little *compendiums? Quotations* must be plentifully gathered and booked in alphabet; to this end, though authors need be little consulted, yet *critics,* and *commentators,* and *lexicons,* carefully must. But above all, those judicious collectors of *bright parts,* and *flowers,* and *observandas,* are to be nicely dwelt on, by some called the *sieves* and *boulters* of learning, though it is left undetermined whether they dealt in *pearls* or meal, and consequently, whether we are more to value that which *passed through,* or what *stayed behind.*

By these methods, in a few weeks, there starts up many a writer capable of managing the profoundest and most universal subjects. For, what though his *head* be empty provided his *commonplace book* be full, and if you will bate him but the circumstances of *method,* and *style,* and *grammar,* and *invention*; allow him but the common privileges of transcribing from others and digressing from himself as often as he shall see occasion; he will desire no more ingredients towards fitting up a treatise that shall make a very comely figure on a bookseller's shelf; there to be preserved neat and clean for a long eternity, adorned with the heraldry of its title fairly inscribed on a label; never to be thumbed or greased by students nor bound to everlasting chains of darkness in a library: but, when the fulness of time is come, shall haply undergo the trial of purgatory in order *to ascend the sky.*

Without these allowances, how is it possible we *modern* wits should ever have an opportunity to introduce our collections, listed under so many thousand heads of a different nature; for want of which, the learned world would be deprived of infinite delight as well as instruction, and we ourselves buried beyond redress in an inglorious and undistinguished oblivion?

From such elements as these, I am alive to behold the day wherein the corporation of authors can outvie all its brethren in the *guild.* A happiness derived to us with a great many others from our Scythian ancestors, among whom the number of *pens* was so infinite that the

Grecian[109] eloquence had no other way of expressing it, than by saying that in the regions far to the *north,* it was hardly possible for a man to travell, the very air was so replete with *feathers.*

The necessity of this digression will easily excuse the length, and I have chosen for it as proper a place as I could readily find. If the judicious reader can assign a fitter, I do here impower him to remove it into any other corner he please. And so I return with great alacrity, to pursue a more important concern.

SECT. VIII

A TALE OF A TUB

The learned Æolists[110] maintain the original cause of all things to be *wind,* from which principle this whole universe was at first produced and into which it must at last be resolved; that the same breath which had kindled and blew *up* the flame of nature, should one day blow it *out.*

Quod procul à nobis flectat fortuna gubernans.

This is what the *adepti* understand by their *anima mundi*; that is to say, the *spirit,* or *breath,* or *wind* of the world; or examine the whole system by the particulars of nature, and you will find it not to be disputed. For whether you please to call the *forma informans* of man by the name of *spiritus, animus, afflatus,* or *anima,* what are all these but several appellations for *mind,* which is the ruling *element* in every compound and into which they all resolve upon their corruption? Further, what is life itself, but as it is commonly called, the *breath* of our nostrils? Whence it is very justly observed by naturalists that *wind* still continues of great emolument in *certain mysteries* not to be named, giving occasion for those happy epithets of *turgidus* and *inflatus,* applied either to the *emittent* or *recipient* organs.

By what I have gathered out of ancient records I find the *compass* of their doctrine took in two and thirty points, wherein it would be tedious to be very particular. However, a few of their most important precepts, deducible from it, are by no means to be omitted, among which the following maxim was of much weight: That since *wind* had the master share as well as operation in every compound, by consequence those beings must be of chief excellence wherein that *primordium* appears most prominently to abound, and therefore *man* is in the highest perfection of all created things, as having, by the great bounty of philosophers, been endued with three distinct *animas* or *winds,* to which the sage Æolists with much liberality have added a fourth of equal necessity as well as ornament with the other three, by this *quartum principium* taking in the four corners of the world. Which gave occasion to that renowned *cabalist Bumbastus,*[111] of placing the body of man in due position to the four *cardinal* points.

In consequence of this, their next principle was that *man* brings with him into the world a peculiar portion or grain of *wind,* which may be called a *quinta essentia,* extracted from the other four. This *quintessence* is of a catholic use upon all emergencies of life, is improveable into all arts and sciences, and may be wonderfully refined as well as enlarged, by certain methods in education. This, when *blown* up to its perfection, ought not to be covetously hoarded up, stifled, or hid under a bushel, but freely communicated to mankind. Upon these reasons and others of equal weight, the wise Æolists affirm the gift of BELCHING to be the noblest act of a rational creature. To cultivate which art and render it more serviceable to mankind, they made use of several methods. At certain seasons of the year, you might behold the priests amongst them, in vast numbers, with their *mouths*[112] *gaping wide against a storm.* At other times were to be seen several hundreds linked together in a circular chain, with every man a pair of bellows applied to his neighbour's breech, by which they blew up each other to the shape and size of a *tun*; and for that reason, with great propriety of speech, did usually call their bodies, their *vessels.* When by these and the like performances they were grown sufficiently replete, they would immediately depart, and disembogue for the public good a plentiful share of their acquirements into their disciples' chaps. For we must here observe that all learning was esteemed among them to be compounded from the same principle. Because first, it is generally affirmed, or confessed, that learning *puffeth men up*; and secondly, they proved it by the following syllogism: *Words are but wind; and learning is nothing but words*; ergo, *learning is nothing but wind.* For this reason, the philosophers among them did in their schools deliver to their pupils all their doctrines and opinions by *eructation,* wherein they had acquired a wonderful eloquence, and of incredible variety. But the great characteristic by which their chief sages were best distinguished, was a certain position of countenance, which gave undoubted intelligence to what degree or proportion the spirit agitated the inward mass. For, after certain gripings, the *wind* and vapours issuing forth, having first by their turbulence and convulsions within caused an earthquake in man's little world, distorted the mouth, bloated the cheeks, and gave the eyes a terrible kind of *relievo.* At which junctures all their *belches* were received for sacred, the sourer the better, and swallowed with infinite consolation by their meagre devotees. And to render these yet more complete, because the breath of man's life is in his nostrils, therefore the choicest, most edifying, and most enlivening *belches,* were very wisely conveyed through that vehicle to give them a tincture as they passed.

Their gods were the four *winds,* whom they worshipped as the spirits that pervade and enliven the universe, and as those from whom alone all *inspiration* can properly be said to proceed. However, the chief of these, to whom they performed the adoration of *latria,* was the *almighty North,* an ancient deity whom the inhabitants of Megalopolis, in Greece, had likewise in highest reverence: *omnium deorum Boream maxime celebrant.*[113] This god, though endued with ubiquity, was yet supposed by the profounder Æolists to possess one peculiar habitation, or (to speak in form) a *cœlum empyræum,* wherein he was more intimately present. This was situated in a certain region well known to the ancient Greeks, by them called Σχοτία, or the *Land of Darkness.* And although many controversies have arisen upon that matter, yet so much is undisputed that from a region of the *like denomination* the most refined Æolists have borrowed their original, from whence, in every age, the zealous among their priesthood have brought over their choicest *inspiration,* fetching it with their own hands from the fountainhead in certain *bladders,* and disploding it among the sectaries in all nations, who did, and do, and ever will, daily gasp and pant after it.

Now, their mysteries and rites were performed in this manner. 'Tis well known among the learned that the virtuosos of former ages had a contrivance for carrying and preserving *winds* in casks or barrels, which was of great assistance upon long sea voyages, and the loss of so useful an art at present is very much to be lamented though, I know not how, with great negligence omitted by Pancirollus.[114] It was an invention ascribed to Æolus himself, from whom this sect is denominated, and who, in honour of their founder's memory, have to this day preserved great numbers of those *barrels,* whereof they fix one in each of their temples, first beating out the top; into this *barrel,* upon solemn days, the priest enters, where having before duly prepared himself by the methods already described a secret funnel is also conveyed from his posteriors to the bottom of the barrel, which admits new supplies of inspiration, from a *northern* chink or cranny. Whereupon, you behold him swell immediately to the shape and size of his *vessel.* In this posture he disembogues whole tempests upon his auditory, as the spirit from beneath gives him utterance, which issuing *ex adytis* and *penetralibus,* is not performed without much pain and gripings. And the wind in breaking forth deals with his face[115] as it does with that of the sea, first *blackening,* then *wrinkling,* and at last *bursting it into a foam.* It is in this guise the sacred Æolist delivers his oracular *belches* to his panting disciples; of whom some are greedily gaping after the sanctified breath, others are all the while hymning out the praises of the *winds,* and, gently wafted to and fro by their own humming, do thus represent the soft breezes of their deities appeased.

It is from this custom of the priests that some authors maintain these Æolists to have been very ancient in the world; because the delivery of their mysteries, which I have just now mentioned, appears exactly the same with that of other ancient oracles whose inspirations were owing to certain subterraneous *effluviums* of *wind,* delivered with the *same* pain to the priest and much about the *same* influence on the people. It is true indeed, that these were frequently managed and directed by *female* officers, whose organs were understood to be better disposed for the admission of those oracular *gusts,* as entering and passing up through a receptacle of greater capacity, and causing also a pruriency by the way, such as with due management hath been refined from a carnal into a spiritual ecstasy. And, to strengthen this profound conjecture, it is further insisted that this custom of *female* priests[116] is kept up still in certain refined colleges of our *modern* Æolists, who are agreed to receive their inspiration, derived through the receptacle aforesaid, like their ancestors the Sybils.

And whereas the mind of man, when he gives the spur and bridle to his thoughts, doth never stop but naturally sallies out into both extremes of high and low, of good and evil, his first flight of fancy commonly transports him to ideas of what is most perfect, finished, and exalted; till, having soared out of his own reach and sight, not well perceiving how near the frontiers of height and depth border upon each other; with the same course and wing he falls down plumb into the lowest bottom of things, like one who travells the *East* into the *West,* or like a straight line drawn by its own length into a circle. Whether a tincture of malice in our natures makes us fond of furnishing every bright idea with its reverse; or whether reason, reflecting upon the sum of things, can like the sun serve only to enlighten one half of the globe, leaving the other half by necessity under shade and darkness; or whether fancy, flying up to the imagination of what is highest and best, becomes overshot, and spent, and weary, and suddenly falls like a dead bird of paradise to the ground; or whether, after all these *metaphysical* conjectures, I have not entirely missed the true reason; the proposition however which hath stood me in so much circumstance is altogether true; that, as the most uncivilized parts of mankind have some way or other climbed up into the conception of a *God* or Supreme Power, so they have seldom forgot to provide their fears with certain ghastly notions, which instead of better have served them pretty tolerably for a *devil.* And this proceeding seems to be natural enough; for it is with men whose imaginations are lifted up very high, after the same rate as with those whose bodies are so; that, as they are delighted with the advantage of a nearer contemplation upwards, so they are equally terrified with the dismal prospect of the precipice below. Thus, in the choice of a *devil,* it hath been the usual method of mankind to single out some being, either in act or in vision, which was in most antipathy to the god they had framed. Thus also the sect of Æolists possessed themselves with a dread and horror and hatred of two malignant natures, betwixt whom and the deities they adored, perpetual enmity was established. The first of these was the *chameleon*[117] sworn foe to *inspiration,* who in scorn devored large influences of their god without refunding the smallest blast by *eructation.* The other was a huge terrible monster called Moulinavent, who with four strong arms waged eternal battle with all their divinities, dexterously turning to avoid their blows and repay them with interest.

Thus furnished, and set out with *gods* as well as *devils,* was the renowned sect of Æolists, which makes at this day so illustrious a figure in the world, and whereof that polite nation of Laplanders are, beyond all doubt, a most authentic branch; of whom I therefore cannot without injustice here omit to make honourable mention, since they appear to be so closely allied in point of interest as well as inclinations with their brother Æolists among us, as not only to buy their *winds* by wholesale from the *same* merchants, but also to retail them after the *same* rate and method, and to customers much alike.

Now, whether the system here delivered was wholly compiled by Jack, or as some writers believe, rather copied from the original at Delphos, with certain additions and emendations suited to times and circumstances; I shall not absolutely determine. This I may affirm, that Jack gave it at least a new turn, and formed it into the same dress and model as it lies deduced by me.

I have long sought after this opportunity of doing justice to a society of men for whom I have a peculiar honour; and whose opinions, as well as practices, have been extremely misrepresented and traduced by the malice or ignorance of their adversaries. For I think it one of the greatest and best of human actions, to remove prejudices and place things in their truest and fairest light; which I therefore boldly undertake without any regards of my own, beside the conscience, the honour, and the thanks.

SECT. IX

A DIGRESSION CONCERNING THE ORIGINAL, THE USE, AND IMPROVEMENT OF MADNESS IN A COMMONWEALTH

Nor shall it anyways detract from the just reputation of this famous sect, that its rise and institution are owing to such an author as I have described Jack to be: a person whose intellectuals were overturned, and his brain shaken out of its natural position, which we commonly suppose to be a distemper and call by the name of *madness or frenzy*. For, if we take a survey of the greatest actions that have been performed in the world under the influence of single men, which are *the establishment of new empires by conquest, the advance and progress of new schemes in philosophy, and the contriving, as well as the propagating, of new religions*; we shall find the authors of them all to have been persons whose natural reason hath admitted great revolutions, from their diet, their education, the prevalency of some certain temper, together with the particular influence of air and climate. Besides, there is something individual in human minds that easily kindles at the accidental approach and collision of certain circumstances, which though of paltry and mean appearance, do often flame out into the greatest emergencies of life. For great turns are not always given by strong hands, but by lucky adaption and at proper seasons; and it is of no import where the fire was kindled if the vapour has once got up into the brain. For the *upper region* of man is furnished like the *middle region* of the air; the materials are formed from causes of the widest difference, yet produce at last the same substance and effect. Mists arise from the earth, steams from dunghills, exhalations from the sea, and smoke from fire; yet all clouds are the same in composition as well as consequences, and the fumes issuing from a jakes will furnish as comely and useful a vapour as incense from an altar. Thus far, I suppose, will easily be granted me; and then it will follow that, as the face of nature never produces rain but when it is overcast and disturbed, so human understanding, seated in the brain, must be troubled and overspread by vapours ascending from the lower faculties to water the invention, and render it fruitful. Now, although these vapours (as it hath been already said) are of as various original as those of the skies, yet the crop they produce differs both in kind and degree, merely according to the soil. I will produce two instances to prove and explain what I am now advancing.

A certain great prince[118] raised a mighty army, filled his coffers with infinite treasures, provided an invincible fleet, and all this without giving the least part of his design to his greatest ministers or his nearest favourites. Immediately the whole world was alarmed; the neighbouring crowns in trembling expectation towards what point the storm would burst; the small politicians everywhere forming profound conjectures. Some believed he had laid a scheme for universal monarchy; others, after much insight, determined the matter to be a project for pulling down the pope and setting up the *reformed* religion, which had once been his own. Some again, of a deeper sagacity, sent him into Asia to subdue the Turk and recover Palestine. In the midst of all these projects and preparations, a certain *state-surgeon*[119] gathering the nature of the disease by these symptoms, attempted the cure, at one blow performed the operation, broke the bag, and out flew the *vapour,* nor did anything want to render it a complete remedy, only that the prince unfortunately happened to die in the performance. Now, is the reader exceeding curious to learn from whence this *vapour* took its rise, which had so long set the nations at a gaze? What secret wheel, what hidden spring, could put into motion so wonderful an engine? It was afterwards discovered that the movement of this whole machine had been directed by an absent *female* whose eyes had raised a protuberancy, and before emission, she was removed into an enemy's country. What should an unhappy prince do in such ticklish circumstances as these? He tried in vain the poet's never-failing receipt of *corpora quæque*; for

Idque petit corpus mens unde est saucia amore:
Unde feritur, eo tendit, gestitque coire. LUCR.

Having to no purpose used all peaceable endeavours, the collected part of the semen, raised and inflamed, became adust, converted to choler, turned head upon the spinal duct, and ascended to the brain. The very same principle that influences a *bully* to break the windows of a whore who has jilted him, naturally stirs up a great prince to raise mighty armies and dream of nothing but sieges, battles, and victories.

[Cunnus] *teterrima belli*
Causa——

The other instance[120] is what I have read somewhere in a very ancient author, of a mighty king, who, for the space of above thirty years, amused himself to take and lose towns; beat armies, and be beaten; drive princes out of their dominions; fright children from their bread and butter; burn, lay waste, plunder, dragoon, massacre subject and stranger, friend and foe, male and female. 'Tis recorded that the philosophers of each country were in grave dispute upon causes natural, moral, and political, to find out where they should assign an original solution of this *phenomenon.* At last, the *vapour* or *spirit* which animated the hero's brain, being in perpetual circulation, seized upon that region of the human body so renowned for furnishing the *zibeta occidentalis,*[121] and gathering there into a tumour, left the rest of the world for that time in peace. Of such mighty consequence it is where those exhalations fix, and of so little from whence they proceed. The same spirits which, in their superior progress, would conquer a kingdom, descending upon the *anus* conclude in a *fistula.*

Let us next examine the great introducers of new schemes in philosophy, and search till we can find from what faculty of the soul the disposition arises in mortal man, of taking it into his head to advance new systems with such an eager zeal, in things agreed on all hands impossible to be known; from what seeds this disposition springs, and to what quality of human nature these grand innovators have been indebted for their number of disciples. Because it is plain that several of the chief among them, both *ancient* and *modern,* were usually mistaken by their adversaries, and indeed by all except their own followers, to have been persons crazed, or out of their wits; having generally proceeded in the common course of their words and actions, by a method very different from the vulgar dictates of *unrefined* reason, agreeing for the most part in their several models with their present undoubted successors in the *academy* of *modern Bedlam* (whose merits and principles I shall further examine in due place). Of this kind were *Epicurus, Diogenes, Apollonius, Lucretius, Paracelsus, Des Cartes,* and others, who if they were now in the world, tied fast, and separate from their followers, would in this our undistinguishing age incur manifest danger of *phlebotomy,* and *whips,* and *chains,* and *dark chambers,* and *straw.* For what man in the natural state or course of thinking, did ever conceive it in his power to reduce the notions of all mankind exactly to the same length, and breadth, and height of his own? Yet this is the first humble and civil design of all innovators in the empire of reason. Epicurus modestly hoped that, one time or other, a certain fortuitous concourse of all men's opinions, after perpetual justlings, the sharp with the smooth, the light and the heavy, the round and the square, would by certain *clinamina* unite in the notions of *atoms* and *void,* as these did in the originals of all things. Cartesius reckoned to see, before he died, the sentiments of all philosophers, like so many lesser stars in his *romantic* system, wrapped and drawn within his own *vortex.* Now I would gladly be informed, how it is possible to account for such imaginations as these in particular men without recourse to my *phenomenon* of *vapours,* ascending from the lower faculties to overshadow the brain, and thence distilling into conceptions for which the narrowness of our mother tongue has not yet assigned any other name besides that of *madness* or *phrenzy.* Let us therefore now conjecture how it comes to pass, that none of these great prescribers do ever fail providing themselves and their notions with a number of implicit disciples. And I think the reason is easy to be assigned: for there is a peculiar *string* in the harmony of human understanding which, in several individuals, is exactly of the same tuning. This, if you can dexterously screw up to its right key and then strike gently upon it, whenever you have the good fortune to light among those of the same pitch they will, by a secret necessary sympathy, strike exactly at the same time. And in this one circumstance lies all the skill or luck of the matter; for if you chance to jar the string among those who are either above or below your own height, instead of subscribing to your doctrine they will tie you fast, call you mad, and feed you with bread and water. It is therefore a point of the nicest conduct to distinguish and adapt this noble talent, with respect to the differences of persons and times. Cicero understood this very well, when writing to a friend in England with a caution, among other matters, to beware of being cheated by our *hackney-coachmen* (who it seems, in those days were as arrant rascals as they are now) has these remarkable words, *Est quod gaudeas te in ista loca venisse, ubi aliquid sapere viderere.*[122] For, to speak a bold truth, it is a fatal miscarriage so ill to order affairs as to pass for a *fool* in one company, when in another you might be treated as a *philosopher*. Which I desire *some certain gentlemen of my acquaintance* to lay up in their hearts as a very seasonable *innuendo*.

This, indeed, was the fatal mistake of that worthy gentleman, my most ingenious friend Mr. W[o]tt[o]n: a person, in appearance, ordained for great designs as well as performances, whether you will consider his *notions* or his *looks*. Surely no man ever advanced into the public with fitter qualifications of body and mind for the propagation of a new religion. Oh, had those happy talents, misapplied to vain philosophy, been turned into their proper channels of *dreams* and *visions*, where *distortion* of mind and countenance are of such sovereign use, the base detracting world would not then have dared to report that something is amiss, that his brain hath undergone an unlucky shake, which even his brother *modernists* themselves, like ungrates, do whisper so loud that it reaches up to the very garret I am now writing in.

Lastly, whoever pleases to look into the fountains of *enthusiasm*, from whence in all ages have eternally proceeded such fattening streams, will find the spring head to have been as *troubled* and *muddy* as the current. Of such great emolument is a tincture of this *vapour* which the world calls *madness*, that without its help the world would not only be deprived of those two great blessings, *conquests* and *systems*, but even all mankind would unhappily be reduced to the same belief in things invisible. Now, the former *postulatum* being held, that it is of no import from what originals this *vapour* proceeds, but either in what *angles* it strikes and spreads over the understanding or upon what *species* of brain it ascends, it will be a very delicate point to cut the feather, and divide the several reasons to a nice and curious reader, how this numerical difference in the brain can produce effects of so vast a difference from the same *vapour*, as to be the sole point of individuation between Alexander the Great, Jack of Leyden, and Monsieur Des Cartes. The present argument is the most abstracted that ever I engaged in; it strains my faculties to their highest stretch; and I desire the reader to attend with the utmost perpensity, for I now proceed to unravel this knotty point.

There is in mankind a certain[123] * * * *
* * * * * * * *
Hic multa * * * * * *
desiderantur. * * * * * *
* * * * * And this I take to be a clear solution of the matter.

Having therefore so narrowly passed through this intricate difficulty, the reader will I am sure agree with me in the conclusion, that if the *moderns* mean by *madness,* only a disturbance or transposition of the brain by force of certain *vapours* issuing up from the lower faculties, then has this *madness* been the parent of all those mighty revolutions that have happened in *empire,* in *philosophy,* and in *religion.* For the brain, in its natural position and state of serenity, disposeth its owner to pass his life in the common forms without any thoughts of subduing multitudes to his own *power,* his *reasons,* or his *visions*; and the more he shapes his understanding by the pattern of human learning, the less he is inclined to form parties after his particular notions, because that instructs him in his private infirmities, as well as in the stubborn ignorance of the people. But when a man's fancy gets *astride* on his reason, when imagination is at cuffs with the senses, and common understanding as well as common sense, is kicked out of doors; the first proselyte he makes is himself, and when that is once compassed the difficulty is not so great in bringing over others, a strong delusion always operating from *without* as vigorously as from *within.* For cant and vision are to the ear and the eye, the same that tickling is to the touch. Those entertainments and pleasures we most value in life are such as *dupe* and play the wag with the senses. For, if we take an examination of what is generally understood by *happiness,* as it has respect either to the understanding or the senses, we shall find all its properties and adjuncts will herd under this short definition: that *it is a perpetual possession of being well deceived.* And first, with relation to the mind or understanding, 'tis manifest what mighty advantages fiction has over truth; and the reason is just at our elbow, because imagination can build nobler scenes and produce more wonderful revolutions than fortune or nature will be at expense to furnish. Nor is mankind so much to blame in his choice thus determining him, if we consider that the debate merely lies between *things past* and *things conceived;* and so the question is only this, whether things that have place in the *imagination,* may not as properly be said to *exist* as those that are seated in the *memory;* which may be justly held in the affirmative, and very much to the advantage of the former since this is acknowledged to be the *womb* of things, and the other allowed to be no more than the *grave.* Again, if we take this definition of happiness and examine it with reference to the senses, it will be acknowledged wonderfully adapt. How fade and insipid do all objects accost us that are not conveyed in the vehicle of *delusion*! How shrunk is everything as it appears in the glass of nature! So that if it were not for the assistance of artificial *mediums,* false lights, refracted angles, varnish, and tinsel, there would be a mighty level in the felicity and enjoyments of mortal men. If this were seriously considered by the world, as I have a certain reason to suspect it hardly will, men would no longer reckon among their high points of wisdom the art of exposing weak sides and publishing infirmities; an employment, in my opinion, neither better nor worse than that of *unmasking,* which I think has never been allowed fair usage, either in the *world* or the *playhouse.*

In the proportion that credulity is a more peaceful possession of the mind than curiosity; so far preferable is that wisdom which converses about the surface, to that pretended philosophy which enters into the depth of things, and then comes gravely back with informations and discoveries that in the inside they are good for nothing. The two senses to which all objects first address themselves are the sight and the touch. These never examine further than the colour, the shape, the size, and whatever other qualities dwell, or are drawn by art, upon the outward of bodies; and then comes reason officiously, with tools for cutting, and opening, and mangling, and piercing, offering to demonstrate that they are not of the same consistence quite through. Now I take all this to be the last degree of perverting Nature, one of whose eternal laws it is, to put her best furniture forward. And therefore, in order to save the charges of all such expensive anatomy for the time to come, I do here think fit to inform the reader that in such conclusions as these, reason is certainly in the right, and that in most corporeal beings which have fallen under my cognizance, the *outside* hath been infinitely preferable to the *in*; whereof I have been further convinced from some late experiments. Last week I saw a woman *flayed,* and you will hardly believe how much it altered her person for the worse. Yesterday I ordered the carcass of a *beau* to be stripped in my presence, when we were all amazed to find so many unsuspected faults under one suit of clothes. Then I laid open his *brain,* his *heart,* and his *spleen;* but I plainly perceived at every operation that the farther we proceeded, we found the defects increase upon us in number and bulk; from all which, I justly formed this conclusion to myself. That whatever philosopher or projector can find out an art to solder and patch up the flaws and imperfections of nature will deserve much better of mankind, and teach us a more useful science than that so much in present esteem, of widening and exposing them (like him who held *anatomy* to be the ultimate end of *physic*). And he whose fortunes and dispositions have placed him in a convenient station to enjoy the fruits of this noble art; he that can with Epicurus content his ideas with the *films* and *images* that fly off upon his senses from the *superficies* of things; such a man, truly wise, creams off Nature, leaving the sour and the dregs for philosophy and reason to lap up. This is the sublime and refined point of felicity, called *the possession of being well deceived;* the serene peaceful state, of being a fool among knaves.

But to return to *madness.* It is certain that, according to the system I have above deduced, every *species* thereof proceeds from a redundancy of *vapours;* therefore, as some kinds of *phrenzy* give double strength to the sinews, so there are of other *species* which add vigour, and life, and spirit to the brain. Now, it usually happens that these active spirits, getting possession of the brain, resemble those that haunt other waste and empty dwellings, which for want of business, either vanish and carry away a piece of the house, or else stay at home, and fling it all out of the windows. By which are mystically displayed the two principal branches of *madness,* and which some philosophers not considering so well as I, have mistook to be different in their causes, over-hastily assigning the first to deficiency, and the other to redundance.

I think it therefore manifest from what I have here advanced, that the main point of skill and address is to furnish employment for this redundancy of *vapour,* and prudently to adjust the seasons of it; by which means it may certainly become of cardinal and catholic emolument in a commonwealth. Thus one man, choosing a proper juncture, leaps into a gulf, from thence proceeds a hero and is called the saver of his country; another achieves the same enterprise but, unluckily timing it, has left the brand of *madness* fixed as a reproach upon his memory. Upon so nice a distinction are we taught to repeat the name of Curtius with reverence and love, that of Empedocles with hatred and contempt. Thus also it is usually conceived that the elder Brutus only personated the *fool* and *madman* for the good of the public; but that was nothing else than a redundancy of the same *vapour* long misapplied, called by the Latins, *ingenium par negotiis*;[124] or, (to translate it as nearly as I can) a sort of *phrenzy,* never in its right element till you take it up in business of the state.

Upon all which and many other reasons of equal weight, though not equally curious, I do here gladly embrace an opportunity I have long sought for, of recommending it as a very noble undertaking to Sir E[dwar]d S[eymou]r, Sir C[hristophe]r M[usgra]ve, Sir J[oh]n B[ow]ls, J[oh]n H[o]w, Esq. and other patriots concerned, that they would move for leave to bring in a bill for appointing commissioners to inspect into Bedlam, and the parts adjacent; who shall be empowered to *send for persons, papers, and records,* to examine into the merits and qualifications of every student and professor, to observe with utmost exactness their several dispositions and behaviour, by which means, duly distinguishing and adapting their talents, they might produce admirable instruments for the several offices in a state, [*ecclesiastical*], *civil,* and *military,* proceeding in such methods as I shall here humbly propose. And I hope the gentle reader will give some allowance to my great solicitudes in this important affair, upon account of the high esteem I have borne that honourable society whereof I had some time the happiness to be an unworthy member.

Is any student tearing his straw in piecemeal, swearing and blaspheming, biting his grate, foaming at the mouth, and emptying his piss-pot in the spectators' faces? Let the right worshipful the *commissioners of inspection* give him a regiment of dragoons, and send him into Flanders among the *rest*. Is another eternally talking, sputtering, gaping, bawling in a sound without period or article? What wonderful talents are here mislaid! Let him be furnished immediately with a green bag and papers and *threepence* in his pocket,[125] and away with him to Westminster Hall. You will find a third gravely taking the dimensions of his kennel, a person of foresight and insight, though kept quite in the dark; for why, like Moses *ecce cornuta*[126] *erat ejus facies*. He walks duly in one pace, entreats your penny with due gravity and ceremony, talks much of hard times, and taxes, and the whore of Babylon, bars up the wooden window of his cell constantly at eight o'clock, dreams of *fire,* and *shoplifters,* and *court-customers,* and *privileged places*. Now what a figure would all these acquirements amount to, if the owner were sent into the *city* among his brethren! Behold a fourth, in much and deep conversation with himself, biting his thumbs at proper junctures, his countenance checkered with business and design; sometimes walking very fast, with his eyes nailed to a paper that he holds in his hands; a great saver of time, somewhat thick of hearing, very short of sight, but more of memory; a man ever in haste, a great hatcher and breeder of business, and excellent at the famous art of *whispering nothing*; a huge idolator of monosyllables and procrastination, so ready to *give* his word to everybody that he never *keeps* it; one that has forgot the common *meaning* of words, but an admirable retainer of the *sound*; extremely subject to the *looseness,* for his *occasions* are perpetually *calling him away*. If you approach his grate in his familiar intervals; "Sir," says he, "give me a penny and I'll sing you a song; but give me the penny first" (hence comes the common saying, and commoner practice, of parting with money for a *song*). What a complete system of *court skill* is here described in every branch of it, and all utterly lost with wrong application! Accost the hole of another kennel, first stopping your nose, you will behold a surly, gloomy, nasty, slovenly mortal, raking in his own dung and dabbling in his urine. The best part of his diet is the reversion of his own ordure which, expiring into steams, whirls perpetually about and at last reinfunds. His complexion is of a dirty yellow with a thin scattered beard, exactly agreeable to that of his diet upon its first declination; like other insects, who having their birth and education in an excrement, from thence borrow their colour and their smell. The student of this apartment is very sparing of his words, but somewhat over-liberal of his breath. He holds his hand out ready to receive your penny, and immediately upon receipt, withdraws to his former occupations. Now, is it not amazing to think, the society of Warwick Lane should have no more concern for the recovery of so useful a member who, if one may judge from these appearances, would become the greatest ornament to that illustrious body? Another student struts up fiercely to your teeth, puffing with his lips, half squeezing out his eyes, and very graciously holds you out his hand to kiss. The *keeper* desires you not to be afraid of this professor, for he will do you no hurt; to him alone is allowed the liberty of the antechamber, and the *orator* of the place gives you to understand that this solemn person is a *tailor* run mad with pride. This considerable student is adorned with many other qualities, upon which at present I shall not further enlarge. . . . . *Hark in your ear*[127] . . . . I am strangely mistaken if all his address, his motions, and his airs, would not then be very natural and in their proper element.

I shall not descend so minutely as to insist upon the vast number of *beaux, fiddlers, poets,* and *politicians,* that the world might recover by such a reformation. But what is more material, besides the clear gain redounding to the commonwealth by so large an acquisition of persons to employ, whose talents and acquirements, if I may be so bold to affirm it, are now buried or at least misapplied; it would be a mighty advantage accruing to the public from this inquiry, that all these would very much excel and arrive at great perfection in their several kinds; which I think is manifest from what I have already shown, and shall enforce by this one plain instance, that even I myself, the author of these momentous truths, am a person whose imaginations are hard-mouthed and exceedingly disposed to run away with his *reason,* which I have observed from long experience to be a very light rider, and easily shook off; upon which account, my friends will never trust me alone without a solemn promise to vent my speculations in this, or the like manner, for the universal benefit of human kind; which perhaps the gentle, courteous, and candid reader, brimful of that *modern* charity and tenderness usually annexed to his *office,* will be very hardly persuaded to believe.

SECT. X

[A FURTHER DIGRESSION]

It is an unanswerable argument of a very refined age, the wonderful civilities that have passed of late years between the nation of *authors* and that of *readers.* There can hardly pop out a *play,* a *pamphlet,* or a *poem,* without a preface full of acknowledgments to the world for the general reception and applause they have given it,[128] which the Lord knows where, or when, or how, or from whom it received. In due deference to so laudable a custom I do here return my humble thanks to *His Majesty,* and both houses of *Parliament*; to the *Lords* of the King's Most Honourable Privy Council; to the reverend the *Judges*; to the *clergy,* and *gentry,* and *yeomanry* of this land; but in a more especial manner to my worthy brethren and friends at Will's Coffeehouse, and Gresham College, and Warwick Lane, and Moorfields, and Scotland Yard, and Westminster Hall, and Guildhall; in short, to all inhabitants and retainers whatsoever, either in court, or church, or camp, or city, or country, for their generous and universal acceptance of this divine treatise. I accept their approbation and good opinion with extreme gratitude, and, to the utmost of my poor capacity, shall take hold of all opportunities to return the obligation.

I am also happy that fate has flung me into so blessed an age for the mutual felicity of *booksellers* and *authors,* whom I may safely affirm to be at this day the two only satisfied parties in England. Ask an *author* how his last piece hath succeeded. Why, truly he thanks his stars, the world has been very favourable, and he has not the least reason to complain; and yet, by G—, he writ it in a week, at bits and starts, when he could steal an hour from his urgent affairs, as it is a hundred to one you may see further in the preface, to which he refers you, and for the rest, to the bookseller. There you go as a customer, and make the same question: he blesses his God the *thing* takes wonderfully, he is just printing a second edition, and has but three left in his shop. You beat down the *price:* "Sir, we shall not differ"—and, in hopes of your custom another time, lets you have it as reasonable as you please, "and pray send as many of your acquaintance as you will, I shall, upon your account, furnish them all at the same rate."

Now, it is not well enough considered to what accidents and occasions the world is indebted for the greatest part of these noble writings which hourly start up to entertain it. If it were not for a *rainy day, a drunken vigil, a fit of the spleen, a course of physic, a sleepy Sunday, an ill run at dice, a long tailor's bill, a beggar's purse, a factious head, a hot sun, costive diet, want of books, and a just contempt of learning*—but for these events, I say, and some others too long to recite (especially *a prudent neglect of taking brimstone inwardly)* I doubt the number of *authors* and of *writings* would dwindle away to a degree most woeful to behold. To confirm this opinion, hear the words of the famous Troglodyte philosopher. "'Tis certain" (said he) "some grains of folly are of course annexed, as part of the composition of human nature, only the choice is left us whether we please to wear them *inlaid* or *embossed,* and we need not go very far to seek how that is usually determined, when we remember it is with human faculties as with liquors, the lightest will be ever at the top."

There is in this famous island of Britain a certain paltry *scribbler,* very voluminous, whose character the reader cannot wholly be a stranger to. He deals in a pernicious kind of writings called *Second Parts,* and usually passes under the name of *The Author of the First.* I easily foresee that as soon as I lay down my pen, this nimble *operator* will have stole it, and treat me as inhumanly as he hath already done Dr. B[lackmo]re, L[estran]ge, and many others who shall here be nameless. I therefore fly, for justice and relief, into the hands of that great *rectifier of saddles,* and *lover of mankind,* Dr. B[en]tly, begging he will take this enormous grievance into his most *modern* consideration; and if it should so happen that the *furniture of an ass,* in the shape of a *Second Part,* must for my sins be clapped by a mistake upon my back, that he will immediately please, in the presence of the world, to lighten me of the burden, and take it home to *his own house* till the *true beast* thinks fit to call for it.

In the meantime I do here give this public notice, that my resolutions are to circumscribe within this discourse the whole stock of matter I have been so many years providing. Since my *vein* is once opened, I am content to exhaust it all at a running for the peculiar advantage of my dear country, and for the universal benefit of mankind. Therefore, hospitably considering the number of my guests, they shall have my whole entertainment at a meal, and I scorn to set up the *leavings* in the cupboard. What the *guests* cannot eat may be given to the *poor*, and the *dogs*[129] under the table may gnaw the *bones*. This I understand for a more generous proceeding, than to turn the company's stomach by inviting them again tomorrow to a scurvy meal of *scraps*.

If the reader fairly considers the strength of what I have advanced in the foregoing section I am convinced it will produce a wonderful revolution in his notions and opinions; and he will be abundantly better prepared to receive and to relish the concluding part of this miraculous treatise. Readers may be divided into three classes—the *superficial*, the *ignorant*, and the *learned;* and I have with much felicity fitted my pen to the genius and advantage of each. The *superficial* reader will be strangely provoked to *laughter*, which clears the breast and the lungs, is sovereign against the *spleen*, and the most innocent of all *diuretics*. The *ignorant* reader (between whom and the former the distinction is extremely nice) will find himself disposed to *stare*; which is an admirable remedy for ill eyes, serves to raise and enliven the spirits, and wonderfully helps *perspiration*. But the reader truly *learned*, chiefly for whose benefit I wake when others sleep, and sleep when others wake, will here find sufficient matter to employ his speculations for the rest of his life. It were much to be wished, and I do here humbly propose for an experiment, that every prince in Christendom will take seven of the *deepest scholars* in his dominions, and shut them up close for *seven* years in *seven* chambers, with a command to write *seven* ample commentaries on this comprehensive discourse. I shall venture to affirm that whatever difference may be found in their several conjectures, they will be all, without the least distortion, manifestly deducible from the text. Meantime it is my earnest request that so useful an undertaking may be entered upon (if their Majesties please) with all convenient speed; because I have a strong inclination, before I leave the world, to taste a blessing which we *mysterious* writers can seldom reach till we have got into our graves: whether it is that *fame,* being a fruit grafted on the body, can hardly grow and much less ripen till the *stock* is in the earth: or whether she be a bird of prey, and is lured among the rest to pursue after the scent of a *carcass*: or whether she conceives her trumpet sounds best and farthest when she stands on a *tomb,* by the advantage of a rising ground and the echo of a hollow vault.

'Tis true indeed, the republic of *dark* authors, after they once found out this excellent expedient of *dying,* have been peculiarly happy in the variety as well as extent of their reputation. For, *night* being the universal mother of things, wise philosophers hold all writings to be *fruitful,* in the proportion they are *dark*; and therefore, the *true illuminated*[130] (that is to say, the *darkest* of all) have met with such numberless commentators, whose *scholiastic* midwifery hath delivered them of meanings that the authors themselves perhaps never conceived, and yet may very justly be allowed the lawful parents of them; the words of such writers being like seed,[131] which, however scattered at random, when they light upon a fruitful ground, will multiply far beyond either the hopes or imagination of the sower.

And therefore, in order to promote so useful a work I will here take leave to glance a few *innuendoes,* that may be of great assistance to those sublime spirits who shall be appointed to labour in a universal comment upon this wonderful discourse. And first,[132] I have couched a very profound mystery in the number of 0's multiplied by *seven,* and divided by *nine.* Also, if a devout brother of the Rosy Cross will pray fervently for sixty-three mornings with a lively faith, and then transpose certain letters and syllables according to prescription in the second and fifth section, they will certainly reveal into a full receipt of the *opus magnum.* Lastly, whoever will be at the pains to calculate the whole number of each letter in this treatise, and sum up the difference exactly between the several numbers, assigning the true natural cause for every such difference, the discoveries in the product will plentifully reward his labour. But then he must beware of *Bythus* and *Sigè,*[133] and be sure not to forget the qualities of *Acamoth; à cujus lacrymis humecta prodit substantia, à risu lucida, à tristitia solida, et à timore mobilis*; wherein Eugenius Philalethes[134] hath committed an unpardonable mistake.

SECT. XI

A TALE OF A TUB

After so wide a compass as I have wandered, I do now gladly overtake and close in with my subject, and shall henceforth hold on with it an even pace to the end of my journey, except some beautiful prospect appears within sight of my way; whereof though at present I have neither warning nor expectation, yet upon such an accident, come when it will, I shall beg my reader's favour and company, allowing me to conduct him through it along with myself. For in *writing* it is as in *travelling:* if a man is in haste to be at home (which I acknowledge to be none of my case, having never so little business as when I am there) if his *horse* be tired with long riding and ill ways or be naturally a jade, I advise him clearly to make the straightest and the commonest road, be it ever so dirty. But then surely we must own such a man to be a scurvy companion at best; he *spatters* himself and his fellow-travellers at every step; all their thoughts, and wishes, and conversation, turn entirely upon the subject of their journey's end; and at every splash, and plunge, and stumble they heartily wish one another at the devil.

On the other side, when a traveller and his *horse* are in heart and plight, when his purse is full and the day before him, he takes the road only where it is clean or convenient; entertains his company there as agreeably as he can; but upon the first occasion carries them along with him to every delightful scene in view, whether of art, of nature, or of both; and if they chance to refuse out of stupidity or weariness, let them jog on by themselves and be d—n'd; he'll overtake them at the next town, at which arriving, he rides furiously through; the men, women, and children run out to gaze, a hundred[135] *noisy curs* run *barking* after him, of which if he honours the boldest with a *lash of his whip*, it is rather out of sport than revenge; but should some *sourer mongrel* dare too near an approach, he receives a *salute* on the chops by an accidental stroke from the courser's heels (nor is any ground lost by the blow) which sends him yelping and limping home.

I now proceed to sum up the singular adventures of my renowned Jack, the state of whose dispositions and fortunes the careful reader does, no doubt, most exactly remember as I last parted with them in the conclusion of a former section. Therefore, his next care must be, from two of the foregoing, to extract a scheme of notions that may best fit his understanding for a true relish of what is to ensue.

Jack had not only calculated the first revolution of his brain so prudently as to give rise to that epidemic sect of Æolists, but succeeding also into a new and strange variety of conceptions, the fruitfulness of his imagination led him into certain notions which, although in appearance very unaccountable, were not without their mysteries and their meanings, nor wanted followers to countenance and improve them. I shall therefore be extremely careful and exact in recounting such material passages of this nature as I have been able to collect, either from undoubted tradition, or indefatigable reading; and shall describe them as graphically as it is possible, and as far as notions of that height and latitude can be brought within the compass of a pen. Nor do I at all question, but they will furnish plenty of noble matter for such whose converting imaginations dispose them to reduce all things into *types*; who can make *shadows*, no thanks to the sun, and then mould them into substances, no thanks to philosophy; whose peculiar talent lies in fixing tropes and allegories to the *letter*, and refining what is literal into figure and mystery.

Jack had provided[136] a fair copy of his father's Will engrossed in form upon a large skin of parchment, and resolving to act the part of a most dutiful son, he became the fondest creature of it imaginable. For although, as I have often told the reader, it consisted wholly in certain plain, easy directions about the management and wearing of their coats, with legacies and penalties in case of obedience or neglect, yet he began to entertain a fancy that the matter was *deeper* and *darker*, and therefore must needs have a great deal more of mystery at the bottom. "Gentlemen," said he, "I will prove this very skin of parchment to be meat, drink, and cloth, to be the philosopher's stone, and the universal medicine." In consequence of which raptures he resolved to make use of it in the necessary, as well as the most paltry occasions of life. He had a way of working it into any shape he pleased, so that it served him for a nightcap when he went to bed, and for an umbrella in rainy weather. He would lap a piece of it about a sore toe, or when he had fits burn two inches under his nose; or if anything lay heavy on his stomach, scrape off and swallow as much of the powder as would lie on a silver penny. They were all infallible remedies. With analogy to these refinements, his common talk and conversation ran wholly in the phrase of his Will,[137] and he circumscribed the utmost of his eloquence within that compass, not daring to let slip a syllable without authority from thence. Once at a strange house he was suddenly taken short upon an urgent juncture, whereon it may not be allowed too particularly to dilate; and being not able to call to mind with that suddenness the occasion required, an authentic phrase for demanding the way to the backside, he chose rather, as the more prudent course, to incur the penalty in such cases usually annexed. Neither was it possible for the united rhetoric of mankind to prevail with him to make himself clean again; because having consulted the Will upon this emergency, he met with a passage[138] near the bottom (whether foisted in by the transcriber, is not known) which seemed to forbid it.

He made it a part of his religion never to say grace to his meat;[139] nor could all the world persuade him, as the common phrase is, to eat his victuals *like a Christian*.[140]

He bore a strange kind of appetite to *snapdragon*,[141] and to the livid snuffs of a burning candle, which he would catch and swallow with an agility wonderful to conceive; and by this procedure, maintained a perpetual flame in his belly, which, issuing in a glowing steam from both his eyes as well as his nostrils and his mouth, made his head appear in a dark night like the skull of an ass wherein a roguish boy hath conveyed a farthing candle, *to the terror of his Majesty's liege subjects*. Therefore, he made use of no other expedient to light himself home, but was wont to say that *a wise man was his own lantern*.

He would shut his eyes as he walked along the streets, and if he happened to bounce his head against a post, or fall into a kennel (as he seldom missed either to do one or both) he would tell the gibing prentices who looked on, that he submitted with entire resignation as to a trip, or a blow of fate, with whom he found by long experience how vain it was either to wrestle or to cuff, and whoever durst undertake to do either would be sure to come off with a swingeing fall or a bloody nose. "It was ordained," said he, "some few days before the Creation, that my nose and this very post should have a rencounter, and therefore nature thought fit to send us both into the world in the same age, and to make us countrymen and fellow-citizens. Now, had my eyes been open it is very likely the business might have been a great deal worse; for how many a confounded slip is daily got by man with all his foresight about him? Besides, the eyes of the understanding see best when those of the senses are out of the way; and therefore blind men are observed to tread their steps with much more caution, and conduct, and judgment, than those who rely with too much confidence upon the virtue of the visual nerve which every little accident shakes out of order, and a drop, or a film, can wholly disconcert; like a lantern among a pack of roaring bullies when they scour the streets, exposing its owner and itself to outward kicks and buffets, which both might have escaped if the vanity of appearing would have suffered them to walk in the dark. But further, if we examine the *conduct* of these boasted lights, it will prove yet a great deal worse than their *fortune.* 'Tis true, I have broke my nose against this post because fortune either forgot, or did not think it convenient, to twitch me by the elbow and give me notice to avoid it. But let not this encourage either the present age, or posterity, to trust their *noses* into the keeping of their *eyes,* which may prove the fairest way of losing them for good and all. For, O ye eyes, ye blind guides, miserable guardians are ye of our frail noses; ye, I say, who fasten upon the first precipice in view, and then tow our wretched willing bodies after you to the very brink of destruction. But, alas, that brink is rotten, our feet slip, and we tumble down prone into a gulf without one hospitable shrub in the way to break the fall—a fall to which not any nose of mortal make is equal, except that of the giant Laurcalco[142] who was Lord of the Silver Bridge. Most properly therefore, O eyes, and with great justice may you be compared to those foolish lights which conduct men through dirt and darkness, till they fall into a deep pit or a noisome bog."

This I have produced as a scantling of Jack's great eloquence and the force of his reasoning upon such abstruse matters.

He was, besides, a person of great design and improvement in affairs of *devotion,* having introduced a new deity who hath since met with a vast number of worshippers, by some called Babel, by others Chaos; who had an ancient temple of Gothic structure upon Salisbury Plain, famous for its shrine and celebration by pilgrims.

When he had some roguish trick to play[143] he would down with his knees, up with his eyes, and fall to prayers, though in the midst of the kennel. Then it was that those who understood his pranks would be sure to get far enough out of his way; and whenever curiosity attracted strangers to laugh or to listen, he would of a sudden, with one hand, out with his *gear* and piss full in their eyes, and with the other all to-bespatter them with mud.

In winter he went always loose and unbuttoned[144] and clad as thin as possible, to let *in* the ambient heat; and in summer lapped himself close and thick to keep it *out.*

In all revolutions of government[145] he would make his court for the office of *hangman* general, and in the exercise of that dignity, wherein he was very dexterous, would make use of no other *vizard*[146] than a *long prayer.*

He had a tongue so musculous and subtile that he could twist it up into his nose and deliver a strange kind of speech from thence. He was also the first in these kingdoms who began to improve the Spanish accomplishment of *braying*; and having large ears, perpetually exposed and arrect, he carried his art to such a perfection, that it was a point of great difficulty to distinguish either by the view or the sound between the *original* and the *copy.*

He was troubled with a disease reverse to that called the stinging of the *tarantula,* and would run dog-mad at the noise of *music,*[147] especially a *pair of bagpipes.* But he would cure himself again by taking two or three turns in Westminster Hall, or Billingsgate, or in a boarding-school, or the Royal Exchange, or a *state coffeehouse.*

He was a person that *feared* no *colours* but mortally *hated* all, and upon that account bore a cruel aversion to *painters;*[148] insomuch that, in his paroxysms, as he walked the streets he would have his pockets loaden with stones to pelt at the *signs.*

Having from this manner of living, frequent occasions to *wash* himself, he would often leap over head and ears into the water though it were in the midst of the winter, but was always observed to come out again much *dirtier,* if possible, than he went in.

He was the first that ever found out the secret of contriving a *soporiferous* medicine to be conveyed in at the *ears;*[149] it was a compound of *sulphur* and *balm of Gilead,* with a little *pilgrim's salve.*

He wore a large plaister of artificial *caustics* on his stomach, with the fervour of which he could set himself a-*groaning,* like the famous *board* upon application of a red-hot iron.

He would stand in the turning of a street, and calling to those who passed by, would cry to one, "Worthy sir, do me the honour of a good slap in the chaps."[150] To another, "Honest friend, pray favour me with a handsome kick on the arse." "Madam, shall I entreat a small box in the ear from your ladyship's fair hands?" "Noble captain, lend a reasonable thwack, for the love of God, with that cane of yours over these poor shoulders." And when he had, by such earnest solicitations, made a shift to procure a basting sufficient to swell up his fancy and his sides, he would return home extremely comforted, and full of terrible accounts of what he had undergone for the *public good.* "Observe this stroke," (said he, showing his bare shoulders) "a plaguy janissary gave it me this very morning at seven o'clock as, with much ado, I was driving off the Great Turk. Neighbours mine, this broken head deserves a plaster; had poor Jack been tender of his noddle you would have seen the Pope, and the French king, long before this time of day among your wives and your warehouses. Dear Christians, the Great Mogul was come as far as Whitechapel, and you may thank these poor sides that he hath not (God bless us) already swallowed up man, woman, and child."

It was highly worth observing the singular effects of that aversion[151] or antipathy which Jack and his brother Peter seemed, even to an affectation, to bear towards each other. Peter had lately done *some rogueries* that forced him to abscond, and he seldom ventured to stir out before night, for fear of bailiffs. Their lodgings were at the two most distant parts of the town from each other; and whenever their occasions or humours called them abroad, they would make choice of the oddest unlikely times, and most uncouth rounds they could invent, that they might be sure to avoid one another: yet, after all this, it was their perpetual fortune to meet. The reason of which is easy enough to apprehend; for the frenzy and the spleen of both having the same foundation, we may look upon them as two pair of compasses, equally extended, and the fixed foot of each remaining in the same centre; which, though moving contrary ways at first, will be sure to encounter somewhere or other in the circumference. Besides, it was among the great misfortunes of Jack to bear a huge personal resemblance with his brother Peter. Their humour and dispositions were not only the same but there was a close analogy in their shape, their size, and their mien. Insomuch, as nothing was more frequent than for a bailiff to seize Jack by the shoulders, and cry "Mr. Peter, you are the king's prisoner." Or, at other times, for one of Peter's nearest friends to accost Jack with open arms, "Dear Peter, I am glad to see thee, pray send me one of your best medicines for the worms." This we may suppose was a mortifying return of those pains and proceedings Jack had laboured in so long. And finding how directly opposite all his endeavours had answered to the sole end and intention which he had proposed to himself, how could it avoid having terrible effects upon a head and heart so furnished as his? However, the poor remainders of his *coat* bore all the punishment; the orient sun never entered upon his diurnal progress without missing a piece of it. He hired a tailor to stitch up the collar so close that it was ready to choke him, and squeezed out his eyes at such a rate as one could see nothing but the white. What little was left of the main substance of the coat, he rubbed everyday for two hours against a rough-cast wall in order to grind away the remnants of *lace* and *embroidery*, but at the same time went on with so much violence that he proceeded a *heathen philosopher*. Yet after all he could do of this kind, the success continued still to disappoint his expectation. For, as it is the nature of rags to bear a kind of mock resemblance to finery, there being a sort of fluttering appearance in both which is not to be distinguished at a distance, in the dark, or by short-sighted eyes; so, in those junctures it fared with Jack and his tatters that they offered to the first view a ridiculous flaunting which, assisting the resemblance in person and air, thwarted all his projects of separation, and left so near a similitude between them as frequently deceived the very disciples and followers of both.

* * * * * * * *

* * * * * * * *

Desunt non- * * * * * *

nulla. * * * * * *

* * * * * * * *

* * * * * * * *

The old Sclavonian proverb said well, that it is with *men* as with *asses*; whoever would keep them fast, must find a very good hold at their ears. Yet I think we may affirm, and it hath been verified by repeated experience, that

Effugiet tamen hæc sceleratus vincula Proteus.

It is good, therefore, to read the maxims of our ancestors with great allowances to times and persons; for if we look into primitive records we shall find that no revolutions have been so great, or so frequent, as those of human *ears*. In former days there was a curious invention to catch and keep them, which I think we may justly reckon among the *artes perditæ;* and how can it be otherwise when, in these latter centuries, the very species is not only diminished to a very lamentable degree but the poor remainder is also degenerated so far as to mock our skilfullest *tenure?* For, if the only slitting of one *ear* in a stag hath been found sufficient to propagate the defect through a whole forest, why should we wonder at the greatest consequences from so many loppings and mutilations to which the *ears* of our fathers, and our own, have been of late so much exposed? 'Tis true indeed, that while this *island* of ours was under the *dominion of grace,* many endeavours were made to improve the growth of *ears* once more among us. The proportion of largeness was not only looked upon as an ornament of the *outward* man, but as a type of grace in the *inward.* Besides, it is held by naturalists that if there be a protuberancy of parts in the *superior* region of the body, as in the *ears* and *nose,* there must be a parity also in the *inferior,* and therefore in that truly pious age, the *males* in every assembly, according as they were gifted, appeared very forward in exposing their *ears* to view, and the regions about them; because Hippocrates tells us,[152] that "when the vein behind the ear happens to be cut, a man becomes a eunuch." And the *females* were nothing backwarder in beholding and edifying by them; whereof those who had already *used the means* looked about them with great concern in hopes of conceiving a suitable offspring by such a prospect; others, who stood candidates for *benevolence,* found there a plentiful choice and were sure to fix upon such as discovered the largest *ears,* that the breed might not dwindle between them. Lastly, the devouter sisters, who looked upon all extraordinary dilatations of that member as protrusions of zeal, or spiritual excrescencies, were sure to honour every head they sat upon as if they had been *marks of grace;* but especially that of the preacher, whose *ears* were usually of the prime magnitude, which upon that account, he was very frequent and exact in exposing with all advantages to the people: in his rhetorical *paroxysms* turning sometimes to *hold forth* the one, and sometimes to *hold forth* the other; from which custom the whole operation of preaching is to this very day, among their professors, styled by the phrase of *holding forth.*

Such was the progress of the *saints* for advancing the size of that member. And it is thought the success would have been every way answerable if, in process of time, a cruel king had not arisen[153] who raised a bloody persecution against all *ears* above a certain standard; upon which, some were glad to hide their flourishing sprouts in a black border, others crept wholly under a periwig; some were slit, others cropped, and a great number sliced off to the stumps. But of this more hereafter in my *General History of Ears,* which I design very speedily to bestow upon the public.

From this brief survey of the falling state of *ears* in the last age, and the small care had to advance their ancient growth in the present, it is manifest how little reason we can have to rely upon a hold so short, so weak, and so slippery; and that whoever desires to catch mankind fast must have recourse to some other methods. Now, he that will examine human nature with circumspection enough, may discover several *handles,* whereof the *six*[154] senses afford one a-piece, beside a great number that are screwed to the passions and some few rivetted to the intellect. Among these last, *curiosity* is one, and of all others affords the firmest grasp; *curiosity,* that spur in the side, that bridle in the mouth, that ring in the nose, of a lazy, an impatient, and a grunting reader. By this *handle* it is that an author should seize upon his readers; which as soon as he hath once compassed, all resistance and struggling are in vain, and they become his prisoners as close as he pleases, till weariness or dulness force him to let go his gripe.

And therefore I, the author of this miraculous treatise, having hitherto beyond expectation maintained, by the aforesaid *handle,* a firm hold upon my gentle readers, it is with great reluctance that I am at length compelled to remit my grasp, leaving them, in the perusal of what remains, to that natural *oscitancy* inherent in the tribe. I can only assure thee, courteous reader, for both our comforts, that my concern is altogether equal to thine for my unhappiness in losing, or mislaying among my papers, the remaining part of these memoirs; which consisted of accidents, turns, and adventures, both new, agreeable, and surprising, and therefore calculated in all due points to the delicate taste of this our noble age. But, alas, with my utmost endeavours I have been able only to retain a few of the heads. Under which there was a full account, how Peter got a *protection* out of the King's Bench; and of a reconcilement[155] between Jack and him, upon a design they had, in a certain *rainy night* to trepan brother Martin into a *sponging-house* and there strip him to the skin. How Martin, with much ado, showed them both a fair pair of heels. How a *new warrant* came out against Peter, upon which, how Jack left him in the lurch, *stole his protection, and made use of it himself.* How Jack's tatters came into fashion in *court* and *city;* how *he got upon a great horse,*[156] *and eat custard.*[157] But the particulars of all these, with several others which have now slid out of my memory, are lost beyond all hopes of recovery. For which misfortune, leaving my readers to condole with each other as far as they shall find it to agree with their several constitutions, but conjuring them by all the friendship that hath passed between us, from the title-page to this, not to proceed so far as to injure their healths for an accident past remedy; I now go on to the ceremonial part of an accomplished writer and therefore, by a courtly *modern,* least of all others to be omitted.

THE CONCLUSION

Going too long is a cause of abortion as effectual, though not so frequent, as *going too short*; and holds true especially in the *labours* of the brain. Well fare the heart of that noble Jesuit[158] who first adventured to confess in print that books must be suited to their several seasons, like dress, and diet, and diversions. And better fare our noble nation for refining upon this among other French modes. I am living fast to see the time when a *book* that misses its tide shall be neglected as the *moon* by day, or like *mackerel* a week after the season. No man hath more nicely observed our climate than the bookseller who bought the copy of this work. He knows to a tittle what subjects will best go off in a *dry year,* and which it is proper to expose foremost when the weatherglass is fallen to *much rain.* When he had seen this treatise and consulted his *almanac* upon it, he gave me to understand that he had maturely considered the two principal things, which were the *bulk* and the *subject,* and found it would never *take* but after a long vacation, and then only in case it should happen to be a hard year for turnips. Upon which I desired to know, *considering my urgent necessities,* what he thought might be acceptable this month. He looked westward and said, "I doubt we shall have a fit of bad weather. However, if you could prepare some pretty little *banter (but not in verse)* or a small treatise upon the——, it would run like wildfire. But *if it hold up,* I have already hired an author to write something against Dr. B[en]tl[e]y, which I am sure will turn to account."

At length we agreed upon this expedient; that when a customer comes for one of these and desires in confidence to know the author, he will tell him very privately as a friend, naming whichever of the wits shall happen to be that week in the vogue; and if Durfey's last play should be in course, I would as lieve he may be the person as Congreve. This I mention, because I am wonderfully well acquainted with the present relish of courteous readers, and have often observed with singular pleasure, that a *fly* driven from a *honey-pot* will immediately, with very good appetite, alight and finish his meal on an *excrement.*

I have one word to say upon the subject of *profound writers,* who are grown very numerous of late and I know very well the judicious world is resolved to list me in that number. I conceive therefore, as to the business of being *profound,* that it is with *writers* as with *wells*—a person with good eyes may see to the bottom of the deepest provided any *water* be there, and that often when there is nothing in the world at the bottom besides *dryness* and *dirt,* though it be but a yard and half underground it shall pass, however, for wondrous *deep,* upon no wiser a reason than because it is wondrous *dark.*

I am now trying an experiment very frequent among modern authors, which is *to write upon nothing;* when the subject is utterly exhausted, to let the pen still move on; by some called the ghost of wit, delighting to walk after the death of its body. And to say the truth, there seems to be no part of knowledge in fewer hands than that of discerning *when to have done.* By the time that an author has writ out a book, he and his readers are become old acquaintance and grow very loth to part; so that I have sometimes known it to be in writing as in visiting, where the ceremony of taking leave has employed more time than the whole conversation before. The conclusion of a treatise resembles the conclusion of human life, which hath sometimes been compared to the end of a feast where few are satisfied to depart, *ut plenus vitæ conviva.* For men will sit down after the fullest meal, though it be only to *doze* or to *sleep* out the rest of the day. But in this latter I differ extremely from other writers, and shall be too proud if by all my labours I can have anyways contributed to the *repose* of mankind, in times[159] so turbulent and unquiet as these. Neither do I think such an employment so very alien from the office of a *wit* as some would suppose. For, among a very polite nation in Greece,[160] there were the same temples built and consecrated to *Sleep* and the *Muses,* between which two deities they believed the strictest friendship was established.

I have one concluding favour to request of my reader; that he will not expect to be equally diverted and informed by every line or every page of this discourse, but give some allowance to the author's spleen and short fits or intervals of dulness, as well as his own; and lay it seriously to his conscience whether, if he were walking the streets in dirty weather or a rainy day, he would allow it fair dealing in folks at their ease from a window to critick his gait, and ridicule his dress at such a juncture.

In my disposure of employments of the brain, I have thought fit to make *invention* the *master,* and to give *method* and *reason* the office of its *lackeys.* The cause of this distribution was, from observing it my peculiar case to be often under a temptation of being *witty* upon occasion where I could be neither *wise,* nor *sound,* nor anything to the matter in hand. And I am too much a servant of the *modern* way to neglect any such opportunities, whatever pains or improprieties I may be at to introduce them. For I have observed that from a laborious collection of seven hundred thirty-eighty *flowers* and *shining hints* of the best *modern* authors, digested with great reading into my book of *commonplaces,* I have not been able after five years to draw, hook, or force, into common conversation any more than a dozen. Of which dozen, the one moiety failed of success by being dropped among unsuitable company, and the other cost me so many strains, and traps, and *ambages* to introduce, that I at length resolved to give it over. Now this disappointment (to discover a secret) I must own gave me the first hint of setting up for an *author,* and I have since found, among some particular friends, that it is become a very general complaint and has produced the same effects upon many others. For I have remarked many a *towardly word* to be wholly neglected or despised in *discourse,* which has passed very smoothly, with some consideration and esteem, after its preferment and sanction in *print.* But now, since by the liberty and encouragement of the press, I am grown absolute master of the occasions and opportunities to expose the talents I have acquired, I already discover that the *issues* of my *observanda* begin to grow too large for the *receipts.* Therefore, I shall here pause a while till I find, by feeling the world's pulse and my own, that it will be of absolute necessity (for us both) to resume my pen.

A DISCOURSE CONCERNING THE MECHANICAL OPERATION OF THE SPIRIT (1704)

TO A FRIEND

A FRAGMENT

THE BOOKSELLER'S ADVERTISEMENT

The following discourse came into my hands perfect and entire. But there being several things in it which the present age would not very well bear, I kept it by me some years, resolving it should never see the light. At length, by the advice and assistance of a judicious friend, I retrenched those parts that might give most offence, and have now ventured to publish the remainder. Concerning the author I am wholly ignorant, neither can I conjecture whether it be the same with that of the two foregoing pieces, the original having been sent me at a different time, and in a different hand. The learned reader will better determine; to whose judgement I entirely submit it.[1]

For T. H. *Esquire, at his Chambers in the Academy of the* Beaux Esprits *in* New Holland.

Sir,

It is now a good while since I have had in my head something not only very material, but absolutely necessary to my health, that the world should be informed in. For to tell you a secret, I am able to contain *it no longer. However, I have been perplexed for some time to resolve what would be the most proper form to send it abroad in. To which end I have three days been coursing through Westminster Hall, and*

St. Paul's Churchyard, and Fleet Street, to peruse titles, and I do not find any which holds so general a vogue as that of A Letter to a Friend. *Nothing is more common than to meet with long epistles addressed to persons and places where, at first thinking, one would be apt to imagine it not altogether so necessary or convenient; such as* a Neighbour at next Door, a mortal Enemy, a perfect Stranger, *or* a Person of Quality in the Clouds; *and these upon subjects in appearance the least proper for conveyance by the post; as* long schemes in philosophy; dark and wonderful mysteries of state; laborious dissertations in criticism and philosophy; advice to parliaments, *and the like.*

Now, Sir, to proceed after the method in present wear—for let me say what I will to the contrary, I am afraid you will publish this letter, as soon as ever it comes to your hands—I desire you will be my witness to the world how careless and sudden a scribble it has been; that it was but yesterday when you and I began accidentally to fall into discourse on this matter; that I was not very well when we parted; that the post is in such haste, I have had no manner of time to digest it into order or correct the style. And if any other modern excuses for haste and negligence shall occur to you in reading, I beg you to insert them, faithfully promising they shall be thankfully acknowledged.

Pray, Sir, in your next letter to the Iroquois Virtuosi, *do me the favour to present my humble service to that illustrious body, and assure them I shall send an account of those phenomena, as soon as we can determine them at Gresham.*

I have not had a line from the Literati *of Tobinambou these three last ordinaries.*

And now, Sir, having dispatched what I had to say of forms, or of business, let me entreat you will suffer me to proceed upon my subject, and to pardon me if I make no further use of the epistolary style till I come to conclude.

SECTION I

'Tis recorded of Mahomet that, upon a visit he was going to pay in Paradise, he had an offer of several vehicles to conduct him upwards, as fiery chariots, winged horses, and celestial sedans; but he refused them all and would be borne to Heaven upon nothing but his *ass*. Now this inclination of Mahomet, as singular as it seems, hath been since taken up by a great number of devout Christians, and doubtless with very good reason. For, since that Arabian is known to have borrowed a moiety of his religious system from the Christian faith, it is but just he should pay reprisals to such as would challenge them; wherein the good people of England, to do them all right, have not been backward. For though there is not any other nation in the world so plentifully provided with carriages for that journey, either as to safety or ease, yet there are abundance of us who will not be satisfied with any other machine beside this of Mahomet.

For my own part I must confess to bear a very singular respect to this animal, by whom I take human nature to be most admirably held forth in all its qualities as well as operations. And therefore whatever in my small reading occurs concerning this our fellow creature, I do never fail to set it down by way of commonplace; and when I have occasion to write upon human reason, politics, eloquence, or knowledge, I lay my *memorandums* before me and insert them with a wonderful facility of application. However, among all the qualifications ascribed to this distinguished brute by ancient or modern authors I cannot remember this talent of bearing his rider to Heaven has been recorded for a part of his character, except in the two examples mentioned already. Therefore I conceive the methods of this art to be a point of useful knowledge in very few hands, and which the learned world would gladly be better informed in. This is what I have undertaken to perform in the following discourse. For, towards the operation already mentioned many peculiar properties are required both in the *rider* and the *ass* which I shall endeavour to set in as clear a light as I can.

But, because I am resolved by all means to avoid giving offence to any party whatever, I will leave off discoursing so closely to the *letter* as I have hitherto done, and go on for the future by way of allegory, though in such a manner that the judicious reader may without much straining make his applications as often as he shall think fit. Therefore, if you please, from henceforward instead of the term *ass* we shall make use of *gifted* or *enlightened teacher*, and the word *rider* we will exchange for that of *fanatic auditory,* or any other denomination of the like import. Having settled this weighty point, the great subject of inquiry before us is to examine by what methods this *teacher* arrives at his *gifts,* or *spirit,* or *light*; and by what intercourse between him and his assembly it is cultivated and supported.

In all my writings I have had constant regard to this great end, not to suit and apply them to particular occasions and circumstances of time, of place, or of person; but to calculate them for universal nature and mankind in general. And of such catholic use I esteem this present disquisition; for I do not remember any other temper of body or quality of mind, wherein all nations and ages of the world have so unanimously agreed as that of a *fanatic* strain, or tincture of *enthusiasm*; which, improved by certain persons or societies of men and by them practised upon the rest, has been able to produce revolutions of the greatest figure in history, as will soon appear to those who know anything of Arabia, Persia, India, or China, of Morocco and Peru. Farther, it has possessed as great a power in the kingdom of knowledge, where it is hard to assign one art or science which has not annexed to it some *fanatic* branch: such are the *Philosopher's Stone, The Grand Elixir,*[2] *The Planetary Worlds, The Squaring of the Circle, The Summum Bonum, Utopian Commonwealths,* with some others of less or subordinate note; which all serve for nothing else but to employ or amuse this grain of *enthusiasm,* dealt into every composition.

But if this plant has found a root in the fields of *empire* and of *knowledge,* it has fixed deeper and spread yet further upon *holy ground.* Wherein, though it hath passed under the general name of *enthusiasm* and perhaps arisen from the same original, yet hath it produced certain branches of a very different nature, however often mistaken for each other. The word in its universal acceptation may be defined, a *lifting up of the soul, or its faculties, above matter.* This description will hold good in general; but I am only to understand it as applied to *religion,* wherein there are three general ways of ejaculating the soul, or transporting it beyond the sphere of matter. The first is the immediate act of God, and is called *prophecy* or *inspiration.* The second is the immediate act of the Devil, and is termed *possession.* The third is the product of natural causes, the effect of strong imagination, spleen, violent anger, fear, grief, pain, and the like. These three have been abundantly treated on by authors and therefore shall not employ my enquiry. But the fourth method of *religious enthusiasm* or launching out the soul, as it is purely an effect of artifice and *mechanic operation,* has been sparingly handled or not at all by any writer; because, though it is an art of great antiquity, yet having been confined to few persons, it long wanted those advancements and refinements which it afterwards met with since it has grown so epidemic and fallen into so many cultivating hands.

It is, therefore, upon this *Mechanical Operation of the Spirit* that I mean to treat, as it is at present performed by our *British Workmen.* I shall deliver to the reader the result of many judicious observations upon the matter, tracing as near as I can the whole course and method of this *trade,* producing parallel instances, and relating certain discoveries that have luckily fallen in my way.

I have said that there is one branch of *religious enthusiasm* which is purely an effect of Nature whereas the part I mean to handle is wholly an effect of art which, however, is inclined to work upon certain natures and constitutions more than others. Besides, there is many an operation which in its original was purely an artifice but through a long succession of ages hath grown to be natural. Hippocrates tells us that among our ancestors the Scythians there was a nation called *Longheads,*[3] which at first began, by a custom among midwives and nurses, of moulding, and squeezing, and bracing up the heads of infants, by which means Nature, shut out at one passage, was forced to seek another, and finding room above, shot upwards in the form of a sugar-loaf; and being diverted that way for some generations, at last found it out of herself, needing no assistance from the nurse's hand. This was the original of the *Scythian Longheads* and thus did custom, from being a second nature, proceed to be a first. To all which there is something very analogous among us of this nation, who are the undoubted posterity of that refined people. For, in the age of our fathers, there arose a generation of men in this island called *Roundheads,* whose race is now spread over three kingdoms, yet in its beginning was merely an operation of art, produced by a pair of scissors, a squeeze of the face, and a black cap. These heads thus formed into a perfect sphere in all assemblies were most exposed to the view of the female sort, which did influence their conceptions so effectually that nature at last took the hint and did it of herself; so that a *Roundhead* has been ever since as familiar a sight among us as a *Longhead* among the Scythians.

Upon these examples and others easy to produce, I desire the curious reader to distinguish first, between an effect grown from *Art* into *Nature,* and one that is natural from its beginning; secondly, between an effect wholly natural, and one which has only a natural foundation but where the superstructure is entirely artificial. For the first and the last of these I understand to come within the districts of my subject. And having obtained these allowances, they will serve to remove any objections that may be raised hereafter against what I shall advance.

The practitioners of this famous art proceed in general upon the following fundamental, that *the corruption of the senses is the generation of the spirit;* because the *senses* in men are so many avenues to the fort of *reason,* which in this operation is wholly blocked up. All endeavours must be therefore used, either to divert, bind up, stupify, fluster, and amuse the *senses,* or else to justle them out of their stations; and while they are either absent or otherwise employed, or engaged in a civil war against each other, the spirit enters and performs its part.

Now the usual methods of managing the senses upon such conjunctures are what I shall be very particular in delivering, as far as it is lawful for me to do; but having had the honour to be initiated into the mysteries of every society, I desire to be excused from divulging any rites wherein the *profane* must have no part.

But here, before I can proceed further, a very dangerous objection must, if possible, be removed: for it is positively denied by certain critics that the *spirit* can by any means be introduced into an assembly of modern saints, the disparity being so great in many material circumstances, between the primitive way of inspiration and that which is practised in the present age. This they pretend to prove from the second chapter of the *Acts* where, comparing both, it appears first, that *the apostles were gathered together with one accord, in one place;* by which is meant an universal agreement in opinion and form of worship; a harmony (say they) so far from being found between any two conventicles among us that it is in vain to expect it between any two heads in the same. Secondly, the *spirit* instructed the apostles in the gift of speaking several languages, a knowledge so remote from our dealers in this art that they neither understand propriety of words or phrases in their own. Lastly (say these objectors) the modern artists do utterly exclude all approaches of the *spirit,* and bar up its ancient way of entering, by covering themselves so close and so industriously a-top. For they will needs have it as a point clearly gained that the *Cloven Tongues* never sat upon the apostles' heads while their hats were on.

Now, the force of these objections seems to consist in the different acceptation of the word *spirit,* which, if it be understood for a supernatural assistance approaching from without, the objectors have reason and their assertions may be allowed; but the *spirit* we treat of here proceeding entirely from within, the argument of these adversaries is wholly eluded. And upon the same account, our modern artificers find it an expedient of absolute necessity to cover their heads as close as they can, in order to prevent perspiration, than which nothing is observed to be a greater spender of Mechanic Light, as we may perhaps further show in convenient place.

To proceed therefore upon the phenomenon of *Spiritual Mechanism,* it is here to be noted that in forming and working up the *spirit,* the assembly has a considerable share as well as the preacher. The method of this *arcanum* is as follows. They violently strain their eyeballs inward, half closing the lids; then, as they sit, they are in a perpetual motion of *see-saw* making long hums at proper periods and continuing the sound at equal height, choosing their time in those intermissions while the preacher is at ebb. Neither is this practice, in any part of it, so singular or improbable as not to be traced in distant regions from reading and observation. For first, *the Jauguis*[4] or enlightened saints of India see all their visions by help of an acquired straining and pressure of the eyes. Secondly, the art of *see-saw* on a beam and swinging by session upon a cord, in order to raise artificial ecstasies, hath been derived to us from our Scythian[5] ancestors where it is practised at this day among the women. Lastly, the whole proceeding as I have here related it is performed by the natives of Ireland with a considerable improvement; and it is granted that this noble nation hath of all others admitted fewer corruptions, and degenerated least from the purity of the old Tartars. Now, it is usual for a knot of Irish, men and women, to abstract themselves from matter, bind up all their senses, grow visionary and spiritual, by influence of a short pipe of tobacco, handed round the company; each preserving the smoke in his mouth till it comes again to his turn to take it in fresh: at the same time there is a consort of a continued gentle hum, repeated and renewed by instinct as occasion requires, and they move their bodies up and down to a degree that sometimes their heads and points lie parallel to the horizon. Meanwhile you may observe their eyes turned up in the posture of one who endeavours to keep himself awake; by which, and many other symptoms among them, it manifestly appears that the reasoning faculties are all suspended and superseded, that imagination hath usurped the seat, scattering a thousand deliriums over the brain. Returning from this digression, I shall describe the methods by which the *spirit* approaches. The eyes being disposed according to art, at first you can see nothing, but after a short pause a small glimmering light begins to appear and dance before you. Then, by frequently moving your body up and down, you perceive the vapours to ascend very fast, till you are perfectly dosed and flustered like one who drinks too much in a morning. Meanwhile the preacher is also at work. He begins a loud hum which pierces you quite through; this is immediately returned by the audience, and you find yourself prompted to imitate them by a mere spontaneous impulse, without knowing what you do. The *interstitia* are duly filled up by the preacher to prevent too long a pause, under which the *spirit* would soon faint and grow languid.

This is all I am allowed to discover about the progress of the *spirit* with relation to that part which is borne by the *assembly*. But in the methods of the preacher to which I now proceed, I shall be more large and particular.

SECTION II

You will read it very gravely remarked in the books of those illustrious and right eloquent penmen, the modern travellers, that the fundamental difference in point of religion between the wild Indians and us, lies in this; that we worship *God,* and they worship the *devil.* But there are certain critics who will by no means admit of this distinction; rather believing, that all nations whatsoever adore the *true God* because they seem to intend their devotions to some invisible power of greatest *goodness* and *ability* to help them, which perhaps will take in the brightest attributes ascribed to the divinity. Others, again, inform us that those idolators adore *two principles,* the *principle of good,* and that of *evil;* which indeed I am apt to look upon as the most universal notion that mankind, by the mere light of nature, ever entertained of things invisible. How this idea hath been managed by the Indians and us, and with what advantage to the understandings of either, may deserve well to be examined. To me, the difference appears little more than this that they are put oftener upon their knees by their *fears,* and we by our *desires;* that the former set them a-*praying,* and us a-*cursing.* What I applaud them for is their discretion in limiting their devotions and their deities to their several districts, nor ever suffering the liturgy of the *white* God to cross or interfere with that of the *black.* Not so with us, who pretending by the lines and measures of our reason to extend the dominion of one invisible power and contract that of the other, have discovered a gross ignorance in the natures of good and evil, and most horribly confounded the frontiers of both. After men have lifted up the throne of their divinity to the *cœlum empyræum,* adorned him with all such qualities and accomplishments as themselves seem most to value and possess: after they have sunk *their principle of evil* to the lowest centre, bound him with chains, loaded him with curses, furnished him with viler dispositions than any *rake-hell* of the town, accouterd him with tail, and horns, and huge claws, and saucer eyes; I laugh aloud to see these reasoners at the same time engaged in wise dispute about certain walks and purlieus, whether they are in the verge of God or the devil, seriously debating whcther such and such influences come into men's minds from above or below, or whether certain passions and affections are guided by the evil spirit or the good.

Dum fas atque nefas exiguo fine libidinum
Discernunt avidi—

Thus do men establish a fellowship of Christ with Belial, and such is the analogy they make between *Cloven Tongues* and *Cloven Feet*. Of the like nature is the disquisition before us. It hath continued these hundred years an even debate whether the deportment and the cant of our English enthusiastic preachers were *possession* or *inspiration*, and a world of argument has been drained on either side, perhaps to little purpose. For, I think it is in *life* as in *tragedy*, where it is held a conviction of great defect, both in order and invention, to interpose the assistance of preternatural power without an absolute and last necessity. However, it is a sketch of human vanity for every individual to imagine the whole universe is interessed in his meanest concern. If he hath got cleanly over a kennel, some angel unseen descended on purpose to help him by the hand; if he hath knocked his head against a post, it was the devil, for his sins, let loose from hell on purpose to *buffet* him. Who that sees a little paltry mortal, droning, and dreaming, and drivelling to a multitude, can think it agreeable to common good sense that either Heaven or Hell should be put to the trouble of influence or inspection upon what he is about? Therefore I am resolved immediately to weed this error out of mankind, by making it clear that this mystery of venting spiritual gifts is nothing but a *trade*, acquired by as much instruction and mastered by equal practice and application, as others are. This will best appear by describing and deducing the whole process of the operation, as variously as it hath fallen under my knowledge or experience.

* * * * * * * *

* * * * * * * *

* * * * * *Here the whole scheme of*
* * * * * *spiritual mechanism was de-*
* * * * * *duced and explained, with an*
* * * * * *appearance of great reading*
* * * * * *and observation; but it was*
* * * * * *thought neither safe nor con-*
* * * * * *venient to print it.*

* * * * * * * *

* * * * * * * *

Here it may not be amiss to add a few words upon the laudable practice of wearing *quilted caps,* which is not a matter of mere custom, humour, or fashion, as some would pretend, but an institution of great sagacity and use; these, when moistened with sweat, stop all perspiration, and by reverberating the heat prevent the spirit from evaporating any way but at the mouth: even as a skilful housewife, that covers her still with a wet clout for the same reason, and finds the same effect. For it is the opinion of choice *virtuosi* that the brain is only a crowd of little animals, but with teeth and claws extremely sharp, and therefore cling together in the contexture we behold, like the picture of Hobbes' *Leviathan,* or like bees in perpendicular swarm upon a tree, or like a carrion corrupted into vermin, still preserving the shape and figure of the mother animal; that all invention is formed by the morsure of two or more of these animals upon certain capillary nerves which proceed from thence, whereof three branches spread into the tongue, and two into the right hand. They hold also, that these animals are of a constitution extremely cold; that their food is the air we attract, their excrement phlegm; and that what we vulgarly call rheums, and colds, and distillations, is nothing else but an epidemical looseness to which that little commonwealth is very subject from the climate it lies under. Further, that nothing less than a violent heat can disentangle these creatures from their hamated station of life, or give them vigour and humour to imprint the marks of their little teeth. That if the morsure be hexagonal, it produces Poetry; the circular gives Eloquence; if the bite hath been conical, the person whose nerve is so affected shall be disposed to write upon Politics; and so of the rest.

I shall now discourse briefly, by what kind of practices the voice is best governed towards the composition and improvement of the *spirit;* for, without a competent skill in tuning and toning each word and syllable and letter to their due cadence, the whole operation is incomplete, misses entirely of its effect on the hearers, and puts the workman himself to continual pains for new supplies without success. For it is to be understood, that in the language of the spirit, *cant* and *droning* supply the place of *sense* and *reason* in the language of men: because in spiritual harangues the disposition of the words according to the art of grammar hath not the least use, but the skill and influence wholly lie in the choice and cadence of the syllables; even as a discreet *composer*, who in setting a song, changes the words and order so often that he is forced to make it *nonsense* before he can make it *music*. For this reason, it hath been held by some that the Art of Canting is ever in greatest perfection when managed by *ignorance;* which is thought to be enigmatically meant by Plutarch when he tells us that the best musical instruments were made from the bones of an *ass*. And the profounder critics upon that passage are of opinion, the word in its genuine signification means no other than a jaw-bone, though some rather think it to have been the *os sacrum*; but in so nice a case I shall not take upon me to decide. The curious are at liberty to *pick* from it whatever they please.

The first ingredient towards the Art of Canting is a competent share of *inward light*; that is to say, a large memory plentifully fraught with theological polysyllables and mysterious texts from holy writ, applied and digested by those methods and mechanical operations already related: the bearers of this *light* resembling lanterns compact of leaves from old Geneva Bibles; which invention, Sir H[u]mphrey Edw[i]n, during his mayoralty, of happy memory, highly approved and advanced, affirming the Scripture to be now fulfilled where it says, *Thy word is a lantern to my feet, and a light to my paths.*

Now, the Art of *Canting* consists in skilfully adapting the voice to whatever words the spirit delivers, that each may strike the ears of the audience with its most significant cadence. The force or energy of this eloquence is not to be found, as among ancient orators, in the disposition of words to a sentence or the turning of long periods, but agreeable to the modern refinements in music, is taken up wholly in dwelling and dilating upon syllables and letters. Thus it is frequent for a single *vowel* to draw sighs from a multitude, and for a whole assembly of saints to sob to the music of one solitary *liquid*. But these are trifles, when even sounds inarticulate are observed to produce as forcible effects. A master workman shall *blow his nose so powerfully* as to pierce the hearts of his people, who are disposed to receive the *excrements* of his brain with the same reverence as the *issue* of it. Hawking, spitting, and belching, the defects of other men's rhetoric, are the flowers and figures and ornaments of his. For, the *spirit* being the same in all, it is of no import through what vehicle it is conveyed.

It is a point of too much difficulty to draw the principles of this famous art within the compass of certain adequate rules. However, perhaps I may one day oblige the world with my critical essay upon the Art of *Canting, philosophically, physically, and musically considered.*

But, among all improvements of the *spirit* wherein the voice hath borne a part, there is none to be compared with that of *conveying the sound through the nose,* which under the denomination of *snuffling*[6] hath passed with so great applause in the world. The originals of this institution are very dark, but having been initiated into the mystery of it, and leave being given me to publish it to the world, I shall deliver as direct a relation as I can.

This art, like many other famous inventions, owed its birth or at least improvement and perfection, to an effect of chance, but was established upon solid reasons and hath flourished in this island ever since with great lustre. All agree that it first appeared upon the decay and discouragement of *bagpipes,* which having long suffered under the mortal hatred of the *brethren,* tottered for a time, and at last fell with *monarchy.* The story is thus related.

As yet *snuffling* was not, when the following adventure happened to a *Banbury saint.* Upon a certain day, while he was far engaged among the tabernacles of the *wicked,* he felt the outward man put into odd commotions, and strangely pricked forward by the inward; an effect very usual among the modern inspired. For, some think that the *spirit* is apt to feed on the *flesh,* like hungry wines upon raw beef. Others rather believe there is a perpetual game at *leap-frog* between both, and sometimes the *flesh* is uppermost, and sometimes the *spirit;* adding that the former, while it is in the state of a *rider,* wears huge Rippon spurs, and when it comes to the turn of being *bearer,* is wonderfully headstrong and hard-mouthed. However it came about, the *saint* felt his *vessel* full *extended* in every part (a very natural effect of strong *inspiration),* and the place and time falling out so unluckily that he could not have the convenience of evacuating upwards by repetition, prayer, or lecture, he was forced to open an inferior vent. In short, he wrestled with the flesh so long that he at length subdued it, coming off with honourable wounds, all *before.* The surgeon had now cured the parts primarily affected, but the disease, driven from its post, flew up into his head; and, as a skilfull general, valiantly attacked in his trenches and beaten from the field, by flying marches withdraws to the capital city, breaking down the bridges to prevent pursuit; so the disease, repelled from its first station, fled before the *Rod* of *Hermes* to the upper region, there fortifying itself; but finding the foe making attacks at the *nose,* broke down the *bridge,* and retired to the headquarters. Now, the naturalists observe that there is in human noses an *idiosyncrasy,* by virtue of which the more the passage is obstructed, the more our speech delights to go through, as the music of a flageolet is made by the *stops.* By this method the twang of the nose becomes perfectly to resemble the *snuffle* of a bagpipe, and is found to be equally attractive of British ears; whereof the saint had sudden experience by practicing his new faculty with wonderful success in the operation of the *spirit.* For, in a short time, no doctrine passed for sound and orthodox unless it were delivered through the nose. Straight, every pastor copied after this original, and those who could not otherwise arrive to a perfection, spirited by a noble zeal, made use of the same experiment to acquire it. So that I think it may be truly affirmed, the *saints* owe their empire to the *snuffling* of one animal as Darius did his to the *neighing* of another, and both stratagems were performed by the same art; for we read how the *Persian beast* acquired his faculty by *covering a mare* the day before.[7]

I should now have done, if I were not convinced that whatever I have yet advanced upon this subject is liable to great exception. For allowing all I have said to be true, it may still be justly objected that there is, in the commonwealth of *artificial enthusiasm,* some real foundation for art to work upon in the temper and complexion of individuals, which other mortals seem to want. Observe but the gesture, the motion, and the countenance, of some choice professors though in their most familiar actions, you will find them of a different race from the rest of human creatures. Remark your commonest pretender to a light *within,* how dark, and dirty, and gloomy he is *without*; as lanterns which, the more light they bear in their bodies, cast out so much the more soot and smoke and fuliginous matter to adhere to the sides. Listen but to their ordinary talk, and look on the mouth that delivers it; you will imagine you are hearing some ancient oracle, and your understanding will be *equally* informed. Upon these and the like reasons, certain objectors pretend to put it beyond all doubt that there must be a sort of preternatural *spirit* possessing the heads of the modern saints; and some will have it to be the *heat* of zeal working upon the *dregs* of ignorance, as other *spirits* are produced from *lees* by the force of fire. Some again think that when our earthly tabernacles are disordered and desolate, shaken and out of repair, the *spirit* delights to dwell within them, as houses are said to be haunted when they are forsaken and gone to decay.

To set this matter in as fair a light as possible, I shall here very briefly deduce the history of *Fanaticism* from the most early ages to the present. And if we are able to fix upon any one material or fundamental point wherein the chief professors have universally agreed, I think we may reasonably lay hold on that and assign it for the great seed or principle of the *spirit.*

The most early traces we meet with of *fanatics* in ancient story are among the Egyptians, who instituted those rites, known in Greece by the names of *Orgia, Panegyres,* and *Dionysia,* whether introduced there by Orpheus or Melampus we shall not dispute at present, nor in all likelihood at anytime for the future.[8] These feasts were celebrated to the honour of Osiris, whom the Grecians called Dionysius and is the same with Bacchus, which has betrayed some superficial readers to imagine that the whole business was nothing more than a set of roaring, scouring companions, overcharged with wine; but this is a scandalous mistake foisted on the world by a sort of modern authors who have too *literal* an understanding and, because antiquity is to be traced *backwards,* do therefore like Jews begin their books at the wrong end, as if learning were a sort of *conjuring.* These are the men who pretend to understand a book by scouting through the *index,* as if a traveller should go about to describe a *palace* when he had seen nothing but the privy; or like certain fortunetellers in North America who have a way of reading a man's destiny by peeping in his *breech.* For, at the time of instituting these mysteries there was not one vine in all Egypt,[9] the natives drinking nothing but *ale;* which liquor seems to have been far more ancient than wine and has the honour of owing its invention and progress not only to the Egyptian Osiris,[10] but to the Grecian Bacchus, who in their famous expedition, carried the receipt of it along with them, and gave it to the nations they visited or subdued. Besides, Bacchus himself was very seldom or never drunk; for it is recorded of him that he was the first inventor of the *mitre,*[11] which he wore continually on his head (as the whole company of bacchanals did) to prevent vapours and the headache after hard drinking. And for this reason (say some) the *Scarlet Whore,* when she makes the kings of the earth drunk with her cup of abomination, is always sober herself though she never balks the glass in her turn, being it seems kept upon her legs by the virtue of her *triple mitre.* Now, these feasts were instituted in imitation of the famous expedition Osiris made through the world, and of the company that attended him, whereof the bacchanalian ceremonies were so many types and symbols. From which account[12] it is manifest that the fanatic rites of these bacchanals cannot be imputed to intoxications by wine, but must needs have had a deeper foundation. What this was, we may gather large hints from certain circumstances in the course of their mysteries. For, in the first place, there was in their processions an entire *mixture and confusion of sexes;* they affected to ramble about hills and deserts. Their garlands were of *ivy* and *vine,* emblems of cleaving and clinging; or of *fir,* the parent of *turpentine.* It is added that they imitated *satyrs,* were attended by *goats* and rode upon *asses,* all companions of great skill and practice in affairs of gallantry. They bore for their ensigns certain curious figures perched upon long poles, made into the shape and size of the *virga genitalis,* with its *appurtenances,* which were so many shadows and emblems of the whole mystery; as well as trophies set up by the female conquerors. Lastly, in a certain town of Attica, the whole solemnity stripped of all its types[13] was performed in *puris naturalibus,* the votaries not flying in coveys but sorted into couples. The same may be farther conjectured from the death of Orpheus, one of the institutors of these mysteries, who was torn in pieces by women because he refused to *communicate his orgies* to them;[14] which others explained by telling us he had castrated himself upon grief for the loss of his wife.

Omitting many others of less note, the next *fanatics* we meet with of any eminence, were the numerous sects of *heretics* appearing in the five first centuries of the *Christian era,* from Simon Magus and his followers to those of Eutyches. I have collected their systems from infinite reading, and comparing them with those of their successors in the several ages since, I find there are certain bounds set even to the irregularities of human thought, and those a great deal narrower than is commonly apprehended. For, as they all frequently interfere even in their wildest ravings, so there is one fundamental point wherein they are sure to meet, as lines in a centre, and that is the *community of women.* Great were their solicitudes in this matter, and they never failed of certain articles in their schemes of worship, on purpose to establish it.

The last *fanatics* of note were those which started up in Germany a little after the *reformation* of Luther, springing as *mushrooms* do at the *end of a harvest;* such were John of Leyden, David George, Adam Neuster, and many others, whose visions and revelations always terminated in *leading about half a dozen sisters apiece,* and making that practice a fundamental part of their system. For human life is a continual navigation, and if we expect our *vessels* to pass with safety through the waves and tempests of this fluctuating world, it is necessary to make a good provision of the *flesh,* as seamen lay in store of *beef* for a long voyage.

Now from this brief survey of some principal sects among the *fanatics* in all ages (having omitted the Mahometans and others, who might also help to confirm the argument I am about) to which I might add several among ourselves, such as the *Family of Love, Sweet Singers of Israel,* and the like, and from reflecting upon that fundamental point in their doctrines about *women,* wherein they have so unanimously agreed; I am apt to imagine that the seed or principle which has ever put men upon *visions* in things *invisible,* is of a corporeal nature; for the profounder chemists inform us that the strongest *spirits* may be extracted from *human flesh.* Besides, the spinal marrow being nothing else but a continuation of the brain, must needs create a very free communication between the superior faculties and those below: and thus the *thorn in the flesh* serves for a *spur* to the *spirit.* I think it is agreed among physicians that nothing affects the head so much as a tentiginous humour, repelled and elated to the upper region, found by daily practice to run frequently up into madness. A very eminent member of the faculty assured me that when the Quakers first appeared, he seldom was without some female patients among them for the *furor* [*Uterinus*]. Persons of a visionary devotion, either men or women, are in their complexion of all others the most amorous; for *zeal* is frequently kindled from the same spark with other fires, and from inflaming brotherly love will proceed to raise that of a gallant. If we inspect into the usual process of modern courtship, we shall find it to consist in a devout turn of the eyes, called *ogling;* an artificial form of canting and whining by rote, every interval for want of other matter made up with a shrug or a hum, a sigh or a groan; the style compact of insignificant words, incoherences, and repetition. These I take to be the most accomplished rules of address to a mistress; and where are these performed with more dexterity than by the *saints*? Nay, to bring this argument yet closer, I have been informed by certain sanguine brethren of the first class that in the height and *orgasmus* of their spiritual exercise, it has been frequent with them * * * * *; immediately after which they found the *spirit* to relax and flag of a sudden with the nerves, and they were forced to hasten to a conclusion. This may be further strengthened by observing, with wonder, how unaccountably all females are attracted by visionary or enthusiastic preachers, though never so contemptible in their *outward men;* which is usually supposed to be done upon considerations purely spiritual without any carnal regards at all. But I have reason to think the *sex* hath certain characteristics by which they form a truer judgment of human abilities and performings than we ourselves can possibly do of each other. Let that be as it will, thus much is certain that, however spiritual intrigues begin, they generally conclude like all others; they may branch upwards toward heaven but the root is in the earth. Too intense a contemplation is not the business of flesh and blood; it must by the necessary course of things, in a little time let go its hold and fall into *matter.* Lovers, for the sake of celestial converse, are but another sort of *Platonics* who pretend to see stars and heaven in ladies' eyes, and to look or think no lower; but the same *pit* is provided for both; and they seem a perfect moral to the story of that philosopher who, while his thoughts and eyes were fixed upon the *constellations,* found himself seduced by his *lower parts* into a *ditch.*

I had somewhat more to say upon this part of the subject but the post is just going, which forces me in great haste to conclude,

Sir,

Yours, &c.

Pray, burn this letter as soon
as it comes to your hands.

A TRITICAL ESSAY UPON THE FACULTIES OF THE MIND (1707)

To - - - - - - -

Sir,

Being so great a Lover of Antiquities, it was reasonable to suppose you would be very much obliged with any Thing that was new. I have been of late offended with many Writers of Essays and moral Discourses, for running into stale Topicks and threadbare Quotations, and not handling their Subject fully and closely: All which Errors I have carefully avoided in the following Essay, which I have proposed as a Pattern for young Writers to imitate. The Thoughts and Observations being entirely new, the Quotations untouched by others, the Subject of mighty Importance, and treated with much Order and Perspicuity: It hath cost me a great deal of Time; and I desire you will accept and consider it as the utmost Effort of my Genius.

A TRITICAL ESSAY, &C.

Philosophers say, that Man is a Microcosm or little World, resembling in Miniature every Part of the great: And, in my Opinion, the Body Natural may be compared to the Body Politick: And if this be so, how can the *Epicureans* Opinion be true, that the Universe was formed by a fortuitous Concourse of Atoms, which I will no more believe, than that the accidental Jumbling of the Letters in the

Alphabet, could fall by Chance into a most ingenious and learned Treatise of Philosophy, *Risum teneatis Amici,* HOR.[1] This false Opinion must needs create many more; it is like an Error in the first Concoction, which cannot be corrected in the second; the Foundation is weak, and whatever Superstructure you raise upon it, must of Necessity fall to the Ground. Thus Men are led from one Error to another, till with *Ixion* they embrace a Cloud instead of *Juno*; or, like the Dog in the Fable, lose the Substance in gaping at the Shadow. For such Opinions cannot cohere; but like the Iron and Clay in the Toes of *Nebuchadnezzar's* Image, must separate and break in Pieces. I have read in a certain Author, that *Alexander* wept because he had no more Worlds to conquer; which he need not have done, if the fortuitous Concourse of Atoms could create one: But this is an Opinion fitter for that many-headed Beast, the Vulgar, to entertain, than for so wise a Man as *Epicurus;* the corrupt Part of his Sect only borrowed his Name, as the Monkey did the Cat's Claw, to draw the Chesnut out of the Fire.

However, the first Step to the Cure is to know the Disease; and although Truth may be difficult to find, because, as the Philosopher observes, she lives in the Bottom of a Well; yet we need not, like blind Men, grope in open Daylight. I hope, I may be allowed, among so many far more learned Men, to offer my Mite, since a Stander-by may sometimes, perhaps, see more of the Game than he that plays it. But I do not think a Philosopher obliged to account for every Phænomenon in Nature; or drown himself with *Aristotle,* for not being able to solve the Ebbing and Flowing of the Tide, in that fatal Sentence he passed upon himself, *Quia te non capio, tu capies me.*[2]

Wherein he was at once the Judge and the Criminal, the Accuser and Executioner. *Socrates,* on the other Hand, who said he knew nothing, was pronounced by the Oracle to be the wisest Man in the World.

But to return from this Digression; I think it as clear as any Demonstration in *Euclid,* that Nature does nothing in vain; if we were able to dive into her secret Recesses, we should find that the smallest Blade of Grass, or most contemptible Weed, has its particular Use; but she is chiefly admirable in her minutest Compositions, the least and most contemptible Insect most discovers the Art of Nature, if I may so call it; although Nature, which delights in Variety, will always triumph over Art: And as the Poet observes,

Naturam expellas furcâ licet, usque recurret. Hor.[3]

But the various Opinions of Philosophers, have scattered through the World as many Plagues of the Mind, as *Pandora's* Box did those of the Body; only with this Difference, that they have not left Hope at the Bottom. And if Truth be not fled with *Astræa,* she is certainly as hidden as the Source of *Nile,* and can be found only in *Utopia.* Not that I would reflect on those wise Sages, which would be a Sort of Ingratitude; and he that calls a Man ungrateful, sums up all the Evil that a Man can be guilty of.

Ingratum si dixeris, omnia dicis.

But what I blame the Philosophers for, (although some may think it a Paradox) is chiefly their Pride; nothing less than an *ipse dixit,* and you mast pin your Faith on their Sleeve. And, although *Diogenes* lived in a Tub, there might be, for ought I know, as much Pride under his Rags, as in the fine spun Garment of the Divine *Plato.* It is reported of this *Diogenes,* that when *Alexander* came to see him, and promised to give him whatever he would ask; the *Cynick* only answered, *Take not from me, what thou canst not give me; but stand from between me and the Light;* which was almost as extravagant as the Philosopher that flung his Money into the Sea, with this remarkable Saying,——

How different was this Man from the Usurer, who being told his Son would spend all he had got, replied, *He cannot take more Pleasure in spending, than I did in getting it.* These Men could see the Faults of each other, but not their own; those they flung into the Bag behind; *Non videmus id manticæ quod in tergo est.* I may, perhaps, be censured for my free Opinions, by those carping *Momus,'* whom Authors worship as the *Indians* do the Devil, for fear. They will endeavour to give my Reputation as many Wounds as the Man in the Almanack; but I value it not; and perhaps, like Flies, they may buz so often about the

Candle, till they burn their Wings. They must pardon me, if I venture to give them this Advice, not to rail at what they cannot understand; it does but discover that self-tormenting Passion of Envy; than which, the greatest Tyrant never invented a more cruel Torment.

Invidia Siculi non invenere Tyranni
Tormentum majus.—— Juven.

I must be so bold, to tell my Criticks and Witlings, that they are no more Judges of this, than a Man that is born blind can have any true Idea of Colours. I have always observed, that your empty Vessels sound loudest: I value their Lashes as little, as the Sea did when *Xerxes* whipped it. The utmost Favour a Man can expect from them, is that which *Polyphemus* promised *Ulysses,* that he would devour him the last: They think to subdue a Writer, as *Cæsar* did his Enemy, with a *Veni, vidi, vici.* I confess, I value the Opinion of the judicious Few, a *Rymer,* a *Dennis,* or a *Walsh;* but for the rest, to give my Judgment at once; I think the long Dispute among the Philosophers about a *Vacuum,* may be determined in the Affirmative, that it is to be found in a Critick's Head. They are, at best, but the Drones of the learned World, who devour the Honey, and will not work themselves; and a Writer need no more regard them, than the Moon does the Barking of a little sensless Cur. For, in spight of their terrible Roaring, you may with half an Eye discover the *Ass* under the *Lyon's* Skin.

BUT to return to our Discourse: *Demosthenes* being asked, what was the first Part of an Orator, replied, *Action:* What was the Second, *Action:* What was the Third, *Action:* And so on *ad infinitum.* This may be true in Oratory; but Contemplation, in other Things, exceeds Action. And, therefore, a wise Man is never less alone, than when he is alone:

Nunquam minus solus, quàm cum solus.

And *Archimedes,* the famous Mathematician, was so intent upon his Problems, that he never minded the Soldier who came to kill him. Therefore, not to detract from the just Praise which belongs to

Orators; they ought to consider that Nature, which gave us two Eyes to see, and two Ears to hear, hath given us but one Tongue to speak; wherein, however, some do so abound; that the *Virtuosi,* who have been so long in Search for the perpetual Motion, may infallibly find it there.

Some Men admire Republicks; because, Orators flourish there most, and are the great Enemies of Tyranny: But my Opinion is, that one Tryant is better than an Hundred. Besides, these Orators inflame the People, whose Anger is really but a short Fit of Madness.

Ira furor brevis est.—— Horat.

After which, Laws are like Cobwebs, which may catch small Flies, but let Wasps and Hornets break through. But in Oratory, the greatest Art is to hide Art.

Artis est celare Artem.

But this must be the Work of Time; we must lay hold on all Opportunities, and let slip no Occasion, else we shall be forced to weave *Penelope's* Web; unravel in the Night what we spun in the Day. And, therefore, I have observed that Time is painted with a Lock before, and bald behind; signifying thereby, that we must take Time (as we say) by the Forelock; for when it is once past, there is no recalling it.

The Mind of Man is, at first, (if you will pardon the Expression) like a *Tabula rasa;* or like Wax, which while it is soft, is capable of any Impression, until Time hath hardened it. And at length Death, that grim Tyrant, stops us in the Midst of our Career. The greatest Conquerors have at last been conquered by Death, which spares none from the Sceptre to the Spade.

Mors omnibus communis.

All Rivers go to the Sea, but none return from it. *Xerxes* wept when he beheld his Army; to consider that in less than an Hundred Years they would all be dead. *Anacreon* was choqued with a

Grape-stone; and violent Joy kills as well as violent Grief. There is nothing in this World constant, but Inconstancy; yet *Plato* thought, that if Virtue would appear to the World in her own native Dress, all Men would be enamoured with her. But now, since Interest governs the World, and Men neglect the Golden Mean, *Jupiter* himself, if he came on the Earth, would be despised, unless it were as he did to *Danaæ,* in a golden Shower. For Men, nowadays, worship the rising Sun, and not the setting.

Donec eris fœlix, multos numerabis amicos.

Thus have I, in Obedience to your Commands, ventured to expose my self to Censure in this Critical Age. Whether I have done Right to my Subject, must be left to the Judgment of the learned Reader: However, I cannot but hope, that my attempting of it may be an Encouragement for some able Pen to perform it with more Success.

AN ARGUMENT TO PROVE THAT THE ABOLISHING OF CHRISTIANITY IN ENGLAND, MAY AS THINGS NOW STAND, BE ATTENDED WITH SOME INCONVENIENCES, AND PERHAPS NOT PRODUCE THOSE MANY GOOD EFFECTS PROPOSED THEREBY (1708)

I AM VERY SENSIBLE WHAT A WEAKNESS AND PRESUMPTION IT IS, TO reason against the general humour and disposition of the world. I remember it was with great justice, and a due regard to the freedom both of the public and the press, forbidden upon severe penalties to write or discourse or lay wagers against the [Union] even before it was confirmed by parliament, because that was looked upon as a design to oppose the current of the people, which, besides the folly of it, is a manifest breach of the fundamental law that makes this majority of opinion the voice of God. In like manner, and for the very same reasons, it may perhaps be neither safe nor prudent to argue against the abolishing of Christianity, at a juncture when all parties seem so unanimously determined upon the point, as we cannot but allow from their actions, their discourses, and their writings. However, I know not how, whether from the affectation of singularity, or the perverseness of human nature, but so it unhappily falls out that I cannot be entirely of this opinion. Nay, though I were sure an order were issued for my immediate prosecution by the Attorney-General, I should still confess that in the present posture of our affairs at home or abroad, I do not yet see the absolute necessity of extirpating the Christian religion from among us.

This perhaps may appear too great a paradox even for our wise and paradoxical age to endure; therefore I shall handle it with all tenderness, and with the utmost deference to that great and profound majority which is of another sentiment.

And yet the curious may please to observe how much the genius of a nation is liable to alter in half an age. I have heard it affirmed for certain by some very old people, that the contrary opinion was even in their memories as much in vogue as the other is now; and that a project for the abolishing of Christianity would then have appeared as singular, and been thought as absurd, as it would be at this time to write or discourse in its defence.

Therefore I freely own that all appearances are against me. The system of the Gospel, after the fate of other systems, is generally antiquated and exploded, and the mass or body of the common people, among whom it seems to have had its latest credit, are now grown as much ashamed of it as their betters; opinions, like fashions, always descending from those of quality to the middle sort, and thence to the vulgar, where at length they are dropped and vanish.

But here I would not be mistaken, and must therefore be so bold as to borrow a distinction from the writers on the other side, when they make a difference betwixt nominal and real Trinitarians. I hope no reader imagines me so weak to stand up in the defence of real Christianity, such as used in primitive times (if we may believe the authors of those ages) to have an influence upon men's belief and actions. To offer at the restoring of that would indeed be a wild project; it would be to dig up foundations; to destroy at one blow all the wit, and half the learning of the kingdom; to break the entire frame and constitution of things; to ruin trade, extinguish arts and sciences with the professors of them; in short, to turn our courts, exchanges, and shops into deserts; and would be full as absurd as the proposal of Horace, where he advises the Romans all in a body to leave their city, and seek a new seat in some remote part of the world, by way of a cure for the corruption of their manners.

Therefore I think this caution was in itself altogether unnecessary, (which I have inserted only to prevent all possibility of cavilling) since every candid reader will easily understand my discourse to be intended only in defence of nominal Christianity; the other having been for some time wholly laid aside by general consent, as utterly inconsistent with all our present schemes of wealth and power.

But why we should therefore cast off the name and title of Christians, although the general opinion and resolution be so violent for it, I confess I cannot (with submission) apprehend the consequence necessary. However, since the undertakers propose such wonderful advantages to the nation by this project, and advance many plausible objections against the systems of Christianity, I shall briefly consider the strength of both, fairly allow them their greatest weight, and offer such answers as I think most reasonable. After which I will beg leave to show what inconveniences may possibly happen by such an innovation, in the present posture of our affairs.

First, one great advantage proposed by the abolishing of Christianity is, that it would very much enlarge and establish liberty of conscience, that great bulwark of our nation and of the Protestant Religion, which is still too much limited by priestcraft, notwithstanding all the good intentions of the legislature, as we have lately found by a severe instance. For it is confidently reported, that two young gentlemen of real hopes, bright wit, and profound judgment, who upon a thorough examination of causes and effects, and by the mere force of natural abilities, without the least tincture of learning, having made a discovery that there was no God, and generously communicating their thoughts for the good of the public, were some time ago, by an unparallelled severity and upon I know not what obsolete law, broke for blasphemy. And as it hath been wisely observed, if persecution once begins, no man alive knows how far it may reach or where it will end.

In answer to all which, with deference to wiser judgments, I think this rather shows the necessity of a nominal religion among us. Great wits love to be free with the highest objects, and if they cannot be allowed a God to revile or renounce, they will speak evil of dignities, abuse the government, and reflect upon the ministry; which I am sure few will deny to be of much more pernicious consequence, according to the saying of Tiberius, *Deorum offensa diis curæ*. As to the particular fact related, I think it is not fair to argue from one instance, perhaps another cannot be produced; yet (to the comfort of all those who may be apprehensive of persecution) blasphemy we know is freely spoke a million of times in every coffeehouse and tavern, or wherever else good company meet. It must be allowed indeed, that to break an English freeborn officer only for blasphemy was, to speak the gentlest of such an action, a very high strain of absolute power. Little can be said in excuse for the general; perhaps he was afraid it might give offence to the allies, among whom, for aught we know, it may be the custom of the country to believe a God. But if he argued, as some have done, upon a mistaken principle that an officer who is guilty of speaking blasphemy, may some time or other proceed so far as to raise a mutiny, the consequence is by no means to be admitted; for surely, the commander of an English army is like to be but ill obeyed whose soldiers fear and reverence him as little as they do a Deity.

It is further objected against the Gospel System, that it obliges men to the belief of things too difficult for freethinkers and such who have shaken off the prejudices that usually cling to a confined education. To which I answer that men should be cautious how they raise objections which reflect upon the wisdom of the nation. Is not everybody freely allowed to believe whatever he pleases and to publish his belief to the world whenever he thinks fit, especially if it serves to strengthen the party which is in the right? Would any indifferent foreigner who should read the trumpery lately written by Asgil, Tindal, Toland, Coward, and forty more, imagine the Gospel to be our rule of faith and to be confirmed by parliaments? Does any man either believe, or say he believes, or desire to have it thought that he says he believes one syllable of the matter? And is any man worse received upon that score, or does he find his want of nominal faith a disadvantage to him in the pursuit of any civil or military employment? What if there be an old dormant statute or two against him, are they not now obsolete, to a degree that Empson and Dudley themselves if they were now alive, would find it impossible to put them in execution?

It is likewise urged that there are, by computation, in this kingdom above ten thousand parsons, whose revenues added to those of my lords the bishops would suffice to maintain at least two hundred young gentlemen of wit and pleasure and free-thinking, enemies to priestcraft, narrow principles, pedantry, and prejudices; who might be an ornament to the Court and Town. And then again, so great a number of able [bodied] divines might be a recruit to our fleet and armies. This indeed appears to be a consideration of some weight. But then, on the other side, several things deserve to be considered likewise: as, first, whether it may not be thought necessary that in certain tracts of country, like what we call parishes, there should be one man at least of abilities to read and write. Then it seems a wrong computation that the revenues of the Church throughout this island would be large enough to maintain two hundred young gentlemen or even half that number, after the present refined way of living; that is, to allow each of them such a rent as in the modern form of speech would make them easy. But still there is in this project a greater mischief behind, and we ought to beware of the woman's folly who killed the hen that every morning laid her a golden egg. For, pray what would become of the race of men in the next age if we had nothing to trust to besides the scrofulous, consumptive productions furnished by our men of wit and pleasure, when, having squandered away their vigour, health and estates, they are forced by some disagreeable marriage to piece up their broken fortunes and entail rottenness and politeness on their posterity? Now, here are ten thousand persons reduced by the wise regulations of Henry the Eighth to the necessity of a low diet and moderate exercise, who are the only great restorers of our breed, without which the nation would in an age or two become one great hospital.

Another advantage proposed by the abolishing of Christianity is the clear gain of one day in seven, which is now entirely lost and consequently the kingdom one seventh less considerable in trade, business, and pleasure; beside the loss to the public of so many stately structures now in the hands of the Clergy, which might be converted into playhouses, exchanges, market-houses, common dormitories, and other public edifices.

I hope I shall be forgiven a hard word if I call this a perfect *cavil.* I readily own there hath been an old custom time out of mind for people to assemble in the churches every *Sunday,* and that shops are still frequently shut in order as it is conceived to preserve the memory of that ancient practise; but how this can prove a hindrance to business or pleasure is hard to imagine. What if the men of pleasure are forced one day in the week to game at home instead of the chocolate-house? Are not the taverns and coffeehouses open? Can there be a more convenient season for taking a dose of physic? Are fewer claps got upon Sundays than other days? Is not that the chief day for traders to sum up the accounts of the week and for lawyers to prepare their briefs? But I would fain know how it can be pretended that the churches are misapplied? Where are more appointments and rendezvous of gallantry? Where more care to appear in the foremost box with greater advantage of dress? Where more meetings for business? Where more bargains driven of all sorts? And where so many conveniences or incitements to sleep?

There is one advantage greater than any of the foregoing proposed by the abolishing of Christianity: that it will utterly extinguish parties among us, by removing those factious distinctions of High and Low Church, of Whig and Tory, Presbyterian and Church of England, which are now so many mutual clogs upon public proceedings, and are apt to prefer the gratifying themselves or depressing their adversaries, before the most important interest of the state.

I confess, if it were certain that so great an advantage would redound to the nation by this expedient I would submit and be silent. But will any man say that if the words *whoring, drinking, cheating, lying, stealing,* were by act of parliament ejected out of the English tongue and dictionaries, we should all awake next morning chaste and temperate, honest and just, and lovers of truth? Is this a fair consequence? Or if the physicians would forbid us to pronounce the words *pox, gout, rheumatism* and *stone,* would that expedient serve like so many *talismans* to destroy the diseases themselves? Are party and faction rooted in men's hearts no deeper than phrases borrowed from religion, or founded upon no firmer principles? And is our language so poor that we cannot find other terms to express them?

Are envy, pride, avarice and ambition such ill nomenclators that they cannot furnish appellations for their owners? Will not *heydukes* and *mamalukes, mandarins* and *patshaws,* or any other words formed at pleasure, serve to distinguish those who are in the ministry, from others who would be in it if they could? What, for instance, is easier than to vary the form of speech, and instead of the word church, make it a question in politics whether the Monument be in danger? Because religion was nearest at hand to furnish a few convenient phrases, is our invention so barren we can find no others? Suppose, for argument sake, that the Tories favoured Margarita, the Whigs Mrs Tofts, and the Trimmers Valentini; would not *Margaritians, Toftians,* and *Valentinians* be very tolerable marks of distinction? The Prasini and Veniti, two most virulent factions in Italy, began (if I remember right) by a distinction of colours in ribbons, which we might do with as good a grace about the dignity of the *blue* and the *green,* and serve as properly to divide the Court, the Parliament, and the Kingdom between them, as any terms of art whatsoever borrowed from religion. And therefore I think there is little force in this objection against Christianity, or prospect of so great an advantage as is proposed in the abolishing of it.

'Tis again objected as a very absurd ridiculous custom, that a set of men should be suffered, much less employed and hired, to bawl one day in seven against the lawfulness of those methods most in use towards the pursuit of greatness, riches and pleasure, which are the constant practise of all men alive on the other six. But this objection is, I think, a little unworthy so refined an age as ours. Let us argue this matter calmly. I appeal to the breast of any polite freethinker whether in the pursuit of gratifying a predominant passion, he hath not always felt a wonderful incitement by reflecting it was a thing forbidden; and therefore we see, in order to cultivate this taste, the wisdom of the nation hath taken special care that the ladies should be furnished with prohibited silks, and the men with prohibited wine. And indeed it were to be wished that some other prohibitions were promoted, in order to improve the pleasures of the town; which for want of such expedients begin already, as I am told, to flag and grow languid, giving way daily to cruel inroads from the spleen.

'Tis likewise proposed as a great advantage to the public, that if we once discard the system of the Gospel, all religion will of course be banished forever, and consequently, along with it, those grievous prejudices of education which under the names of virtue, conscience, honour, justice, and the like, are so apt to disturb the peace of human minds, and the notions whereof are so hard to be eradicated by right reason or free-thinking, sometimes during the whole course of our lives.

Here first I observe how difficult it is to get rid of a phrase, which the world is once grown fond of, though the occasion that first produced it be entirely taken away. For some years past, if a man had but an ill-favoured nose, the deep thinkers of the age would some way or other contrive to impute the cause to the prejudice of his education. From this fountain were said to be derived all our foolish notions of justice, piety, love of our country, all our opinions of God or a future state, Heaven, Hell, and the like. And there might formerly perhaps have been some pretence for this charge. But so effectual care hath been since taken to remove those prejudices by an entire change in the methods of education, that (with honour I mention it to our polite innovators) the young gentlemen who are now on the scene seem to have not the least tincture of those infusions or string of those weeds; and, by consequence, the reason for abolishing nominal Christianity upon that pretext is wholly ceased.

For the rest, it may perhaps admit a controversy, whether the banishing of all notions of religion whatsoever would be convenient for the vulgar. Not that I am in the least of opinion with those who hold religion to have been the invention of politicians, to keep the lower part of the world in awe by the fear of invisible powers; unless mankind were then very different from what it is now. For I look upon the mass or body of our people here in England, to be as freethinkers, that is to say, as staunch unbelievers, as any of the highest rank. But I conceive some scattered notions about a superior power to be of singular use for the common people, as furnishing excellent materials to keep children quiet when they grow peevish, and providing topics of amusement in a tedious winter night.

Lastly, 'tis proposed as a singular advantage that the abolishing of Christianity will very much contribute to the uniting of Protestants, by enlarging the terms of communion so as to take in all sorts of dissenters who are now shut out of the pale upon account of a few ceremonies which all sides confess to be things indifferent; that this alone will effectually answer the great ends of a scheme for comprehension, by opening a large noble gate at which all bodies may enter; whereas the chaffering with dissenters, and dodging about this or t'other ceremony, is but like opening a few wickets and leaving them ajar, by which no more than one can get in at a time, and that not without stooping, and sideling, and squeezing his body.

To all this I answer that there is one darling inclination of mankind, which usually affects to be a retainer to religion, though she be neither its parent, its godmother, nor its friend; I mean the spirit of opposition, that lived long before Christianity and can easily subsist without it. Let us for instance examine wherein the opposition of sectaries among us consists, we shall find Christianity to have no share in it at all. Does the Gospel any where prescribe a starched squeezed countenance, a stiff formal gait, a singularity of manners and habit, or any affected forms and modes of speech different from the reasonable part of mankind? Yet, if Christianity did not lend its name to stand in the gap and to employ or divert these humours, they must of necessity be spent in contraventions to the laws of the land, and disturbance of the public peace. There is a portion of enthusiasm assigned to every nation, which, if it hath not proper objects to work on, will burst out and set all into a flame. If the quiet of a state can be bought by only flinging men a few ceremonies to devour, it is a purchase no wise man would refuse. Let the mastiffs amuse themselves about a sheepskin stuffed with hay, provided it will keep them from worrying the flock. The institution of convents abroad seems in one point a strain of great wisdom, there being few irregularities in human passions which may not have recourse to vent themselves in some of those orders, which are so many retreats for the speculative, the melancholy, the proud, the silent, the politic, and the morose, to spend themselves and evaporate the noxious particles; for each of whom we in this island are forced to provide a several sect of religion to keep them quiet. And whenever Christianity shall be abolished, the legislature must find some other expedient to employ and entertain them. For what imports it how large a gate you open, if there will be always left a number who place a pride and a merit in not coming in?

Having thus considered the most important objections against Christianity and the chief advantages proposed by the abolishing thereof, I shall now with equal deference and submission to wiser judgments as before, proceed to mention a few inconveniences that may happen if the Gospel should be repealed, which perhaps the projectors may not have sufficiently considered.

And first, I am very sensible how much the gentlemen of wit and pleasure are apt to murmur, and be choqued at the sight of so many daggled-tail parsons that happen to fall in their way, and offend their eyes; but at the same time these wise reformers do not consider what an advantage and felicity it is for great wits to be always provided with objects of scorn and contempt, in order to exercise and improve their talents and divert their spleen from falling on each other or on themselves; especially when all this may be done without the least imaginable danger to their persons.

And to urge another argument of a parallel nature, if Christianity were once abolished how would the freethinkers, the strong reasoners, and the men of profound learning, be able to find another subject so calculated in all points whereon to display their abilities? What wonderful productions of wit should we be deprived of, from those whose genius by continual practise hath been wholly turned upon raillery and invectives against religion, and would therefore never be able to shine or distinguish themselves upon any other subject? We are daily complaining of the great decline of wit among us, and would we take away the greatest, perhaps the only topic we have left? Who would ever have suspected Asgil for a wit, or Toland for a philosopher, if the inexhaustible stock of Christianity had not been at hand to provide them with materials? What other subject through all art or nature could have produced Tindal for a profound author, or furnished him with readers? It is the wise choice of the subject that alone adorns and distinguishes the writer. For, had a hundred such pens as these been employed on the side of religion, they would have immediately sunk into silence and oblivion.

Nor do I think it wholly groundless, or my fears altogether imaginary, that the abolishing of Christianity may perhaps bring the Church in danger, or at least put the senate to the trouble of another securing vote. I desire I may not be mistaken. I am far from presuming to affirm or think that the Church is in danger at present, or as things now stand, but we know not how soon it may be so when the Christian religion is repealed. As plausible as this project seems, there may a dangerous design lurk under it. Nothing can be more notorious than that the Atheists, Deists, Socinians, Anti-Trinitarians, and other subdivisions of freethinkers, are persons of little zeal for the present ecclesiastical establishment. Their declared opinion is for repealing the Sacramental Test; they are very indifferent with regard to ceremonies; nor do they hold the *jus divinum* of Episcopacy. Therefore this may be intended as one politic step towards altering the constitution of the Church established, and setting up Presbytery in the stead, which I leave to be further considered by those at the helm.

In the last place, I think nothing can be more plain than that by this expedient we shall run into the evil we chiefly pretend to avoid, and that the abolishment of the Christian religion will be the readiest course we can take to introduce popery. And I am the more inclined to this opinion because we know it has been the constant practice of the Jesuits to send over emissaries with instructions to personate themselves members of the several prevailing sects amongst us. So it is recorded that they have at sundry times appeared in the guise of Presbyterians, Anabaptists, Independents, and Quakers, according as any of these were most in credit; so, since the fashion hath been taken up of exploding religion, the popish missionaries have not been wanting to mix with the freethinkers, among whom Toland, the great oracle of the Antichristians, is an Irish priest, the son of an Irish priest; and the most learned and ingenious author of a book called *The Rights of the Christian Church,* was in a proper juncture reconciled to the Romish faith, whose true son (as appears by a hundred passages in his treatise) he still continues. Perhaps I could add some others to the number; but the fact is beyond dispute, and the reasoning they proceed by is right. For, supposing Christianity to be extinguished, the people will never be at ease till they find out some other method of worship, which will as infallibly produce superstition, as this will end in popery.

And therefore, if notwithstanding all I have said it still be thought necessary to have a bill brought in for repealing Christianity, I would humbly offer an amendment, that instead of the word Christianity, may be put Religion in general; which I conceive will much better answer all the good ends proposed by the projectors of it. For, as long as we leave in being a God and his Providence, with all the necessary consequences which curious and inquisitive men will be apt to draw from such premises, we do not strike at the root of the evil though we should ever so effectually annihilate the present scheme of the Gospel. For, of what use is freedom of thought if it will not produce freedom of action, which is the sole end, how remote soever in appearance, of all objections against Christianity? And therefore the freethinkers consider it as a sort of edifice, wherein all the parts have such a mutual dependence on each other that if you happen to pull out one single nail, the whole fabric must fall to the ground. This was happily expressed by him who had heard of a text brought for proof of the Trinity, which in an ancient manuscript was differently read; he thereupon immediately took the hint, and by a sudden deduction of a long sorites most logically concluded "Why, if it be as you say, I may safely whore and drink on, and defy the parson." From which, and many the like instances easy to be produced, I think nothing can be more manifest than that the quarrel is not against any particular points of hard digestion in the Christian system, but against religion in general, which, by laying restraints on human nature, is supposed the great enemy to the freedom of thought and action.

Upon the whole, if it shall still be thought for the benefit of Church and State that Christianity be abolished, I conceive however it may be more convenient to defer the execution to a time of peace, and not venture in this conjuncture to disoblige our allies who, as it falls out, are all Christians, and many of them by the prejudices of their education so bigoted as to place a sort of pride in the appellation. If upon being rejected by them, we are to trust an alliance with the Turk, we shall find ourselves much deceived. For, as he is too remote, and generally engaged in war with the Persian emperor, so his people would be more scandalized at our infidelity than our Christian neighbours. For they are not only strict observers of religious worship, but what is worse, believe a God; which is more than is required of us even while we preserve the name of Christians.

To conclude, whatever some may think of the great advantages to trade by this favourite scheme, I do very much apprehend that in six months time after the Act is passed for the extirpation of the Gospel, the Bank and East India Stock may fall at least one *percent.* And since that is fifty times more than ever the wisdom of our age thought fit to venture for the preservation of Christianity, there is no reason we should be at so great a loss merely for the sake of destroying it.

THE EXAMINER NO. 14 (THURSDAY, NOVEMBER 9, 1710)

E quibus hi vacuas implent Sermonibus aures,
Hi narrata ferunt alio: mensuraque ficti
Crescit, & auditis aliquid novus adjicit autor,
Illic Credulitas, illic temerarius Error,
Vanaque Lætitia est, consternatique Timores,
Seditioque recens, dubioque autore susurri.[1]

I AM PREVAILED ON, THROUGH THE IMPORTUNITY OF FRIENDS, TO interrupt the Scheme I had begun in my last Paper, by an Essay upon the Art of *Political Lying.* We are told, *The Devil is the Father of Lyes,* and *was a Lyar from the beginning;* so that, beyond Contradiction, the Invention is old: And, which is more, his first Essay of it was purely *Political,* employed in undermining the Authority of his Prince, and seducing a third Part of the Subjects from their Obedience. For which he was driven down from Heaven, where (as *Milton* expresseth it) he had been VICEROY of a great *Western Province;* and forced to exercise his Talent in inferior Regions among *other fallen Spirits,* or *poor deluded Men,* whom he still daily tempts to *his own Sin,* and will ever do so till he be *chained in the bottomless Pit.*

But although the Devil be the Father of *Lyes,* he seems, like other great Inventors, to have lost much of his Reputation, by the continual Improvements that have been made upon him.

Who first reduced *Lying* into an Art, and adapted it to *Politicks,* is not so clear from History; although I have made some diligent Enquiries: I shall therefore consider it only according to the modern System, as it hath been cultivated these twenty Years past in the Southern Part of our own Island.

The Poets tell us, That after the Giants were overthrown by the Gods, the *Earth* in revenge produced her last Offspring, which was *Fame.* And the Fable is thus interpreted; That when Tumults and Seditions are quieted, Rumours and false Reports are plentifully spread through a Nation. So that by this Account, *Lying* is the last Relief of a *routed, earth-born, rebellious Party* in a State. But here, the Moderns have made great Additions, applying this Art to the gaining of Power, and preserving it, as well as revenging themselves after they have lost it: As the same Instruments are made use of by Animals to feed themselves when they are hungry, and bite those that tread upon them.

But the same Genealogy cannot always be admitted for *Political Lying;* I shall therefore desire to refine upon it, by adding some Circumstances of its Birth and Parents. A *Political Lye* is sometimes born out of a discarded Statesman's Head, and thence delivered to be nursed and dandled by the *Mob.* Sometimes it is produced a Monster, and *licked* into Shape; at other Times it comes into the World compleatly formed, and is spoiled in the *licking.* It is often born an Infant in the regular Way, and requires Time to mature it: And often it sees the Light in its full Growth, but dwindles away by Degrees. Sometimes it is of noble Birth; and sometimes the Spawn of a *Stock-jobber. Here,* it screams aloud at opening the Womb; and *there,* it is delivered with a *Whisper.* I know a *Lye* that now disturbs half the Kingdom with its Noise, which although too proud and great at present to own its Parents, I can remember in its *Whisper-hood.* To conclude the Nativity of this Monster; when it comes into the World without a *Sting,* it is stillborn; and whenever it loses its *Sting,* it dies.

No Wonder, if an Infant so miraculous in its Birth, should be destined for great Adventures: And accordingly we see it hath been the *Guardian Spirit* of a *prevailing Party* for almost twenty Years. It can conquer Kingdoms without Fighting, and sometimes with the Loss of a Battle: It gives and resumes Employments; can sink a Mountain to a Mole-hill, and raise a Mole-hill to a Mountain; hath presided for many Years at Committees of Elections; can wash a *Black-a-moor* white; make a Saint of an Atheist, and a Patriot of a Profligate; can furnish *Foreign Ministers* with Intelligence; and raise or let fall the Credit of the Nation. This Goddess flies with a huge *Looking-glass* in her Hands to dazzle the Crowd, and make them see, according as she turns it, their Ruin in their Interest, and their Interest in their Ruin. In this Glass you will behold your best Friends clad in Coats powdered with *Flower-de-Luce's* and *Triple Crowns*; their Girdles hung round with *Chains,* and *Beads,* and *Wooden Shoes*: And your worst Enemies adorned with the Ensigns of *Liberty, Property, Indulgence, Moderation,* and a *Cornucopia in* their Hands. Her large Wings, like those of a flying Fish, are of no Use but while they are moist; she therefore dips them in *Mud,* and soaring aloft scatters it in the Eyes of the Multitude, flying with great Swiftness; but at every Turn is forced to stoop in *dirty Ways* for new Supplies.

I have been sometimes thinking, if a Man had the Art of the *Second Sight* for seeing *Lyes,* as they have in *Scotland* for seeing Spirits; how admirably he might entertain himself in this Town; to observe the different Shapes, Sizes and Colours, of those Swarms of *Lyes* which buz about the Heads of *some People,* like Flies about a Horse's Ears in Summer: Or those Legions hovering every Afternoon in *Exchange-Alley,* enough to darken the Air; or over a Club of discontented Grandees, and thence sent down in Cargoes to be scattered at Elections.

There is one essential Point wherein a *Political Lyar* differs from others of the Faculty; That he ought to have but a short Memory, which is necessary according to the various Occasions he meets with every Hour, of differing from himself, and swearing to both Sides of a Contradiction, as he finds the Persons disposed, with whom he hath to deal. In describing the Virtues and Vices of Mankind, it is convenient, upon every Article, to have some eminent Person in our Eye, from whence we copy our Description. I have strictly observed this Rule; and my Imagination this Minute represents before me a certain[2] *Great Man* famous for this Talent, to the constant Practice of which he owes his twenty Years Reputation of the most skilful Head in *England,* for the Management of nice Affairs. The Superiority of his

Genius consists in nothing else but an inexhaustible Fund of *Political Lyes,* which he plentifully distributes every Minute he speaks, and by an unparallelled Generosity forgets, and consequently contradicts the next half Hour. He never yet considered whether any Proposition were True or False, but whether it were convenient for the present Minute or Company to affirm or deny it; so that if you think to refine upon him, by interpreting every Thing he says, as we do Dreams by the contrary, you are still to seek, and will find your self equally deceived, whether you believe or no: The only Remedy is to suppose that you have heard some inarticulate Sounds, without any Meaning at all. And besides, that will take off the Horror you might be apt to conceive at the Oaths wherewith he perpetually Tags both ends of every *Proposition:* Although at the same Time, I think, he cannot with any Justice be taxed for Perjury, when he invokes *God* and *Christ*; because he hath often fairly given publick Notice to the World, that he believes in neither.

Some People may think that such an Accomplishment as this, can be of no great Use to the Owner or his Party, after it hath been often practised, and is become notorious; but they are widely mistaken: Few *Lyes* carry the Inventor's Mark; and the most prostitute Enemy to Truth may spread a thousand without being known for the Author. Besides, as the vilest Writer hath his Readers, so the greatest *Lyar* hath his Believers; and it often happens, that if a *Lye* be believed only for an Hour, it hath done its Work, and there is no farther Occasion for it. *Falshood flies,* and *Truth* comes *limping* after it; so that when Men come to be undeceived, it is too late, the Jest is over, and the Tale has had its Effect: Like a Man who has thought of a good Repartee, when the Discourse is changed, or the Company parted: Or, like a Physician who hath found out an infallible Medicine after the Patient is dead.

Considering that natural Disposition in many Men to *Lye,* and in Multitudes to *Believe*; I have been perplexed what to do with that Maxim, so frequent in every Bodies Mouth, That *Truth will at last prevail.* Here, has this Island of ours, for the greatest Part of twenty Years lain under the Influence of such Counsels and Persons, whose Principle and Interest it was to corrupt our Manners, blind our

Understandings, drain our Wealth, and in Time destroy our Constitution both in Church and State; and we at last were brought to the very Brink of Ruin; yet by the Means of perpetual Misrepresentations, have never been able to distinguish between our Enemies and Friends. We have seen a great Part of the Nation's Money got into the Hands of those, who by their Birth, Education and Merit, could pretend no higher than to wear our Liveries. While others, who by their Credit, Quality and Fortune, were only able to give Reputation and Success to the Revolution, were not only laid aside, as dangerous and useless; but loaden with the Scandal of *Jacobites,* Men of *Arbitrary Principles,* and *Pensioners* to *France*; while Truth, who is said to *lie in a Well,* seemed now to be buried there under a heap of Stones. But I remember it was a usual Complaint among the *Whigs,* that the Bulk of Landed-Men was not in their Interests, which some of the Wisest looked on as an ill Omen; and we saw it was with the utmost Difficulty that they could preserve a Majority, while the Court and Ministry were on their Side; till they had learned those admirable Expedients for deciding Elections, and influencing distant Boroughs, by *powerful Motives* from the City. But all this was meer Force and Constraint, however upheld by most dextrous Artifice and Management; until the People began to apprehend their *Properties,* their *Religion,* and the *Monarchy* itself in Danger; then we saw them greedily laying hold on the first Occasion to interpose. But of this mighty Change in the Dispositions of the People, I shall discourse more at large in some following Paper; wherein I shall endeavour to undeceive or discover those deluded or deluding Persons, who hope or pretend, it is only a short Madness in the Vulgar, from which they may soon recover. Whereas, I believe, it will appear, to be very different in its Causes, its Symptoms, and its Consequences; and prove a great Example to illustrate the Maxim I lately mentioned, That *Truth* (however sometimes late) *will at last prevail.*

TO THE TRADESMEN, SHOPKEEPERS, FARMERS, AND COMMON-PEOPLE IN GENERAL, OF THE KINGDOM OF IRELAND (1724)[1]

Brethren, Friends, Countrymen, and Fellow-subjects

WHAT I INTEND NOW TO SAY TO YOU, IS, NEXT TO YOUR DUTY TO God, and the Care of your Salvation, of the greatest Concern to your selves, and your Children; your *Bread* and *Cloathing,* and every common Necessary of Life entirely depend upon it. Therefore I do most earnestly exhort you as *Men,* as *Christians,* as *Parents,* and as *Lovers of your Country,* to read this Paper with the utmost Attention, or get it read to you by others; which that you may do at the less Expence, I have ordered the Printer to sell it at the lowest Rate.

It is a great Fault among you, that when a Person writes with no other Intention than *to do you Good, you will not be at the Pains to read his Advices:* One Copy of this Paper may serve a Dozen of you, which will be less than a Farthing apiece. It is your Folly, that you have no common or general Interest in your View, not even the Wisest among you; neither do you know or enquire, or care who are your Friends, or who are your Enemies.

About four Years ago, a little Book was written to advise all People to wear the[2] *Manufactures of this our own Dear Country:* It had no other Design, said nothing against the *King* or *Parliament,* or *any* Person whatsoever, yet the POOR PRINTER[3] was prosecuted two Years, with the utmost Violence; and even some WEAVERS themselves, for whose Sake it was written, being upon the JURY, FOUND HIM GUILTY. This would be enough to discourage any Man from endeavouring to do you Good, when you will either neglect him, or fly in his Face for his Pains; and when he must expect only *Danger to himself,* and to be fined and imprisoned, perhaps to his Ruin.

However, I cannot but warn you once more of the manifest Destruction before your Eyes, if you do not behave your selves as you ought.

I will therefore first tell you the *plain Story of the Fact;* and then I will lay before you, how you ought to act in common Prudence, and according to the *Laws of your Country.*

The Fact is thus; It having been many Years since COPPER HALF PENCE or FARTHINGS were last Coined in this *Kingdom,* they have been for some Time very scarce, and many *Counterfeits* passed about under the Name of RAPS: Several Applications were made to *England,* that we might have Liberty to *Coin New Ones,* as in former Times we did; but they did not succeed. At last one Mr. WOOD, *a mean ordinary Man, a Hard-Ware Dealer,* procured a *Patent* under His MAJESTY'S BROAD SEAL, to coin 108000*l.* in *Copper* for this *Kingdom;* which Patent however did not oblige anyone here to take them, unless they pleased. Now you must know, that the HALF PENCE and FARTHINGS in *England* pass for very little more than they are worth: And if you should beat them to Pieces, and sell them to the *Brazier,* you would not lose much above a Penny in a Shilling. But Mr. WOOD made his HALF PENCE of such *Base Metal,* and so much smaller than the *English* ones, that the *Brazier* would hardly give you above a *Penny* of good Money for a *Shilling* of his; so that this sum of 108000*l.* in good Gold and Silver, must be given for TRASH that will not be worth above *Eight* or *Nine Thousand Pounds* real Value. But this is not the Worst; for Mr. WOOD, when he pleases, may by Stealth send over *another* 108000*l.* and buy *all our Goods for Eleven Parts in Twelve,* under the Value. For Example, if a *Hatter* sells a Dozen of *Hats* for *Five Shillings* a-piece, which amounts to *Three Pounds,* and receives the Payment in Mr. WOOD'S Coin, he really receives only the Value of *Five Shillings.*

Perhaps you will wonder how such an *ordinary Fellow* as this Mr. Wood could have so much Interest as to get his Majesty's Broad Seal for so great a Sum of bad Money, to be sent to this poor Country; and that all the *Nobility* and *Gentry* here could not obtain the same Favour, and let us make our own Half Pence, as we used to do. Now I will make that Matter very plain. We are at a great Distance from the *King's Court* and have no body there to solicit for us, although a great Number of *Lords* and *Squires,* whose Estates are here, and are our Countrymen, spend all their *Lives* and *Fortunes* there. But this same Mr. Wood was able to attend constantly for his own Interest; he is an Englishman and had Great Friends, and it seems knew very well *where to give Money* to those that would speak to Others that could speak to the King, and would tell a Fair Story. And His Majesty, and perhaps the great Lord or Lords who advised him, might think it was for our *Country's Good;* and so, as the Lawyers express it, the King was deceived in his Grant; which often happens in *all Reigns.* And I am sure if His Majesty knew that such a Patent, if it should take Effect according to the Desire of Mr. Wood, would utterly ruin this Kingdom, which hath given such great Proofs of its *Loyalty;* he would immediately recall it, and perhaps shew his Displeasure to Some Body or Other: *But a Word to the Wise is enough.* Most of you must have heard with what Anger our *Honourable House of Commons* received an Account of this Wood's Patent. There were several *Fine Speeches* made upon it, and plain Proofs, that it was all a Wicked Cheat from the *Bottom to the Top;* and several *smart Votes* were printed, which that same Wood had the Assurance to answer likewise in *Print,* and in so confident a Way, as if he were *a better Man than our whole Parliament* put together.

This Wood, as soon as his *Patent* was passed, or soon after, sends over a great many *Barrels of those* Half Pence, to *Cork* and other *Sea-Port Towns,* and to get them off, offered an *Hundred Pounds* in his *Coin* for *Seventy* or *Eighty* in *Silver:* But the *Collectors* of the King's Customs very honestly refused to take them, and so did almost everybody else. And since the Parliament hath condemned them, and desired the King that they might be stopped, all the *Kingdom* do abominate them.

But WOOD is still working *under hand* to force his HALF PENCE upon us; and if he can by help of his *Friends* in *England* prevail so far as to get an Order that the *Commissioners* and *Collectors* of the *King's* Money shall receive them, and that the *Army* is to be paid with them, then he thinks *his Work shall be done.* And this is the Difficulty you will be under in such a *Case:* For the common Soldier when he goes to the *Market* or *Alehouse,* will offer this Money, and if it be refused, perhaps he will *swagger* and *hector,* and *threaten* to *beat* the *Butcher* or *Ale-wife,* or take the Goods by Force, and throw them the bad HALF PENCE. In this and the like Cases, the *Shopkeeper,* or *Victualler,* or *any other Tradesman* has no more to do, than to demand ten times the Price of his Goods, if it is to be paid in WOOD'S Money; for Example, Twenty Pence of that Money for a *Quart of Ale,* and so in all things else, and not part with his Goods till he gets the *Money.*

For suppose you go to an *Alehouse* with that base Money, and the *Landlord* gives you a Quart for Four of these HALF PENCE, what must the *Victualler* do? His *Brewer* will not be paid in that Coin, or if the *Brewer* should be such a Fool, the *Farmers* will not take it from them for their[4] *Bere,* because they are bound by their Leases to pay their Rents in Good and Lawful Money of *England,* which this is not, nor of *Ireland* neither, and the *Squire their Landlord* will never be so bewitched to take such *Trash* for his Land; so that it must certainly stop somewhere or other, and wherever it stops it is the same Thing, and we are all undone.

The common Weight of these HALF PENCE is between four and five to an *Ounce;* suppose five, then three Shillings and four Pence will weigh a Pound, and consequently *Twenty Shillings* will weigh *Six Pounds Butter Weight.* Now there are many hundred *Farmers* who pay Two hundred Pounds a Year Rent: Therefore when one of these *Farmers* comes with his Half-Year's Rent, which is One hundred Pound, it will be at least Six hundred Pound weight, which is Three Horses Load.

If a *Squire* has a mind to come to Town to buy Cloaths and Wine and Spices for himself and Family, or perhaps to pass the Winter here; he must bring with him five or six Horses loaden with *Sacks* as the *Farmers* bring their Corn; and when his Lady comes in her Coach to our Shops, it must be followed by a Car loaded with Mr. WOOD's Money. And I hope we shall have the Grace to take it for no more than it is worth.

They say SQUIRE CONOLLY has *Sixteen Thousand Pounds a Year;* now if he sends for his *Rent* to Town, *as it is likely he does,* he must have Two *Hundred and Fifty Horses* to bring up his *Half Year's Rent,* and two or three great *Cellars* in his House for Stowage. But what the Bankers will do I cannot tell. For I am assured, that some great Bankers keep by them *Forty Thousand Pounds* in ready Cash to answer all Payments, which Sum in Mr. WOOD's Money, would require Twelve Hundred Horses to carry it.

For my own Part, I am already resolved what to do; I have a pretty good Shop of *Irish Stuffs* and *Silks,* and instead of taking Mr. WOOD's bad Copper, I intend to Truck with my Neighbours the *Butchers,* and *Bakers,* and *Brewers,* and the rest, *Goods for Goods,* and the little *Gold* and *Silver* I have, I will keep by me like my *Heart's Blood* till better Times, or until I am just ready to starve, and then I will buy Mr. WOOD's Money, as my Father did the Brass Money in King *James'* Time; who could buy *Ten Pound* of it with a *Guinea,* and I hope to get as much for a *Pistole,* and so purchase *Bread* from those who will be such Fools as to sell it me.

These *Half pence,* if they once pass, will soon be *Counterfeit,* because it may be cheaply done, the *Stuff* is so *Base.* The *Dutch* likewise will probably do the same thing, and send them over to us to pay for our *Goods*; and Mr. WOOD will never be at rest, but coin on: So that in some Years we shall have at least five Times 108000*l.* of this *Lumber.* Now the current Money of this Kingdom is not reckoned to be above Four Hundred Thousand Pounds in all; and while there is a *Silver* Six-Pence left, these *Bloodsuckers* will never be quiet.

When once the *Kingdom* is reduced to such a Condition, I will tell you what must be the End: The *Gentlemen of Estates* will all turn off their *Tenants* for want of Payment; because, as I told you before, the *Tenants* are obliged by their Leases to pay *Sterling,* which is Lawful Current Money of *England;* then they will turn their own *Farmers, as too many of them do already,* run *all* into *Sheep*[5] where they can, keeping only such other *Cattle* as are necessary; then they will be their own

Merchants, and send their *Wool,* and *Butter,* and *Hides,* and *Linnen* beyond Sea for ready *Money,* and *Wine,* and *Spices,* and *Silks.* They will keep only a few miserable *Cottagers.* The *Farmers* must *Rob* or *Beg,* or leave their *Country.* The *Shopkeepers* in this and every other Town, must *Break* and *Starve:* For it is the *Landed-man* that maintains the *Merchant,* and *Shopkeeper,* and *Handicrafts-Man.*

But when the *Squire* turns *Farmer* and *Merchant* himself, all the good Money he gets from abroad, he will hoard up to send for *England,* and keep some poor *Taylor* or *Weaver,* and the like, in his own House, who will be glad to get Bread at any Rate.

I should never have done, if I were to tell you all the Miseries that we shall undergo, if we be so *Foolish* and *Wicked* as to take this *Cursed Coin.* It would be very hard, if all *Ireland* should be put into *One Scale,* and *this sorry Fellow* WOOD *into the other:* That Mr. WOOD should weigh down *this whole Kingdom,* by which *England* gets above a Million of good Money every Year clear into their *Pockets:* And that is more than the *English* do by *all the World besides.*

But your *great Comfort is,* that, as his Majesty's *Patent* doth not oblige you to take this *Money,* so the *Laws* have not given the Crown a Power of forcing the *Subjects* to take what *Money* the *King* pleases: For then by the same Reason we might be bound to take *Pebble-stones,* or *Cockle-shells,* or *stamped Leather* for *Current Coin;* if ever we should happen to live under an ill *Prince;* who might likewise by the same Power make a *Guinea* pass for Ten Pounds, a *Shilling* for Twenty Shillings, and so on; by which he would in a short Time get all the *Silver* and *Gold* of the *Kingdom* into his own Hands, and leave us nothing but *Brass* or *Leather,* or what he pleased. Neither is anything reckoned more *Cruel* or *Oppressive* in the *French Government,* than their common Practice of calling in all their Money after they have sunk it very low, and then coining it a-new at a much higher Value; which however is not the Thousandth Part so wicked as this *abominable Project* of Mr. *Wood.* For the *French* give their Subjects *Silver* for *Silver,* and *Gold* for *Gold;* but this *Fellow* will not so much as give us good *Brass* or *Copper* for our *Gold* and *Silver,* nor even a Twelfth Part of their Worth.

Having said this much, I will now go on to tell you the Judgments of some great *Lawyers* in this Matter; whom I fee'd on purpose for your Sakes, and got their *Opinions* under their *Hands,* that I might be sure I went upon good Grounds.

A famous Law-Book *called the* Mirrour of Justice,[6] *discoursing of the Charters (or Laws) ordained by our* Ancient Kings, *declares the* Law *to be as follows: It was ordained that no* King *of this Realm should* Change, *or* Impair *the* Money, or *make any other* Money *than of* Gold or Silver *without the Assent of all the Counties, that is,* as my Lord *Coke says, without the Assent of* Parliament.

This Book is very Ancient, and of great Authority for the Time in which it was wrote, and with that Character is often quoted by that great Lawyer my Lord *Coke.*[7] By the Laws of *England,* the several Metals are divided into *Lawful* or *true Metal* and *unlawful* or *false Metal;* the Former comprehends *Silver* or *Gold,* the Latter all *Baser Metals:* That the Former is only to pass in Payments, appears by an Act of *Parliament* made the Twentieth Year of *Edward* the *First,* called the *Statute concerning the passing of Pence;* which I give you here as I got it translated into *English;* For some of our *Laws* at that time were, as I am told, writ in *Latin: Whoever in Buying or Selling presumeth to refuse an Half-penny or Farthing of Lawful Money, bearing the Stamp which it ought to have, let him be seized on as a Contemner of the King's Majesty, and cast into Prison.*

By this *Statute,* no Person is to be reckoned a *Contemner* of the *King's Majesty,* and for that Crime to be *committed to Prison;* but he who refuseth to accept the King's Coin made of *Lawful Metal:* by which as I observed before, *Silver* and *Gold* only are intended.

That this is the true *Construction* of the *Act,* appears not only from the plain Meaning of the Words, but from my Lord *Coke's* Observation upon it. By this Act (says he) it appears, that no Subject can be forced to take in *Buying* or *Selling* or other *Payments,* any Money made but of lawful Metal; that is, of *Silver* or *Gold.*

The Law of *England* gives the King all Mines of *Gold* and *Silver,* but not the Mines of other *Metals;* the Reason of which *Prerogative* or *Power,* as it is given by my Lord *Coke,* is because Money can be made of *Gold* and *Silver;* but not of other Metals.

Pursuant to this Opinion, *Half pence* and *Farthings* were anciently made of *Silver,* which is evident from the Act of *Parliament* of *Henry* the

IVth Chap. 4. whereby it is enacted as follows: *Item, for the great Scarcity that is at present within the Realm of* England *of Half pence and Farthings of* Silver; *it is ordained and established, that the Third Part of all the* Money *of* Silver Plate *which shall be brought to the* Bullion, *shall be made in* Half pence *and* Farthings. This shews that by the Words *Half-penny* and *Farthing* of Lawful Money in that Statute concerning the *passing of* Pence, is meant a small Coin in *Half-pence* and *Farthings* of *Silver.*

This is further manifest from the Statute of the Ninth Year of *Edward* the III[d] Chap. 3. which enacts, *That no sterling* Halfpenny *or* Farthing *be Molten for to make Vessels, or any other thing by the Goldsmiths, nor others, upon Foreiture of the* Money *so molten (or melted).*

By another Act in this *King's* Reign, *Black Money* was not to be current in *England.* And by an Act made in the Eleventh Year of his Reign, Chap. 5. *Galley Half pence* were not to pass: What kind of *Coin* these were I do not know; but I presume they were made of *Base Metal.* And these Acts were no New *Laws,* but further Declarations of the old *Laws* relating to the Coin.

Thus the *Law* stands in Relation to *Coin.* Nor is there any Example to the contrary, except one in *Davis' Reports;* who tells us, that in the time of *Tyrone's* Rebellion, *Queen Elizabeth* ordered *Money* of *mixt Metal* to be coined in the Tower of *London,* and sent over hither for Payment of the *Army;* obliging all People to receive it; and Commanding, that all *Silver Money* should be taken only as *Bullion,* that is, for as much as it weighed. *Davis* tells us several Particulars in this Matter too long here to trouble you with, and that the *Privy Council* of this *Kingdom* obliged a *Merchant* in *England* to receive this *mixt Money* for Goods transmitted hither.

But this Proceeding is rejected by all the best Lawyers, as contrary to Law, the *Privy Council* here having no such legal Power. And besides it is to be considered, that the *Queen* was then under great Difficulties by a Rebellion in this *Kingdom* assisted from *Spain.* And, whatever is done in great Exigences and dangerous Times, should never be an Example to proceed by in Seasons of *Peace* and *Quietness.*

I will now, my dear Friends, to save you the Trouble, set before you in short, what the *Law* obliges you to do; and what it does not oblige you to.

First, you are obliged to take all Money in Payments which is coined by the *King*, and is of the *English* Standard or Weight; provided it be of *Gold* or *Silver.*

Secondly, you are not obliged to take any Money which is not of *Gold* or *Silver;* not only the *Half pence* or *Farthings* of *England,* but of any other Country. And it is meerly for Convenience, or Ease, that you are content to take them; because the Custom of coining *Silver Half pence* and *Farthings* hath long been left off; I suppose, on Account of their being subject to be lost.

Thirdly, Much less are you obliged to take those *Vile Half pence* of that same Wood, by which you must lose almost *Eleven-Pence* in every Shilling.

Therefore, my Friends, stand to it One and All: Refuse this *Filthy Trash.* It is no Treason to rebel against Mr. *Wood.* His *Majesty* in his Patent obliges no body to take these *Half pence:* Our *Gracious Prince* hath no such ill Advisers about him; or if he had, yet you see the Laws have not left it in the *King's* Power, to force us to take any Coin but what is Lawful, of right Standard, *Gold* and *Silver.* Therefore you have nothing to fear.

And let me in the next Place apply my self particularly to you who are the poorer Sort of *Tradesmen:* Perhaps you may think you will not be so great Losers as the Rich, if these *Half pence* should pass; because you seldom see any *Silver,* and your Customers come to your Shops or Stalls with nothing but *Brass;* which you likewise find hard to be got. But you may take my Word, whenever this Money gains Footing among you, you will be utterly undone. If you carry these *Half pence* to a Shop for *Tobacco* or *Brandy,* or any other Thing you want; the Shopkeeper will advance his Goods accordingly, or else he must break and leave the *Key under the Door.* Do you think I will sell you a Yard of Ten-penny Stuff for Twenty of Mr. *Wood's Half pence?* No, not under Two Hundred at least; neither will I be at the Trouble of counting, but weigh them in a Lump. I will tell you one Thing further; that if Mr. *Wood's* Project should take, it will ruin even our Beggars: For when I give a Beggar a Half-penny, it will quench his Thirst, or go a good Way to fill his Belly; but the Twelfth Part of a Half-penny will do him no more Service than if I should give him three Pins out of my Sleeve.

In short; these *Half pence* are like the *accursed Thing,* which, as the *Scripture* tells us, the *Children of Israel* were forbidden to touch. They will run about like the *Plague* and destroy everyone who lays his Hands upon them. I have heard *Scholars* talk of a Man who told the King that he had invented a Way to torment People by putting them into a *Bull* of Brass with Fire under it: But the *Prince* put the *Projector* first into his own *Brazen Bull* to make the Experiment. This very much resembles the Project of Mr. *Wood*; and the like of this may possibly be Mr. *Wood's* Fate; that the *Brass* he contrived to torment this *Kingdom* with, may prove his own Torment, and his Destruction at last.

N. B. The Author of this Paper is informed by Persons who have made it their Business to be exact in their Observations on the true Value of these *Half pence;* that any Person may expect to get a Quart of Two-penny Ale for Thirty Six of them.

I desire that all Families may keep this Paper carefully by them to refresh their Memories whenever they shall have farther Notice of Mr. *Wood's* Half pence, or any other the like Imposture.

A LETTER TO THE WHOLE PEOPLE OF IRELAND. BY M. B. DRAPIER. AUTHOR OF THE LETTER TO THE SHOPKEEPERS, &C. (1724)

My Dear Countrymen,

Having already written three letters upon so disagreeable a subject as Mr. Wood *and his* halfpence*; I conceived my task was at an end. But I find that cordials must be frequently applied to weak constitutions,* political *as well as* natural. *A people long used to hardships lose by degrees the very notions of liberty; they look upon themselves as creatures at mercy, and that all impositions laid on them by a stronger hand, are, in the phrase of the* Report, legal *and* obligatory. *Hence proceeds that* poverty *and* lowness of spirit, *to which a* kingdom *may be subject as well as a* particular person. *And when* Esau came fainting from the field at the point to die, *it is no wonder that he* sold his birthright for a mess of pottage.

I thought I had sufficiently shown to all who could want instruction, by what methods they might safely proceed whenever this coin *should be offered to them; and I believe there hath not been for many ages an example of any kingdom so firmly united in a point of great importance, as this of ours is at present against that detestable fraud. But however, it so happens that some weak people begin to be alarmed anew, by rumours industriously spread.* Wood *prescribes to the newsmongers in London what they are to write. In one of their papers published here by some obscure printer (and probably with no good design) we are told that "the Papists in Ireland have entered into an association against his coin," although it be notoriously known that they never once offered to stir in the matter; so that the two Houses of Parliament, the privy-council, the great number of corporations, the lord mayor and aldermen of Dublin, the grand juries, and principal gentlemen of several counties, are stigmatized in a lump under the name of "Papists."*

This impostor and his crew do likewise give out that, by refusing to receive his dross for sterling, we "dispute the King's prerogative, are grown ripe for rebellion, and ready to shake off the dependency of Ireland upon the crown of England." To countenance which reports he hath published a paragraph in another newspaper to let us know that "the Lord Lieutenant is ordered to come over immediately to settle his halfpence."

I entreat you, my dear countrymen, not to be under the least concern upon these and the like rumours, which are no more than the last howls of a dog dissected alive, as I hope he hath sufficiently been. These calumnies are the only reserve that is left him. For surely our continued and (almost) unexampled loyalty will never be called in question for not suffering ourselves to be robbed of all that we have, by one obscure ironmonger.

As to disputing the King's prerogative, *give me leave to explain to those who are ignorant, what the meaning of that word* prerogative *is.*

The Kings of these realms enjoy several powers wherein the laws have not interposed. So they can make war and peace without the consent of Parliament; and this is a very great prerogative. *But if the Parliament doth not approve of the war, the King must bear the charge of it out of his own purse, and this is as great a check on the crown. So the King hath a* prerogative *to coin money without consent of Parliament. But he cannot compel the subject to take that money except it be sterling, gold or silver; because herein he is limited by law. Some princes have indeed extended their* prerogative *further than the law allowed them: wherein however, the lawyers of succeeding ages, as fond as they are of* precedents, *have never dared to justify them. But to say the truth, it is only of late times that* prerogative *hath been fixed and ascertained. For whoever reads the histories of England will find that some former Kings, and these none of the worst, have upon several occasions ventured to control the laws with very little ceremony or scruple, even later than the days of Queen Elizabeth. In her reign that pernicious counsel of sending* base money *hither, very narrowly failed of losing the kingdom, being complained of by the lord-deputy, the council, and the whole body of the English here. So that soon after her death it was recalled by her successor, and lawful money paid in exchange.*

Having thus given you some notion of what is meant by the King's prerogative, *as far as a* tradesman *can be thought capable of explaining it, I will only add the opinion of the great Lord Bacon, that "as God governs the world by the settled laws of nature which he hath made, and never transcends these laws, but upon high important occasions; so among earthly princes, those are the wisest and the best who govern by the known laws of the country, and seldomest make use of their* prerogative."

Now, here you may see that the vile accusation of Wood *and his accomplices, charging us with "disputing the King's prerogative" by refusing his brass, can have no place, because compelling the subject to take any coin which is not sterling, is no part of the King's* prerogative, *and I am very confident if it were so, we should be the last of his people to dispute it, as well from that inviolable loyalty we have always paid to His Majesty, as from the treatment we might in such a case justly expect from some, who seem to think we have neither* common sense *nor* common senses. *But God be thanked, the best of them are only our* fellow-subjects, *and not our* masters. *One great merit I am sure we have, which those of English birth can have no pretence to; that our ancestors reduced this kingdom to the obedience of ENGLAND; for which we have been rewarded with a worse climate, the privilege of being governed by laws to which we do not consent, a ruined trade, a House of* Peers *without* jurisdiction, *almost an incapacity for all employments; and the dread of* Wood's *halfpence.*

But we are so far from disputing the King's prerogative *in coining, that we own he has power to give a patent to any man for setting his royal image and superscription upon whatever materials he pleases; and liberty to the patentee to offer them in any country from England to Japan, only attended with one small limitation, That* nobody alive is obliged to take them.

Upon these considerations I was ever against all recourse to England for a remedy against the present impending evil, especially when I observed that the addresses of both Houses, after long expectance, produced nothing but a REPORT altogether in favour of WOOD; upon which I made some observations in a former letter, and might at least have made as many more; for it is a paper of as singular a nature as I ever beheld.

But I mistake; for before this Report *was made, His Majesty's* most gracious answer *to the House of Lords was sent over and printed, wherein there are these words, "granting the patent for coining halfpence and farthings AGREEABLE TO THE PRACTICE OF HIS ROYAL PREDECESSORS, &c." That King Charles 2d. and King James 2d. (AND THEY ONLY) did grant patents for this purpose, is indisputable, and I have shown it at large. Their patents were passed under the great seal of IRELAND by references to IRELAND, the copper to be coined in IRELAND, the patentee was bound on demand to receive his coin back in IRELAND, and pays silver and gold in return.* Wood's *patent was made under the great seal of ENGLAND, the brass coined in ENGLAND, not the least reference made to IRELAND, the sum immense, and the patentee under no obligation to receive it again and give good money for it. This I only mention, because in my private thoughts I have sometimes made a query, whether the* penner *of those words in His Majesty's* most gracious answer, *"agreeable to the practice of his royal predecessors," had maturely considered the several circumstances which, in my poor opinion, seem to make a difference.*

Let me now say something concerning the other great cause of some people's fear, as Wood *has taught the London newswriter to express it, that "his Excellency the Lord Lieutenant is coming over to settle* Wood's *halfpence."*

We know very well that the Lords Lieutenants for several years past have not thought this kingdom worthy the honour of their residence *longer than was absolutely necessary for the King's business, which consequently* wanted no speed in the dispatch*; and therefore it naturally fell into most men's thoughts, that a new governor coming at an* unusual *time must portend some* unusual *business to be done, especially if the common report be true, that the Parliament prorogued to I know not when, is by a new summons (revoking that prorogation) to assemble soon after his arrival. For which extraordinary proceeding the lawyers on t'other side the water have, by great good fortune, found two precedents.*

All this being granted, it can never enter into my head that so little a creature *as* Wood *could find credit enough with the King and his ministers, to have the Lord Lieutenant of Ireland sent hither in a hurry upon his errand.*

For let us take the whole matter nakedly as it lies before us, without the refinements of some people, with which we have nothing to do. Here is a patent granted under the great seal of England, upon false suggestions, to one William Wood *for coining copper halfpence for Ireland. The* Parliament *here, upon apprehensions of the worst consequences from the said patent, address the King to have it recalled; this is refused, and a committee of the privy-council* report *to His Majesty that* Wood *has performed the conditions of his patent. He then is left to do the best he can with his halfpence, no man being obliged to receive them; the people here, being likewise left to themselves, unite as one man, resolving they will have nothing to do with his ware. By this plain account of the fact it is manifest that the King and his ministry are wholly out of the case, and the matter is left to be disputed between him and us. Will any man therefore attempt to persuade me that a Lord Lieutenant is to be dispatched over in great haste, before the ordinary time, and a Parliament summoned by anticipating a prorogation, merely to put an hundred thousand pounds into the pocket of a* sharper, *by the ruin of a most loyal kingdom?*

But supposing all this to be true. By what arguments could a Lord Lieutenant prevail on the same Parliament which addressed with so much zeal and earnestness against this evil, to pass it into a law? I am sure their opinion of Wood *and his project is not mended since the last prorogation. And supposing those* methods *should be used which* detractors *tell us have been sometimes put in practice for* gaining votes, *it is well known that in this kingdom there are few employments to be given, and if there were more, it is* as well known *to whose share they must fall.*

But because great numbers of you are altogether ignorant in the affairs of your country, I will tell you some reasons why there are so few employments to be disposed of in this kingdom. All considerable offices for life here are possessed by those to whom the reversions were granted, and these have been generally followers of the chief governors, or persons who had interest in the Court of England. So the Lord Berkeley of Stratton holds that great office of master of the rolls*; the Lord Palmerstown is* first remembrancer *worth near 2000l.* per ann. *One Dodington, secretary to the Earl of Pembroke,* begged *the reversion of* clerk of the pells *worth 2500l. a year, which he now enjoys by the death of the Lord Newtown. Mr. Southwell is secretary of state, and the Earl of Burlington lord high treasurer of Ireland by inheritance. These are only a few among many others which I have been told of, but cannot remember. Nay the reversion of several employments during pleasure are granted the same way. This among many others, is a circumstance whereby the kingdom of Ireland is distinguished from all other nations upon earth; and makes it so difficult an affair to get into a civil employ that Mr. Addison was forced to purchase an old obscure place, called* keeper of the records of *Bermingham's* Tower, *of ten pounds a year, and to get a salary of 400l. annexed to it, though all the records there are not worth half-a-crown, either for curiosity or use. And we lately saw a* favourite secretary *descend to be* master of the revels, *which by his* credit and extortion *he hath made* pretty considerable. *I say nothing of the under-treasurership worth about 8000l. a year, nor the commissioners of the revenue, four of whom generally live in England; for I think none of these are granted in reversion. But the jest is, that I have known upon occasion some of these absent officers as* keen *against the interest of Ireland, as if they had never been indebted to her for a* single groat.

I confess, I have been sometimes tempted to wish that this project of Wood *might succeed; because I reflected with some pleasure what a* jolly crew *it would bring over among us of* lords *and* squires, *and* pensioners *of* both sexes, *and officers* civil *and* military, *where we should live together as merry and sociable as beggars; only with this one abatement, that we should neither have* meat *to feed, nor* manufactures *to clothe us, unless we could be content to prance about in* coats of mail, *or eat brass as ostriches do iron.*

I return from this digression to that which gave me the occasion of making it. And I believe you are now convinced, that if the Parliament of Ireland were as temptable *as any* other *assembly* within a mile of *Christendom (which God forbid) yet the* managers *must of necessity fail for want of* tools *to work with. But I will yet go one step further, by supposing that a hundred new employments were erected on purpose to gratify* compilers. *Yet still an insuperable difficulty would remain; for it happens, I know not how, that* money *is neither* Whig *nor* Tory, *neither of* town *nor* country party*; and it is not improbable that a gentleman would rather choose to live upon his* own estate *which brings him* gold *and* silver, *than with the addition of an* employment, *when his* rents *and* salary *must both be paid in* Wood*'s brass at above eighty* percent. *discount.*

For these and many other reasons, I am confident you need not be under the least apprehensions from the sudden expectation of the Lord Lieutenant, *while we continue in our present hearty disposition; to alter which there is no suitable temptation can possibly be offered. And if, as I have often asserted from the best authority, the* law *hath not left a power in the crown to force any money except sterling upon the subject, much less can the crown* devolve *such a* power *upon* another.

This I speak with the utmost respect to the person *and* dignity *of his Excellency the Lord Carteret, whose character hath been given me by a gentleman that hath known him from his first appearance in the world. That gentleman describes him as a young nobleman of great accomplishments, excellent learning, regular in his life, and of much spirit and vivacity. He hath since, as I have heard, been employed abroad, was principal secretary of state; and is now about the 37th year of his age appointed Lord Lieutenant of Ireland. From such a governor this kingdom may reasonably hope for as much prosperity as,* under so many discouragements, *it can be capable of receiving.*

It is true indeed, that within the memory of man, there have been governors of so much dexterity as to carry points of terrible consequence to this kingdom, by their power with those who were in office *and by their arts in managing or deluding others with* oaths, affability, *and even with* dinners. *If* Wood's *brass had in those times been upon the anvil, it is obvious enough to conceive what methods would have been taken.* Depending *persons would have been told in plain terms, that it was a "service expected from them, under pain of the public business being put into more complying hands." Others would be allured by* promises. *To the* country gentlemen *(besides* good words*)* burgundy *and* closeting. *It would perhaps have been hinted how "kindly it would be taken to comply with a royal patent, though it were not compulsory," that if any inconveniences ensued, it might be made up with other "graces or favours hereafter." That "gentlemen ought to consider whether it were prudent or safe to disgust England." They would be desired to "think of some good bills for encouraging of trade, and setting the poor to work, some further acts against Popery and for uniting Protestants." There would be solemn engagements that we should "never be troubled with above forty thousand pounds in his coin, and all of the best and weightiest sort, for which we should only give our manufactures in exchange, and keep our gold and silver at home." Perhaps a "seasonable report of some invasion would have been spread in the most proper juncture," which is a great smoother of rubs in public proceedings; and we should have been told that "this was no time to create differences when the kingdom was in danger."*

These, I say, and the like methods would in corrupt times have been taken to let in this deluge of brass among us; and I am confident would even then have not succeeded, much less under the administration of so excellent a person as the Lord Carteret, and in a country where the people of all ranks, parties and denominations are convinced to a man, that the utter undoing of themselves and their posterity forever, will be dated from the admission of that execrable coin; that if it once enters, it can be no more confined to a small or moderate quantity, than the plague *can be confined to a few families, and that no* equivalent *can be given by any earthly power, any more than a dead carcass can be recovered to life by a cordial.*

There is one comfortable circumstance in this universal opposition to Mr. Wood, *that the people sent over hither from England to* fill up our vacancies ecclesiastical, civil and military, *are all on our side.* Money, *the great* divider *of the world, hath by a strange revolution been the great* uniter *of a most* divided *people. Who would leave a hundred pounds a year in England* (a country of freedom) *to be paid a thousand in Ireland out of* Wood's *exchequer? The* gentleman *they have lately made* primate *would never quit his seat in an English House of Lords, and his preferments at Oxford and Bristol, worth twelve hundred pounds a year, for four times the denomination here, but not half the value; therefore I expect to hear he will be as good an Irishman, upon* this article, *as any of his brethren, or even of* us *who have had the* misfortune *to be born in this island. For those, who, in the common phrase, do not "come hither to learn the language," would never change a better country for a worse, to receive* brass *instead of* gold.

Another slander spread by Wood *and his emissaries is that by opposing him, we discover an inclination to "shake off our dependence upon the crown of England." Pray observe how important a person is this same* William Wood, *and how the public weal of two kingdoms is involved in his private interest. First, all those who refuse to take his coin* are Papists, *for he tells us that "none but Papists are associated against him." Secondly, they "dispute the King's prerogative." Thirdly, "they are ripe for rebellion." And fourthly, they are going to "shake off their dependence upon the crown of England." That is to say, "they are going to choose another king." For there can be no other meaning in this expression, however some may pretend to strain it.*

And this gives me an opportunity of explaining to those who are ignorant, another point which hath often swelled in my breast. *Those who come over hither to us from England, and some* weak *people among ourselves, whenever in discourse we make mention of* liberty *and* property, *shake their heads and tell us that Ireland is a "depending kingdom," as if they would seem, by this phrase, to intend that the people of Ireland is in some state of slavery or dependence different from those of England. Whereas a "depending kingdom" is a* modern term of art, *unknown, as I have heard, to all ancient* civilians *and* writers upon government; *and Ireland is on the contrary called in some statutes an "imperial crown," as held only from God; which is as high a style as any kingdom is capable of receiving. Therefore by this expression, a "depending kingdom," there is no more understood than that by a statute made here in the* 33^{d} *year of Henry* 8th*, "The King and his successors are to be kings imperial of this realm as united and knit to the imperial crown of England." I have looked over all the English and Irish statutes without finding any law that makes Ireland* depend *upon England, any more than England does upon Ireland. We have indeed obliged ourselves to have the* same king with them, *and consequently they are obliged to have the* same king with us. *For the law was made by* our own Parliament, *and our ancestors then were not such* fools (whatever they were in the preceding reign) *to bring themselves under I know not what* dependence, *which is now talked of without any ground of* law, reason *or* common sense.

Let whoever think otherwise, I M. B. Drapier, *desire to be excepted, for I declare, next under God, I* depend *only on the King my sovereign, and on the laws of my own country; and I am so far from* depending *upon the people of England, that if they should ever* rebel *against my sovereign (which God forbid) I would be ready at the first command from His Majesty to take arms against them, as some of* my *countrymen did against* theirs *at Preston. And if such a rebellion should prove so successful as to fix the* Pretender *on the throne of England, I would venture to transgress that* statute *so far as to lose every drop of my blood to hinder him from being* King *of Ireland.*

'Tis true indeed, that within the memory of man, the Parliaments of England have sometimes *assumed the power of binding this kingdom by laws enacted there, wherein they were at first openly opposed (as far as* truth, reason *and* justice *are capable of* opposing*) by the famous Mr. Molineux, an English gentleman born here, as well as by several of the greatest patriots and* best Whigs *in England. But the* love and torrent *of power prevailed. Indeed the arguments on both sides were invincible. For in* reason, *all* government *without the consent of the* governed *is the* very definition of slavery. *But in* fact, eleven men well armed will certainly subdue one single man in his shirt. *But I have done. For those who have used* power *to cramp* liberty *have gone so far as to resent even the* liberty *of*

complaining, *although a man upon the rack was never known to be refused the liberty of* roaring *as loud as he thought fit.*

And as we are apt to sink too much *under* unreasonable *fears, so we are too soon inclined to be* raised *by groundless hopes (according to the nature of all* consumptive *bodies like ours). Thus, it hath been given about for several days past that* somebody *in England empowered a second* somebody *to write to a third* somebody *here, to assure us that we "should no more be troubled with those halfpence." And this is reported to have been done by the* same person, *who was said to have sworn some months ago that he would "ram them down our throats" (though I doubt they would* stick in our stomachs*); but whichever of these reports is true or false, it is no concern of ours. For* in this point *we have nothing to do with English* ministers, *and I should be sorry it lay in their power to* redress *this grievance or to* enforce *it; for the "Report of the Committee" hath given me a* surfeit. *The remedy is wholly in your own hands; and therefore I have digressed a little in order to refresh and continue that* spirit *so seasonably raised amongst you, and to let you see, that by the laws of GOD, of NATURE, of NATIONS, and of your own Country, you ARE and OUGHT to be as FREE a people as your brethren in England.*

If the pamphlets published at London by Wood *and his* journeymen *in defence of his cause were reprinted here, and that our countrymen could be persuaded to read them, they would convince you of his wicked design more than all I shall ever be able to say. In short, I make him a perfect* saint *in comparison of what he appears to be from the writings of those whom he* hires *to justify his* project. *But he is so far* master of the field (let others guess the reason) *that no London printer dare publish any paper written in favour of Ireland, and here nobody hath yet been so* bold *as to publish anything in* favour *of* him.

There was a few days ago a pamphlet sent me of near 50 pages written in favour of Mr. Wood *and his coinage, printed in London; it is not worth answering, because probably it will never be published here. But it gave me an occasion to reflect upon an unhappiness we lie under, that the people of England are utterly ignorant of our case; which however is no wonder since it is a point they do not in the least concern themselves about, farther than perhaps as a subject of discourse in a coffeehouse when they have nothing else to talk of. For I have reason to believe that no minister ever gave himself the trouble of reading any papers written in our defence, because I suppose* their opinions are already determined, *and are formed wholly upon the reports of* Wood *and his accomplices; else it would be impossible that any man could have the impudence to write such a pamphlet as I have mentioned.*

Our neighbours, whose understandings are just upon a level with ours *(which perhaps are none of the* brightest*) have a strong contempt for most nations, but especially for Ireland. They look upon us as a sort of* savage *Irish, whom our ancestors conquered several hundred years ago, and if I should describe the Britons to you as they were in Cæsar's time, when they* painted their bodies, or clothed themselves with the skins of beasts, *I would act full as reasonably as they do. However they are so far to be excused in relation to the present subject, that, hearing only* one side of the cause, *and having neither opportunity nor curiosity to examine the* other, *they* believe a lie *merely for their ease, and conclude because Mr.* Wood *pretends to have* power, *he hath also* reason *on his side.*

Therefore to let you see how this case is represented in England by Wood *and his adherents, I have thought it proper to extract out of that pamphlet a few of those notorious falsehoods in point of* fact *and* reasoning *contained therein; the knowledge whereof will confirm my countrymen in their* own *right sentiments, when they will see by comparing both, how much their* enemies are in the wrong.

First, the writer positively asserts, "That Wood's *halfpence were current among us for several months with the universal approbation of all people, without one single gainsayer, and we all to a man thought ourselves happy in having them."*

Secondly, he affirms, "That we were drawn into a dislike of them only by some cunning evil-designing men among us, who opposed this patent of Wood *to get another for themselves."*

Thirdly, That "those who most declared at first against Wood's *patent were the very men who intended to get another for their own advantage."*

Fourthly, That "our Parliament and privy-council, the Lord Mayor and aldermen of Dublin, the grand juries and merchants, and in short the whole kingdom, nay the very dogs" (as he expresseth it) "were fond of those halfpence, till they were inflamed by those few designing persons aforesaid."

Fifthly, he says directly, That "all those who opposed the halfpence were Papists and enemies to King George."

Thus far I am confident the most ignorant among you can safely swear from your own knowledge, that the author is a most notorious liar in every article; the direct contrary being so manifest to the whole kingdom that if occasion required, we might get it confirmed under five hundred thousand hands.

Sixthly, he would persuade us, that "if we sell five shillings worth of our goods or manufactures for two shillings and fourpence worth of copper, although the copper were melted down, and that we could get five shillings in gold or silver for the said goods; yet to take the said two shillings and fourpence in copper would be greatly for our advantage."

And Lastly, he makes us a very fair offer, as empowered by Wood, *that "if we will take off two hundred thousand pounds in his halfpence for our goods, and likewise pay him three* percent *interest for thirty years for an hundred and twenty thousand pounds (at which he computes the coinage above the intrinsic value of the copper) for the loan of his coin, he will after that time give us good money for what halfpence will be then left."*

Let me place this offer in as clear a light as I can, to show the unsupportable villainy and impudence of that incorrigible wretch. First (says he) "I will send two hundred thousand pounds of my coin into your country; the copper I compute to be in real value eighty thousand pounds, and I charge you with an hundred and twenty thousand pounds for the coinage; so that you see, I lend you an hundred and twenty thousand pounds for thirty years, for which you shall pay me three percent. *That is to say three thousand six hundred pounds* per ann. *which in thirty years will amount to an hundred and eight thousand pounds. And when these thirty years are expired, return me my copper and I will give you good money for it."*

This is the proposal made to us by Wood *in that pamphlet written by one of his* commissioners*; and the author is supposed to be the same infamous Coleby one of his* underswearers *at the* committee of council, *who was tried for* robbing the treasury here, *where he was an under-clerk.*

By this proposal he will first receive two hundred thousand pounds, in goods or sterling, for as much copper as he values at eighty thousand pounds, but in reality not worth thirty thousand pounds. Secondly, he will receive for interest an hundred and eight thousand pounds. And when our children come thirty years hence to return his halfpence upon his executors (for before that time he will be probably gone to his own place*) those executors will very reasonably reject them as raps and counterfeits, which probably they will be, and millions of them of his own coinage.*

Methinks I am fond of such a dealer *as this who mends everyday upon our hands, like a Dutch reckoning, where if you dispute the unreasonableness and exorbitance of the bill, the landlord shall bring it up every time with new additions.*

Although these and the like pamphlets published by Wood *in London be altogether unknown here, where nobody could read them without as much* indignation *as* contempt *would allow, yet I thought it proper to give you a specimen how the* man *employs his time, where he rides alone without one creature to contradict him; while OUR FEW FRIENDS there wonder at our silence, and the English in general, if they think of this matter at all, impute our refusal to* wilfulness *or* disaffection *just as* Wood *and his* hirelings *are pleased to represent.*

But although our arguments are not suffered to be printed in England, yet the consequence will be of little moment. Let Wood *endeavour to* persuade *the people* there *that we ought to* receive *his coin, and let me* convince *our people* here *that they ought to* reject *it under pain of our utter undoing. And then let him do his* best *and his* worst.

Before I conclude, I must beg leave in all humility to tell Mr. Wood, *that he is guilty of great* indiscretion, *by causing so honourable a name as that of Mr. W[alpole] to be mentioned so often, and* in such a manner, upon his occasion. A short paper printed at Bristol and reprinted here reports Mr. Wood to say, that he "wonders at the impudence and insolence of the Irish in refusing his coin, and what he will do when Mr. W[alpole] comes to town." Where, by the way, he is mistaken, for it is the true English people of Ireland who refuse it, although we take it for granted that the Irish will do so too whenever they are asked. He orders it to be printed in another paper, that "Mr. W[alpole] will cram this brass down our throats." Sometimes it is given out that we must "either take these halfpence or eat our brogues." And, in another newsletter but of yesterday we read that the same great man "hath sworn to make us swallow his coin in fireballs."

This brings to my mind the known story of a Scotchman, who receiving sentence of death, with all the circumstances of hanging, beheading, quartering, embowelling and the like, cried out, "What need all this COOKERY?" And I think we have reason to ask the same question; for if we believe Wood, here is a dinner getting ready for us, and you see the bill of fare, and I am sorry the drink was forgot, which might easily be supplied with melted lead and flaming pitch.

What vile words are these to put into the mouth of a great councillor, in high trust with His Majesty, and looked upon as a prime minister. If Mr. Wood hath no better a manner of representing his patrons, when I come to be a great man he shall never be suffered to attend at my levee. This is not the style of a great minister, it savours too much of the kettle and the furnace, and came entirely out of Mr. Wood's forge.

As for the threat of making us eat our brogues, we need not be in pain; for if his coin should pass, that unpolite covering for the feet would no longer be a national reproach; because then we should have neither shoe nor brogue left in the kingdom. But here the falsehood of Mr. Wood is fairly detected; for I am confident Mr. W[alpole] never heard of a brogue in his whole life.

As to "swallowing these halfpence in fireballs," it is a story equally improbable. For to execute this operation the whole stock of Mr. Wood's coin and metal must be melted down and moulded into hollow balls with wild-fire, no bigger than a reasonable throat can be able *to swallow. Now the metal he hath prepared, and already coined, will amount to at least fifty millions of halfpence to be* swallowed *by a million and a half of people; so that allowing two halfpence to each* ball, *there will be about seventeen* balls *of* wildfire *a-piece to be swallowed by every person in this kingdom. And to administer this dose there cannot be conveniently fewer than fifty thousand* operators, *allowing one* operator *to every thirty, which, considering the* squeamishness *of some stomachs and the* peevishness *of* young children, *is but reasonable. Now, under correction of better judgments, I think the trouble and charge of such an experiment would exceed the profit; and therefore I take this* report *to be* spurious, *or at least only a new* scheme *of Mr.* Wood *himself, which to make it pass the better in Ireland he would father upon a* minister of state.

But I will now demonstrate beyond all contradiction that Mr. W[alpole] is against this project of Mr. Wood, *and is an entire friend to Ireland, only by this one invincible argument, That he has the universal opinion of being a wise man, an able minister, and in all his proceedings pursuing the* true interest *of the* King his master, *and that, as his* integrity *is above all* corruption, *so is his* fortune *above all* temptation. *I reckon therefore we are perfectly safe from that* corner, *and shall never be under the necessity of contending with so* formidable a power, *but be left to possess our* brogues *and* potatoes *in* peace, *as* remote from thunder as we are from *Jupiter.*

I am,
My dear countrymen,
Your loving fellow-subject,
fellow-sufferer, and humble servant.
M. B.
Oct. 13. 1724

A MODEST PROPOSAL FOR PREVENTING THE CHILDREN OF POOR PEOPLE FROM BEING A BURTHEN TO THEIR PARENTS OR THE COUNTRY, AND FOR MAKING THEM BENEFICIAL TO THE PUBLIC (1729)

IT IS A MELANCHOLY OBJECT TO THOSE WHO WALK THROUGH THIS great town, or travel in the country, when they see the *streets,* the *roads,* and *cabin-doors* crowded with *beggars* of the female sex, followed by three, four, or six children, *all in rags,* and importuning every passenger for an alms. These *mothers* instead of being able to work for their honest livelihood, are forced to employ all their time in strolling to beg sustenance for their *helpless infants* who, as they grow up, either turn *thieves* for want of work, or leave their *dear Native Country to fight for the Pretender* in Spain, or sell themselves to the Barbadoes.

I think it is agreed by all parties that this prodigious number of children, in the arms, or on the backs, or at the *heels* of their *mothers,* and frequently of their fathers, is *in the present deplorable state of the kingdom,* a very great additional grievance; and therefore whoever could find out a fair, cheap and easy method of making these children sound useful members of the commonwealth would deserve so well of the public, as to have his statue set up for a preserver of the nation.

But my intention is very far from being confined to provide only for the children of *professed beggars,* it is of a much greater extent, and shall take in the whole number of infants at a certain age, who are born of parents in effect as little able to support them as those who demand our charity in the streets.

As to my own part, having turned my thoughts for many years upon this important subject, and maturely weighed the several *schemes of other projectors,* I have always found them grossly mistaken in their computation. It is true a child *just dropped from its dam* may be supported by her milk for a solar year with little other nourishment, at most not above the value of two shillings, which the mother may certainly get, or the value in *scraps,* by her lawful occupation of *begging.* And it is exactly at one year old that I propose to provide for them in such a manner as, instead of being a charge upon their *parents,* or the *parish,* or *wanting food and raiment* for the rest of their lives, they shall, on the contrary, contribute to the feeding and partly to the clothing of many thousands.

There is likewise another great advantage in my scheme, that it will prevent those *voluntary abortions,* and that horrid practice of *women murdering their bastard children,* alas! Too frequent among us, sacrificing the *poor innocent babes,* I doubt, more to avoid the expense than the shame, which would move tears and pity in the most savage and inhuman breast.

The number of souls in this kingdom being usually reckoned one million and a half, of these I calculate there may be about two hundred thousand couple whose wives are breeders, from which number I subtract thirty thousand couples who are able to maintain their own children, although I apprehend there cannot be so many under *the present distresses of the kingdom,* but this being granted, there will remain an hundred and seventy thousand breeders. I again subtract fifty thousand for those women who miscarry, or whose children die by accident, or disease within the year. There only remain an hundred and twenty thousand children of poor parents annually born. The question therefore is, how this number shall be reared and provided for, which, as I have already said, under the present situation of affairs is utterly impossible by all the methods hitherto proposed, for we can *neither employ them in handicraft,* or *agriculture;* we neither build houses (I mean in the country) nor cultivate land: they can very seldom pick up a livelihood *by stealing* till they arrive at six years old, except where they are of towardly parts, although I confess they learn the rudiments much earlier, during which time they can however be properly looked upon only as *probationers,* as I have been informed by a principal gentleman in the County of Cavan, who protested to me that he never knew above one or two instances under the age of six, even in a part of the kingdom *so renowned for the quickest proficiency in that art.*

I am assured by our merchants that a boy or a girl, before twelve years old, is no saleable commodity, and even when they come to this age, they will not yield above three pounds, or three pounds and half-a-crown at most on the Exchange, which cannot turn to account either to the parents or the kingdom, the charge of nutriment and rags having been at least four times that value.

I shall now therefore humbly propose my own thoughts, which I hope will not be liable to the least objection.

I have been assured by a very knowing American of my acquaintance in London, that a young healthy child, well nursed, is at a year old a most delicious, nourishing, and wholesome food, whether *stewed, roasted, baked,* or *boiled,* and I make no doubt that it will equally serve in a *fricassee,* or a *ragout.*

I do therefore humbly offer it to *public consideration,* that of the hundred and twenty thousand children, already computed, twenty thousand may be reserved for breed, whereof only one fourth part to be males, which is more than we allow to *sheep, black-cattle,* or *swine;* and my reason is that these children are seldom the fruits of marriage, *a circumstance not much regarded by our savages;* therefore *one male* will be sufficient to serve *four females.* That the remaining hundred thousand may at a year old be offered in sale to the *persons of quality* and *fortune,* through the kingdom, always advising the mother to let them suck plentifully of the last month, so as to render them plump and fat for a good table. A child will make two dishes at an entertainment for friends, and when the family dines alone the fore or hind quarter will make a reasonable dish, and seasoned with a little pepper or salt will be very good boiled on the fourth day, especially in *winter.*

I have reckoned upon a medium, that a child just born will weigh 12 pounds, and in a solar year if tolerably nursed increaseth to 28 pounds.

I grant this food will be somewhat dear, and therefore very *proper for landlords,* who, as they have already devoured most of the parents, seem to have the best title to the children.

Infants' flesh will be in season throughout the year, but more plentiful in *March,* and a little before and after, for we are told by a grave author, an eminent French physician, that *fish being a prolific diet,* there are more children born in *Roman Catholic countries* about nine months after *Lent,* than at any other season; therefore reckoning a year after *Lent,* the markets will be more glutted than usual, because the number of *Popish infants* is at least three to one in this kingdom, and therefore it will have one other collateral advantage by lessening the number of *Papists* among us.

I have already computed the charge of nursing a beggar's child (in which list I reckon all *cottagers, labourers,* and four fifths of the *farmers)* to be about two shillings *per annum,* rags included, and I believe no gentleman would repine to give ten shillings for the *carcass of a good fat child,* which, as I have said, will make four dishes of excellent nutritive meat, when he hath only some particular friend, or his own family to dine with him. Thus the Squire will learn to be a good landlord, and grow popular among his tenants, the mother will have eight shillings net profit, and be fit for work till she produces another child.

Those who are more thrifty (*as I must confess the times require*) may flay the carcass; the skin of which, artificially dressed, will make admirable *gloves for ladies,* and *summer boots for fine gentlemen.*

As to our City of Dublin, shambles may be appointed for this purpose in the most convenient parts of it, and butchers we may be assured will not be wanting, although I rather recommend buying the children alive, and dressing them hot from the knife, as we do *roasting pigs.*

A very worthy person, *a true lover of his country,* and whose virtues I highly esteem, was lately pleased in discoursing on this matter, to offer a refinement upon my scheme. He said that many gentlemen of this kingdom, having of late destroyed their deer, he conceived that the want of venison might be well supplied by the bodies of young lads and maidens not exceeding fourteen years of age, nor under twelve, so great a number of both sexes in every country being now ready to starve for want of work and service: and these to be disposed of by their parents if alive, or otherwise by their nearest relations. But with due deference to so excellent a friend and so deserving a patriot, I cannot be altogether in his sentiments; for as to the males, my American acquaintance assured me from frequent experience that their flesh was generally tough and lean, like that of our school-boys, by continual exercise, and their taste disagreeable, and to fatten them would not answer the charge. Then as to the females, it would I think with humble submission, *be a loss to the public,* because they soon would become breeders themselves. And besides, it is not improbable that some scrupulous people might be apt to censure such a practice (although indeed very unjustly) as a little bordering upon cruelty, which, I confess, hath always been with me the strongest objection against any project, however so well intended.

But in order to justify my friend, he confessed that this expedient was put into his head by the famous *Psalmanazar,* a native of the island Formosa, who came from thence to London above twenty years ago, and in conversation told my friend that in his country when any young person happened to be put to death, the executioner sold the carcass to *persons of quality,* as a prime dainty, and that in his time, the body of a plump girl of fifteen, who was crucified for an attempt to poison the emperor, was sold to his Imperial *Majesty's Prime Minister of State,* and other great *Mandarins* of the Court, *in joints from the gibbet,* at four hundred crowns. Neither indeed can I deny, that if the same use were made of several plump young girls in this town, who, without one single groat to their fortunes, cannot stir abroad without a chair, and appear at the *playhouse* and *assemblies* in foreign fineries which they never will pay for, the kingdom would not be the worse.

Some persons of a desponding spirit are in great concern about that vast number of poor people who are aged, diseased, or maimed, and I have been desired to employ my thoughts what course may be taken to ease the nation of so grievous an encumbrance. But I am not in the least pain upon that matter, because it is very well known that they are everyday *dying,* and *rotting,* by *cold* and *famine,* and *filth,* and *vermin,* as fast as can be reasonably expected. And as to the younger labourers they are now in almost as hopeful a condition. They cannot get work, and consequently pine away for want of nourishment, to a degree that if at anytime they are accidentally hired to common labour, they have not strength to perform it; and thus the country and themselves are happily delivered from the evils to come.

I have too long digressed, and therefore shall return to my subject. I think the advantages by the proposal which I have made are obvious and many, as well as of the highest importance.

For *first,* as I have already observed, it would greatly lessen the *number of Papists,* with whom we are yearly overrun, being the principal breeders of the nation as well as our most dangerous enemies, and who stay at home on purpose with a design to *deliver the kingdom to the Pretender,* hoping to take their advantage by the absence of *so many good Protestants,* who have chosen rather to leave their country than stay at home and pay tithes against their conscience to an *Episcopal curate.*

Secondly, the poorer tenants will have something valuable of their own, which by law may be made liable to distress, and help to pay their landlord's rent, their corn and cattle being already seized, and *money a thing unknown.*

Thirdly, whereas the maintenance of an hundred thousand children, from two years old and upwards, cannot be computed at less than ten shillings a piece *per annum,* the nation's stock will be thereby increased fifty thousand pounds *per annum,* besides the profit of a new dish introduced to the tables of all *gentlemen of fortune* in the kingdom who have any refinement in taste; and the money will circulate among ourselves, the goods being entirely of our own growth and manufacture.

Fourthly, the constant breeders, besides the gain of eight shillings *sterling per annum* by the sale of their children, will be rid of the charge of maintaining them after the first year.

Fifthly, this food would likewise bring great *custom to taverns,* where the vintners will certainly be so prudent as to procure the best receipts for dressing it to perfection, and consequently have their houses frequented by all the *fine gentlemen,* who justly value themselves upon their knowledge in good eating; and a skilful cook, who understands how to oblige his guests, will contrive to make it as expensive as they please.

Sixthly, this would be a great inducement to marriage, which all wise nations have either encouraged by rewards, or enforced by laws and penalties. It would increase the care and tenderness of mothers toward their children, when they were sure of a settlement for life to the poor babes, provided in some sort by the public to their annual profit instead of expense. We should see an honest emulation among the married women, *which of them could bring the fattest child to the market.* Men would become as *fond* of their wives, during the time of their pregnancy, as they are now of their *mares* in foal, their *cows* in calf, or *sows* when they are ready to farrow; nor offer to beat or kick them (as it is too *frequent* a practice) for fear of a miscarriage.

Many other advantages might be enumerated. For instance, the addition of some thousand carcasses in our exportation of barrelled beef; the propagation of *swine's flesh* and improvement in the art of making good *bacon,* so much wanted among us by the great destruction of *pigs,* too frequent at our tables, which are no way comparable in taste, or magnificence to a well-grown, fat yearling child, which roasted whole will make a considerable figure at a *Lord Mayor's feast,* or any other public entertainment. But this and many others I omit, being studious of brevity.

Supposing that one thousand families in this city, would be constant customers for infants' flesh, besides others who might have it at *merry-meetings,* particularly *weddings* and *christenings,* I compute that Dublin would take off annually about twenty thousand carcasses, and the rest of the kingdom (where probably they will be sold somewhat cheaper) the remaining eighty thousand.

I can think of no one objection that will possibly be raised against this proposal, unless it should be urged that the number of people will be thereby much lessened in the kingdom. This I freely own, and it was indeed one principal design in offering it to the world. I desire the reader will observe, that I calculate my remedy *for this one individual Kingdom of IRELAND, and for no other that ever was, is, or, I think, ever can be upon earth.* Therefore let no man talk to me of other expedients: *Of taxing our absentees at five shillings a pound: Of using neither clothes, nor household furniture, except what is of our own growth and manufacture: Of utterly rejecting the materials and instruments that promote foreign luxury: Of curing the expensiveness of pride, vanity, idleness, and gaming in our women: Of introducing a vein of parsimony, prudence and temperance: Of learning to love our Country, wherein we differ even from LAPLANDERS, and the inhabitants of TOPINAMBOO: Of quitting our animosities and factions, nor act any longer like the Jews, who were murdering one another at the very moment their city was taken: Of being a little cautious not to sell our country and consciences for nothing: Of teaching landlords to have at least one degree of mercy toward their tenants. Lastly of putting a spirit of honesty, industry and skill into our shopkeepers, who, if a resolution could now be taken to buy only our native goods, would immediately unite to cheat and exact upon us in the price, the measure, and the goodness, nor could ever yet be brought to make one fair proposal of just dealing, though often and earnestly invited to it.*

Therefore I repeat, let no man talk to me of these and the like expedients, till he hath at least some glimpse of hope that there will ever be some hearty and sincere attempt to put them in practice.

But as to myself, having been wearied out for many years with offering vain, idle, visionary thoughts, and at length utterly despairing of success, I fortunately fell upon this proposal, which as it is wholly new, so it hath something solid and real, of no expense and little trouble, full in our own power, and whereby we can incur no danger in *disobliging England.* For this kind of commodity will not bear exportation, the flesh being of too tender a consistence to admit a long continuance in salt, *although perhaps I could name a country which would be glad to eat up our whole nation without it.*

After all, I am not so violently bent upon my own opinion as to reject any offer proposed by wise men, which shall be found equally innocent, cheap, easy and effectual. But before something of that kind shall be advanced in contradiction to my scheme, and offering a better, I desire the author, or authors, will be pleased maturely to consider two points. *First,* as things now stand, how they will be able to find food and raiment for an hundred thousand useless mouths and backs. And *secondly,* there being a round million of creatures in human figure throughout this kingdom, whose whole subsistence put into a common stock would leave them in debt two millions of pounds *sterling;* adding those who are beggars by profession, to the bulk of farmers, cottagers and labourers with their wives and children, who are beggars in effect; I desire those *politicians* who dislike my overture and may perhaps be so bold to attempt an answer, that they will first ask the parents of these mortals, whether they would not at this day think it a great happiness to have been sold for food at a year old, in the manner I prescribe; and thereby have avoided such a perpetual scene of misfortunes as they have since gone through, by the *oppression of landlords,* the impossibility of paying rent without money or trade, the want of common sustenance, with neither house nor clothes to cover them from the inclemencies of the weather, and the most inevitable prospect of entailing the like, or greater miseries upon their breed forever.

I profess in the sincerity of my heart that I have not the least personal interest in endeavouring to promote this necessary work, having no other motive than the *public good of my country, by advancing our trade, providing for infants, relieving the poor, and giving some pleasure to the rich.* I have no children, by which I can propose to get a single penny; the youngest being nine years old, and my wife past child-bearing.

DIRECTIONS TO SERVANTS RULES THAT CONCERN ALL SERVANTS IN GENERAL (1735)

WHEN YOUR MASTER OR LADY CALLS A SERVANT BY NAME, IF THAT servant be not in the way, none of you are to answer, for then there will be no end of your drudgery: and masters themselves allow, that if a servant comes when he is called, it is sufficient.

When you have done a fault, be always pert and insolent, and behave yourself as if you were the injured person; this will immediately put your master or lady off their mettle.

If you see your master wronged by any of your fellow-servants, be sure to conceal it, for fear of being called a telltale. However, there is one exception, in case of a favourite servant, who is justly hated by the whole family; who therefore are bound, in prudence, to lay all the faults they can upon the favourite.

The cook, the butler, the groom, the market-man, and every other servant who is concerned in the expenses of the family, should act as if his master's whole estate ought to be applied to that servant's particular business. For instance, if the cook computes his master's estate to be a thousand pounds a year, he reasonably concludes that a thousand pounds a year will afford meat enough, and therefore he need not be saving; the butler makes the same judgment, so may the groom and the coachman, and thus every branch of expense will be filled to your master's honour.

When you are chid before company (which, with submission to our masters and ladies, is an unmannerly practice) it often happens that some stranger will have the good nature to drop a word in your excuse; in such a case you have a good title to justify yourself, and may rightly conclude, that whenever he chides you afterwards on other occasions, he may be in the wrong; in which opinion you will be the better confirmed by stating the case to your fellow-servants in your own way, who will certainly decide in your favour: therefore, as I have said before, whenever you are chidden, complain as if you were injured.

It often happens, that servants sent on messages are apt to stay out somewhat longer than the message requires, perhaps two, four, six, or eight hours, or some such trifle, for the temptation to be sure was great, and flesh and blood cannot always resist. When you return, the master storms, the lady scolds; stripping, cudgelling, and turning off is the word. But here you ought be provided with a set of excuses, enough to serve on all occasions. For instance, your uncle came fourscore miles to town this morning, on purpose to see you, and goes back by break of day tomorrow; a brother-servant, that borrowed money of you when he was out of place, was running away to Ireland; you were taking leave of an old fellow-servant, who was shipping for Barbados: your father sent a cow for you to sell, and you could not find a chapman till nine at night; you were taking leave of a dear cousin who is to be hanged next Saturday; you wrenched your foot against a stone, and were forced to stay three hours in a shop before you could stir a step; some nastiness was thrown on you out of a garret-window, and you were ashamed to come home before you were cleaned, and the smell went off; you were pressed for the sea-service, and carried before a justice of peace, who kept you three hours before he examined you, and you got off with much a-do; a bailiff, by mistake, seized you for a debtor, and kept you the whole evening in a sponging-house; you were told your master had gone to a tavern, and came to some mischance, and your grief was so great, that you inquired for his honour in a hundred taverns between Pall Mall and Temple Bar.

Take all tradesmen's parts against your master, and when you are sent to buy anything, never offer to cheapen it, but generously pay the full demand. This is highly for your master's honour; and may be some shillings in your pocket; and you are to consider, if your master hath paid too much, he can better afford the loss than a poor tradesman.

Never submit to stir a finger in any business, but that for which you were particularly hired. For example, if the groom be drunk or absent, and the butler be ordered to shut the stable door, the answer is ready, "An please your honour, I don't understand horses." If a corner of the hanging wants a single nail to fasten it, and the footman be directed to tack it up, he may say he doth not understand that sort of work, but his honour may send for the upholsterer.

Masters and ladies are usually quarrelling with the servants for not shutting the doors after them; but neither masters nor ladies consider that those doors must be open before they can be shut, and that the labour is double to open and shut the doors; therefore the best, the shortest, and easiest way is to do neither. But if you are so often teased to shut the door, that you cannot easily forget it, then give the door such a clap at your going out, as will shake the whole room, and make everything rattle in it, to put your master and lady in mind that you observe their directions.

If you find yourself to grow into favour with your master or lady, take some opportunity in a very mild way to *give them warning*; and when they ask the reason, and seem loth to part with you, answer, that you would rather live with them than anybody else, but a poor servant is not to be blamed if he strives to better himself; that service is no inheritance; that your work is great, and your wages very small. Upon which, if your master hath any generosity, he will add five or ten shillings a quarter rather than let you go. But if you are baulked, and have no mind to go off, get some fellow-servant to tell your master that he had prevailed upon you to stay.

Whatever good bits you can pilfer in the day, save them to junket with your fellow-servants at night, and take in the butler, provided he will give you drink.

Write your own name and your sweetheart's, with the smoke of a candle, on the roof of the kitchen or the servants' hall, to show your learning.

If you are a young, sightly fellow, whenever you whisper your mistress at the table, run your nose full in her cheek, or if your breath be good, breathe full in her face; this I know to have had very good consequences in some families.

Never come till you have been called three or four times; for none but dogs will come at the first whistle; and when the master calls "Who's there?" no servant is bound to come; for *Who's there* is no body's name.

When you have broken all your earthen drinking-vessels below stairs (which is usually done in a week) the copper pot will do as well; it can boil milk, heat porridge, hold small beer, or, in case of necessity, serve for a jordan; therefore apply it indifferently to all these uses; but never wash or scour it, for fear of taking off the tin.

Although you are allowed knives for the servants' hall at meals, yet you ought to spare them, and make use only of your master's.

Let it be a constant rule, that no chair, stool, or table in the servants' hall or the kitchen, shall have above three legs, which hath been the ancient and constant practice in all the families I ever knew, and is said to be founded upon two reasons; first, to show that servants are ever in a tottering condition; secondly, it was thought a point of humility, that the servants' chairs and tables should have at least one leg fewer than those of their masters. I grant there hath been an exception to this rule with regard to the cook, who, by old custom, was allowed an easy chair to sleep in after dinner; and yet I have seldom seen them with above three legs. Now this epidemical lameness of servants' chairs is, by philosophers, imputed to two causes, which are observed to make the greatest revolutions in states and empires; I mean love and war. A stool, a chair, or a table is the first weapon taken up in a general romping or skirmish; and after a peace, the chairs, if they be not very strong, are apt to suffer in the conduct of an amour, the cook being usually fat and heavy, and the butler a little in drink.

I could never endure to see maid-servants so ungenteel as to walk the streets with their petticoats pinned up; it is a foolish excuse to allege their petticoats will be dirty, when they have so easy a remedy as to walk three or four times down a clean pair of stairs after they come home.

When you step to tattle with some crony servant in the same street, leave your own street-door open, that you may get in without knocking when you come back; otherwise your mistress may know you are gone out, and you will be chidden.

I do most earnestly exhort you all to unanimity and concord. But mistake me not: you may quarrel with each other as much as you please, only bear in mind that you have a common enemy, which is your master and lady, and you have a common cause to defend. Believe an old practitioner; whoever, out of malice to a fellow-servant, carries a tale to his master, should be ruined by a general confederacy against him.

The general place of rendezvous for all servants, both in winter and summer, is the kitchen; there the grand affairs of the family ought to be consulted, whether they concern the stable, the dairy, the pantry, the laundry, the cellar, the nursery, the dining room, or my lady's chamber: there, as in your own proper element, you can laugh, and squall, and romp, in full security.

When any servant comes home drunk, and cannot appear, you must all join in telling your master that he is gone to bed very sick; upon which your lady will be so good-natured as to order some comfortable thing for the poor man or maid.

When your master and lady go abroad together, to dinner, or on a visit for the evening, you need leave only one servant in the house, unless you have a black-guard boy to answer at the door, and attend the children, if there be any. Who is to stay at home is to be determined by short and long cuts, and the stayer at home may be comforted by a visit from a sweetheart, without danger of being caught together. These opportunities must never be missed, because they come but sometimes; and you are always safe enough while there is a servant in the house.

When your master or lady comes home, and wants a servant who happens to be abroad, your answer must be, that he is just that minute stept out, being sent for by a cousin who is dying.

If your master calls you by name, and you happen to answer at the fourth call, you need not hurry yourself; and if you be chidden for staying, you may lawfully say, you came no sooner, because you did not know what you were called for.

When you are chidden for a fault, as you go out of the room, and down stairs, mutter loud enough to be plainly heard; this will make him believe you are innocent.

Whoever comes to visit your master or lady when they are abroad, never burthen your memory with the person's name, for indeed you have too many other things to remember. Besides, it is a porter's business, and your master's fault that he doth not keep one; and who can remember names? And you will certainly mistake them, and you can neither write nor read.

If it be possible, never tell a lie to your master or lady, unless you have some hopes that they cannot find it out in less than half an hour.

When a servant is turned off, all his faults must be told, although most of them were never known by his master or lady; and all mischiefs done by others, charge to him. And when they ask any of you why you never acquainted them before, the answer is, "Sir, (or Madam) really I was afraid it would make you angry; and besides, perhaps you might think it was malice in me." Where there are little masters and misses in a house, they are usually great impediments to the diversions of the servants; the only remedy is to bribe them with *goody goodies*, that they may not tell tales to papa and mamma.

I advise you of the servants, whose masters live in the country, and who expect vales, always to stand rank and file when a stranger is taking his leave; so that he must of necessity pass between you; and he must have more confidence, or less money than usual, if any of you let him escape; and according as he behaves himself, remember to treat him the next time he comes.

If you be sent with ready money to buy anything at a shop, and happen at that time to be out of pocket (which is very usual), sink the money and take up the goods on your master's account. This is for the honour of your master and yourself; for he becomes a man of credit at your recommendation.

When your lady sends for you up to her chamber, to give you any orders, be sure to stand at the door, and keep it open, fiddling with the lock all the while she is talking to you, and keep the button in your hand, for fear you should forget to shut the door after you.

If your master or lady happen once in their lives to accuse you wrongfully, you are a happy servant; for you have nothing more to do, than for every fault you commit while you are in their service, to put them in mind of that false accusation, and protest yourself equally innocent in the present case.

When you have a mind to leave your master, and are too bashful to break the matter for fear of offending him, your best way is to grow rude and saucy of a sudden, and beyond your usual behaviour, till he finds it necessary to turn you off; and when you are gone, to revenge yourself, give him and his lady such a character to all your brother servants who are out of place, that none will venture to offer their service.

Some nice ladies who are afraid of catching cold, having observed that the maids and fellows below stairs often forget to shut the door after them, as they come in or go out into the back yards, have contrived that a pulley and rope with a large piece of lead at the end, should be so fixed, as to make the door shut of itself, and require a strong hand to open it; which is an immense toil to servants whose business may force them to go in and out fifty times in a morning. But ingenuity can do much, for prudent servants have found out an effectual remedy against this insupportable grievance, by tying up the pulley in such a manner that the weight of the lead shall have no effect; however, as to my own part, I would rather choose to keep the door always open, by laying a heavy stone at the bottom of it.

The servants' candlesticks are generally broken, for nothing can last forever. But you may find out many expedients; you may conveniently stick your candle in a bottle, or with a lump of butter against the wainscot, or in a powder-horn, or in an old shoe, or in a cleft stick, or in the barrel of a pistol, or upon its own grease on a table, in a coffeecup or a drinking-glass, a horn can, a teapot, a twisted napkin, a mustard-pot, an ink-horn, a marrowbone, a piece of dough, or you may cut a hole in the loaf, and stick it there.

When you invite the neighbouring servants to junket with you at home in an evening, teach them a peculiar way of tapping or scraping at the kitchen-window, which you may hear, but not your master or lady, whom you must take care not to disturb or frighten at such unseasonable hours.

Lay all faults on a lapdog, a favourite cat, a monkey, a parrot, a child, or on the servant who was last turned off; by this rule you will excuse yourself, do no hurt to anybody else, and save your master or lady from the trouble and vexation of chiding.

When you want proper instruments for any work you are about, use all expedients you can invent rather than leave your work undone. For instance, if the poker be out of the way, or broken, stir up the fire with the tongs; if the tongs be not at hand, use the muzzle of the bellows, the wrong end of the fire-shovel, the handle of the fire-brush, the end of a mop, or your master's cane. If you want paper to singe a fowl, tear the first book you see about the house. Wipe your shoes, for want of a clout, with the bottom of a curtain, or a damask napkin. Strip your livery lace for garters. If the butler wants a jordan, in case of need he may use the great silver cup.

There are several ways of putting out candles, and you ought to be instructed in them all. You may run the candle end against the wainscot, which puts the snuff out immediately; you may lay it on the floor, and tread the snuff out with your foot; you may hold it upside down, until it is choked with its own grease; or cram it into the socket of the candlestick; you may whirl it round in your hand till it goes out: when you go to bed, after you have made water, you may dip your candle end into the chamberpot: you may spit on your finger and thumb, and pinch the snuff until it goes out. The cook may run the candle's nose into the meal-tub, or the groom into a vessel of oats, or a lock of hay, or a heap of litter; the housemaid may put out her candle by running it against a looking-glass, which nothing cleans so well as candle-snuff; but the quickest and best of all methods is to blow it out with your breath, which leaves the candle clear, and readier to be lighted.

There is nothing so pernicious in families as a telltale, against whom it must be the principal business of you all to unite: whatever office he serves in, take all opportunities to spoil the business he is about, and to cross him in everything. For instance, if the butler be the telltale, break his glasses whenever he leaves the pantry door open; or lock the cat or the mastiff in it, who will do as well: mislay a fork or a spoon so as he may never find it. If it be the cook, whenever she turns her back, throw a lump of soot or a handful of salt in the pot, or smoking coals into the dripping-pan, or daub the roast meat with the back of the chimney, or hide the key of the jack. If a footman be suspected, let the cook daub the back of his new livery; or when he is going up with a dish of soup, let her follow him softly with a ladleful, and dribble it all the way up stairs to the dining room, and then let the housemaid make such a noise that her lady may hear it. The waiting-maid is very likely to be guilty of this fault, in hopes to ingratiate herself: in this case the laundress must be sure to tear her smocks in the washing, and yet wash them but half; and when she complains, tell all the house that she sweats so much, and her flesh is so nasty, that she fouls a smock more in one hour, than the kitchen-maid does in a week.

A CHARACTER, PANEGYRIC, AND DESCRIPTION OF THE LEGION CLUB (1736)

As I stroll the city, oft I
See a building large and lofty,
Not a bow-shot from the college;
Half the globe from sense and knowledge;
By the prudent architect
Placed against the church direct,
Making good my grandam's jest,
Near the church—you know the rest.
  Tell us what this pile contains?
Many heads that hold no brains. 10
These demoniacs let me dub
With the name of *Legion Club.*
Such assemblies, you would swear,
Meet when butchers bait a bear:
Such a noise and such haranguing,
When a brother thief is hanging:
Such a rout and such a rabble
Run to hear Jackpudden gabble:
Such a crowd their ordure throws
On a far less villain's nose. 20
  Could I from the building's top

Hear the rattling thunder drop,
While the devil upon the roof
(If the devil be thunder-proof)
Should, with poker fiery-red,
Crack the stones, and melt the lead;
Drive them down on ev'ry skull,
While the den of thieves is full;
Quite destroy that harpies' nest—
How might then our isle be blest! 30
For divines allow, that God
Sometimes makes the devil his rod;
And the gospel will inform us,
He can punish crimes enormous.
Yet should Swift endow the schools
For his *lunatics* and *fools*,
With a rood or two of land,
I allow the pile may stand.
You perhaps will ask me, "Why so?"
But it is with this proviso: 40
Since the House is like to last,
Let the royal grant be pass'd,
That the Club have leave to dwell
Each within his proper cell,
With a passage left to creep in
And a hole above for peeping.
Let them, when they once get in,
Sell the nation for a pin;
While they sit a-picking straws,
Let them rave at making laws; 50
While they never hold their tongue,
Let them dabble in their dung:
Let them form a grand committee
How to plague and starve the city;
Let them stare and storm and frown
When they see a clergy-gown;
Let them, ere they crack a louse,

Call for th' Orders of the House;
Let them, with their gosling quills
Scribble senseless heads of bills; 60
We may, while they strain their throats,
Wipe our arses with their Votes.
Let Sir Tom, that rampant ass,
Stuff his guts with flax and grass;
But before the priest he fleeces,
Tear the Bible all to pieces:
At the parsons, Tom, "Halloo-Boy,"
Worthy offspring of a shoe-boy,
Footman, traitor, vile seducer,
Perjur'd rebel, bribed accuser. 70
Lay thy paltry priv'lege aside,
From Papist sprung, and regicide;
Fall a-working like a mole,
Raise the dirt about your hole.
Come, assist me, Muse obedient!
Let us try some new expedient;
Shift the scene for half an hour,
Time and place are in thy pow'r.
Thither, gentle Muse, conduct me;
I shall ask, and you instruct me. 80
See, the Muse unbars the gate;
Hark, the monkeys, how they prate!
All ye gods who rule the soul:[1]
Styx, through Hell whose waters roll!
Let me be allow'd to tell
What I heard in yonder Hell.
Near the door an entrance gapes,[2]
Crowded round with antic shapes,
Poverty, and *Grief*, and *Care*,
Causeless *Joy*, and true *Despair*, 90
Discord periwigg'd with snakes,[3]
See the dreadful strides she takes!
By this odious crew beset,[4]

I began to rage and fret,
And resolv'd to break their pates,
Ere we enter'd at the gates;
Had not Clio in the nick[5]
Whisper'd me, *Let down your stick.*
What! Said I, is this the *mad-house?*
These, she answer'd are but shadows, 100
Phantoms bodiless and vain,
Empty visions of the brain.
 In the porch Briareus stands,[6]
Shows a bribe in all his hands:
Briareus the Secretary,
But we mortals call him Cary.
When the rogues their country fleece,
They may hope for pence apiece.
 Clio, who had been so wise
To put on a fool's disguise, 110
To bespeak some approbation
And be thought a near relation,
When she saw three hundred brutes
All involved in wild disputes,
Roaring, till their lungs were spent,
PRIVILEGE OF PARLIAMENT,
Now a new misfortune feels,
Dreading to be laid by th' heels.
Never durst a Muse before
Enter that infernal door; 120
Clio, stifled with the smell,
Into spleen and vapours fell,
By the Stygian steams that flew
From the dire infectious crew.
Not the stench of Lake Avernus
Could have more offended her nose;
Had she flown but o'er the top,
She must feel her pinions drop.
And by exhalations dire,

Though a goddess, must expire. 130
In a fright she crept away,
Bravely I resolved to stay.
When I saw the Keeper frown,
Tipping him with half-a-crown,
Now, said I, we are alone,
Name your heroes one by one.
   Who is that hell-featured brawler,
Is it Satan? No; 'tis Waller.
In what figure can a bard dress
Jack, the grandson of Sir Hardress? 140
Honest keeper, drive him further,
In his looks are Hell and murther;
See his scowling visage drop,
Just as when he murther'd Throp.
   Keeper, show me where to fix
On the puppy pair of Dicks:
By their lantern jaws and leathern,
You might swear they both were brethren:
Dick Fitzbaker, Dick the player,
Old acquaintance, are you there? 150
Dear companions, hug and kiss,
Toast *old Glorious* in your piss;
Tie them, keeper, in a tether,
Let them stare and stink together;
Both are apt to be unruly,
Lash them daily, lash them duly;
Though 'tis hopeless to reclaim them,
Scorpion rods, perhaps, may tame them.
   Keeper, yon old dotard smoak
Sweetly snoring in his cloak: 160
Who is he? 'Tis humdrum Wynne,
Half encompass'd with his kin.
There observe the tribe of Bingham,
For he never fails to bring 'em;
While he sleeps the whole debate,

They submissive round him wait;
Yet would gladly see the hunks
In his grave, and search his trunks.
See, they gently twitch his coat,
Just to yawn and give his vote, 170
Always firm in his vocation,
For the court against the nation.
  Those are Allens, Jack and Bob,
First in every dirty job,
Son and brother to a queer
Brain-sick brute, they call a peer.
We must give them better quarter,
For their ancestor trod mortar,
And at Howth, to boast his fame,
On a chimney cut his name. 180
  There sit Clements, Dilks, and Carter
Who for Hell would die a martyr:
Such a triplet could you tell
Where to find on this side Hell?
Gallows Carter, Dilks, and Clements,
Souse them in their own ex-crements.
Every mischief's in their hearts;
If they fail, 'tis want of parts.
  Bless us! Morgan, art thou there, man?
Bless mine eyes! Art thou the chairman? 190
Chairman to yon damn'd committee!
Yet I look on thee with pity;
Dreadful sight, the learned Morgan
Metamorphos'd to a Gorgon!
For thy horrid looks, I own,
Half convert me into stone.
Hast thou been so long at school
Now to turn a factious fool?
Alma Mater was thy mother,
Every young divine thy brother. 200
O thou disobedient varlet,

Treat thy mother like a harlot!
Thou, ungrateful to thy teachers
Who are all grown rev'rend preachers!
Morgan, would it not surprise one?
Turn thy nourishment to poison!
When you walk among your books,
They reproach you with their looks;
Bind them fast, or from the shelves
They'll come down and right themselves: 210
Homer, Plutarch, Virgil, Flaccus,
All in arms, prepare to back us.
Soon repent, or put to slaughter
Every Greek and Roman author.
Will you, in your factious phrase
Send the clergy all to graze;
And to make your project pass,
Leave them not a blade of grass?
How I want thee, hum'rous Hogarth!
Thou, I hear, a pleasant rogue art. 220
Were but you and I acquainted,
Ev'ry monster should be painted:
You should try your graving tools
On this odious group of fools;
Draw the beasts as I describe 'em,
Form their features while I gibe 'em;
Draw them like; for I assure you,
You will need no *car'catura;*
Draw them so that we may trace
All the soul in ev'ry face. 230
Keeper, I must now retire,
You have done what I desire:
But I feel my spirits spent
With the noise, the sight, the scent.
"Pray, be patient; you shall find
Half the best are still behind!
You have hardly seen a score;

I can show two hundred more."
   Keeper, I have seen enough.
Taking then a pinch of snuff, 240
I concluded, looking round 'em,
May their god, the devil, confound 'em!

ENDNOTES

A FULL AND TRUE ACCOUNT OF THE BATTEL FOUGHT LAST FRIDAY, BETWEEN THE ANTIENT AND THE MODERN BOOKS IN ST. JAMES' LIBRARY (1697)

[1] "Riches produceth pride; pride is war's ground, &c." *Vide* Ephem. de Mary Clarke; opt. edit.

[2] Their title-pages.

[3] The Honourable Mr. Boyle, in the preface to his edition of Phalaris, says he was refused a manuscript by the library-keeper, *"pro solita humanitate suâ."*

[4] According to the modern paradox.

[5] These are pamphlets, which are not bound or covered.

[6] *Vid.* Homer.

[7] Sir John Denham's poems are very unequal, extremely good and very indifferent; so that his detractors said he was not the real author of *Cooper's Hill.*

[8] *Vid.* Homer.

[9] I do not approve the author's judgment in this, for I think Cowley's Pindarics are much preferable to his *Mistress.*

[10] The person here spoken of is famous for letting fly at everybody without distinction, and using mean and foul scurrilities.

[11] *Vid.* Homer de Thersite.

[12] This is according to Homer, who tells the dreams of those who were killed in their sleep.

[13] *Vid.* Homer.

[14] *Vid.* Homer.

[15] This is also after the manner of Homer; the woman's getting a painful livelihood by spinning, has nothing to do with the similitude, nor would be excusable without such an authority.

A TALE OF A TUB (1704)

[1] The Citation out of Irenæus in the title-page, which seems to be all *gibberish,* is a form of initiation used anciently by the Marcosian Heretics. W. WOTTON.

It is the usual style of decried writers to appeal to Posterity, who is here represented as a prince in his nonage, and Time as his governor; and the author begins in a way very frequent with him, by personating other writers who sometimes offer such reasons and excuses for publishing their works, as they ought chiefly to conceal and be ashamed of.

[2] Comptroller.

[3] Out of guardianship.

[4] This I think the author should have omitted, it being of the very same nature with the *School of Hobby-horses,* if one may venture to censure one who is so severe a censurer of others, perhaps with too little distinction.

[5] Horace. Something extraordinary, new and never hit upon before.

[6] Reading Prefaces, &c.

[7] Plutarch.

[8] *Vide* Xenophon.

[9] Spleen. *Hor.*

[10] Juno and Venus are money and a mistress, very powerful bribes to a judge, if scandal says true. I remember such reflections were cast about that time, but I cannot fix the person intended here.

[11] But to return, and view the cheerful skies;
In this the task and mighty labour lies.

[12] Is the *mountebank's stage,* whose orators the author determines either to the *gallows* or a *conventicle.*

[13] In the open air, and in streets where the greatest resort is.

[14] Lucret. Lib. 2.

[15] 'Tis certain then, that *voice* that thus can wound,
Is all *material; body* every *sound.*

[16] The two principal qualifications of a fanatic preacher are his inward light, and his head full of maggots; and the two different fates of his writings are to be burnt, or worm-eaten.

[17] Here is pretended a defect in the manuscript; and this is very frequent with our author either when he thinks he cannot say anything worth reading, or when he has no mind to enter on the subject, or when it is a matter of little moment; or perhaps to amuse his reader (whereof he is frequently very fond) or lastly, with some satirical intention.

[18] *Will's* Coffeehouse, was formerly the place where the poets usually met, which though it be yet fresh in memory, yet in some years may be forgot, and want this explanation.

[19] *Viz.* About moving the earth.

[20] Virtuoso experiments, and modern comedies.

[21] The Author seems here to be mistaken, for I have seen a Latin edition of *Reynard the Fox,* above a hundred years old, which I take to be the original; for the rest, it has been thought by many people to contain some satyrical design in it.

[22] He lived a thousand.

[23] Viz. In the year 1698.

[24] This is I suppose to be understood of Mr. W[o]tt[o]n's *Discourse of Ancient and Modern Learning.*

[25] Here the author seems to personate L'Estrange, Dryden, and some others, who, having passed their lives in vice, faction, and falsehood, have the impudence to talk of merit and innocence and sufferings.

[26] In King Charles the Second's time, there was an account of a Presbyterian plot, found in a meal-tub, which then made much noise.

[27] The title-page in the original was so torn, that it was not possible to recover several titles which the author here speaks of.

[28] See Virgil translated, &c.

[29] By these three sons, Peter, Martin, and Jack; Popery, the Church of England, and our Protestant dissenters, are designed. W. WOTTON.

[30] By his *coats* which he gave his sons, the Garments of the Israelites. W. WOTTON.

An error (with submission) of the learned commentator; for by the coats are meant the *Doctrine and Faith of Christianity*, by the Wisdom of the divine Founder fitted to all times, places, and circumstances. LAMBIN.

[31] *The New Testament.*

[32] Their mistresses are the Duchess d'Argent, Mademoiselle de Grands Titres, and the Countess d'Orgueil, i.e., *covetousness, ambition,* and *pride;* which were the three great vices that the ancient fathers inveighed against as the first corruptions of Christianity. W. WOTTON.

[33] This is an occasional satire upon dress and fashion, in order to introduce what follows.

[34] By this *idol* is meant a tailor.

[35] The Ægyptians worshipped a monkey, which animal is very fond of eating lice, styled here, creatures that feed on human gore.

[36] Alluding to the word *microcosm,* or a little world, as man hath been called by philosophers.

[37] The first part of the Tale is the History of Peter; thereby Popery is exposed: everybody knows the Papists have made great additions to Christianity; that indeed is the great exception which the Church of England makes against them; accordingly Peter begins his pranks with *adding a shoulder-knot to his coat.* W. WOTTON.

[38] His description of the cloth of which the coat was made, has a farther meaning than the words may seem to import, "The coats their father had left them were of very good cloth, and besides so neatly sewn, you would swear it had been all of a piece; but, at the same time, very plain with little or no ornament." This is the distinguishing character of the Christian religion: *Christiana religio absoluta et simplex* was Ammianus Marcellinus' description of it, who was himself a heathen. W. WOTTON.

[39] By this is understood the first introducing of pageantry, and unnecessary ornaments in the Church, such as were neither for convenience nor edification; as a *shoulder-knot,* in which there is neither symmetry nor use.

[40] When the Papists cannot find anything which they want in Scripture they go to *Oral Tradition:* thus Peter is introduced dissatisfied with the tedious way of looking for all the letters of any word which he has occasion for in the *Will,* when neither the constituent syllables, nor much less the whole word, were there *in terminis.* W. WOTTON.

[41] [*Quibusdam veteribus codicibus.*] Some ancient manuscripts.

[42] I cannot tell whether the author means any new innovation by this word, or whether it be only to introduce the new methods of forcing and perverting scripture.

[43] The next subject of our author's wit is the *glosses* and *interpretations of scripture,* very many absurd ones of which are allowed in the most authentic books of the Church of Rome. W. WOTTON.

[44] By this is meant *tradition,* allowed to have equal authority with the scripture, or rather greater.

[45] This is *purgatory,* whereof he speaks more particularly hereafter, but here, only to show how scripture was perverted to prove it, which was done by giving equal authority with the *canon* to *Apocrypha,* called here a *codicil annexed.*

It is likely the author, in everyone of these changes in the brothers' dresses, refers to some particular error in the Church of Rome, though it is not easy, I think, to apply them all: but by this of *flame-coloured satin* is manifestly intended *purgatory;* by *gold lace* may perhaps be understood the lofty ornaments and plate in the churches; the *shoulder-knots* and *silver fringe* are not so obvious, at least to me; but the Indian figures of men, women, and children, plainly relate to the pictures in the Romish churches, of God like an old man, of the Virgin Mary, and our Saviour as a child.

[46] This shows the time the author writ, it being about fourteen years since those two persons were reckoned the fine gentlemen of the town.

[47] That is, to take care of hell, and in order to do that, to subdue and extinguish their lusts.

[48] I believe this refers to that part of the Apocrypha where mention is made of Tobit and his dog.

[49] This is certainly the further introducing the pomps of habit and ornament.

[50] The images of saints, the blessed Virgin, and our Saviour as an infant.

Ibid. Images in the Church of Rome give him but too fair a handle. *The brothers remembered,* &c. The allegory here is direct. W. WOTTON.

[51] The Papists formerly forbade the people the use of scripture in a vulgar tongue; Peter therefore *locks up his father's will in a strong box, brought out of Greece or Italy.* Those countries are named because the New Testament is written in Greek; and the vulgar Latin, which is

the authentic edition of the Bible in the Church of Rome, is in the language of old Italy. W. WOTTON.

[52] The popes, in their decretals and bulls, have given their sanction to very many gainful doctrines which are now received in the Church of Rome, that are not mentioned in scripture, and are unknown to the primitive church. Peter accordingly pronounces *ex cathedra,* that *points tagged with silver were absolutely jure paterno,* and so they wore them in great numbers. W. WOTTON.

[53] This was Constantine the Great, from whom the popes pretend a donation of St. Peter's patrimony, which they have never been able to produce.

[54] The bishops of Rome enjoyed their privileges in Rome at first by the favour of emperors, whom at last they shut out of their own capital city, and then forged a donation from Constantine the Great, the better to justify what they did. In imitation of this, Peter *having run something behind-hand in the world obtained leave of a certain lord,* &c. W. WOTTON.

[55] See Wotton *of Ancient and Modem Learning.*

[56] Satire and Panegyric upon Critics.

[57] Lib. 4.

[58] *Vide excerpta ex eo apud Photium.*

[59] Lib. 4. [129].

[60] Near Helicon, and round the learned hill,
Grow trees, whose blossoms with their odour kill.

[61] A quotation after the manner of a great author. Vide Bently's *Dissertation,* &c.

[62] That is, Purgatory.

[63] *Penance* and *absolution* are played upon under the notion of a *sovereign remedy for the worms,* especially in the spleen, which by observing Peter's prescription would void sensibly by perspiration, ascending through the brain, &c. W. WOTTON.

[64] Here the author ridicules the penances of the Church of Rome, which may be made as easy to the sinner as he pleases, provided he will pay for them accordingly.

[65] By his *whispering-office* for the relief of eavesdroppers, physicians, bawds, and privy-councillors, he ridicules auricular confession; and the priest who takes it, is described by the ass' head. W. WOTTON.

[66] This I take to be the office of Indulgences, the gross abuses whereof first gave occasion for the Reformation.

[67] I believe are all the monkeries and ridiculous processions, &c., among the papists.

[68] Holy water, he calls an *universal pickle,* to preserve houses, gardens, towns, men, women, children, and cattle, wherein he could preserve them as sound as insects in amber. W. WOTTON.

[69] This is easily understood to be holy water, composed of the same ingredients with many other pickles.

[70] And because holy water differs only in consecration from common water, therefore he tells us that his pickle by the powder of *pimperlim-pimp* receives new virtues, though it differs not in sight nor smell from the common pickle, which preserves beef, and butter, and herrings. W. WOTTON.

[71] The *papal hulk* are ridiculed by name, so that here we are at no loss for the author's meaning. W. WOTTON.

Ibid. Here the author has kept the name, and means the pope's Bulls, or rather his fulminations and excommunications of heretical princes, all signed with lead and the seal of the fisherman.

[72] These are the fulminations of the pope, threatening hell and damnation to those princes who offend him.

[73] That is, kings who incur his displeasure.

[74] This is a copy of a general pardon, signed *servus servorum.*

Ibid. Absolution *in articulo mortis,* and the tax *cameræ apostolicæ,* are jested upon in Emperor Peter's letter. W. WOTTON.

[75] The Pope is not only allowed to be the Vicar of Christ, but by several divines is called God upon Earth, and other blasphemous tides.

[76] The triple crown.

Ibid. The Pope's universal monarchy, and his triple crown, and fisher's ring. W. WOTTON.

[77] The keys of the Church.

[78] Neither does his arrogant way of requiring men to kiss his slipper escape reflection. W. WOTTON.

[79] This word properly signifies a sudden jerk, or lash of a horse, when you do not expect it.

[80] The Celibacy of the Romish clergy is struck at in Peter's beating his own and brothers' wives-out of doors. W. WOTTON.

[81] The Pope's refusing the cup to the laity, persuading them that the blood is contained in the bread, and that the bread is the real and entire body of Christ.

[82] *Transubstantiation.* Peter turns his bread into mutton, and according to the popish doctrine of concomitants, his wine too, which in his way he calls *palming his damned crusts upon the brothers for mutton.* W. WOTTON.

[83] By this *Rupture* is meant the *Reformation.*

[84] The ridiculous multiplying of the Virgin Mary's *milk* among the papists, under the allegory of a *cow,* which gave as much milk at a meal as would fill three thousand churches. W. WOTTON.

[85] By this *sign-post* is meant the *cross* of our Blessed Saviour.

[86] The chapel of Loretto, which travelled from the Holy Land to Italy. He falls here only upon the ridiculous inventions of popery. The Church of Rome intended by these things to gull silly, superstitious people, and rook them of their money; the world had been too long in slavery, and our ancestors gloriously redeemed us from that yoke. The Church of Rome therefore ought to be exposed, and he deserves well of mankind that does expose it. W. WOTTON.

[87] Translated the scriptures into the vulgar tongues.
[88] Administered the cup to the laity at the communion.
[89] Allowed the marriages of priests.
[90] Directed penitents not to trust to pardons and absolutions procured for money, but sent them to implore the mercy of God, from whence alone remission is to be obtained.
[91] By Peter's dragoons is meant the civil power, which those princes who were bigotted to the Romish superstition employed against the reformers.
[92] The Pope shuts all who dissent from him, out of the Church.
[93] The learned person, here meant by our author, hath been endeavouring to annihilate so many ancient writers that, until he is pleased to stop his hand, it will be dangerous to affirm whether there have been ever any ancients in the world.
[94] This is an imaginary island, of kin to that which is called the *Painters' Wives Island,* placed in some unknown part of the ocean, merely at the fancy of the map-maker.
[95] Homerus omnes res humanas poematis complexus est. *Xenoph. in conviv.*
[96] A treatise written about fifty years ago, by a Welsh gentleman of Cambridge. His name, as I remember, was Vaughan, as appears by the answer to it writ by the learned Dr. Henry More. It is a piece of the most unintelligible *fustian,* that perhaps was ever published in any language.
[97] Mr. W[o]tt[o]n (to whom our author never gives any quarter) in his comparison of ancient and modern learning, numbers divinity, law, &c., among those parts of knowledge wherein we excel the ancients.
[98] Martin Luther.
[99] John Calvin.
[100] Points tagged with silver are those doctrines that promote the greatness and wealth of the church, which have been therefore woven deepest into the body of popery.
[101] That is, *Calvin,* from *calvus,* bald.
[102] All those who pretend to inward light.
[103] Jack of Leyden, who gave rise to the Anabaptists.
[104] The Huguenots.
[105] The Gueuses, by which name some Protestants in Flanders were called.
[106] John Knocks, the reformer of Scotland.
[107] Ctesiæ fragm. apud Photium.
[108] Herodot. L. 4. [2].
[109] Herodot. L. 4. [7 and 31].
[110] All pretenders to inspiration whatsoever.
[111] This is one of the names of Paracelsus; he was called Christophorus, Theophrastus, Paracelsus, Bumbastus.
[112] This is meant of those seditious preachers, who blow up the seeds of rebellion, &c.
[113] Pausan. L. 8.

[114] An author who writ *De Artibus perditis* &c., of arts lost, and of arts invented.

[115] This is an exact description of the changes made in the face by Enthusiastic preachers.

[116] Quakers, who suffer their women to preach and pray.

[117] I do not well understand what the Author aims at here, anymore than by the terrible Monster mentioned in the following lines, called *Moulinavent,* which is the French word for a windmill.

[118] This was Harry the Great of France.

[119] Ravillac, who stabbed Henry the Great in his coach.

[120] This is meant of the present French king.

[121] Paracelsus, who was so famous for chemistry, tried an experiment upon human excrement to make a perfume of it; which, when he had brought to perfection, he called *zibeta occidentalis,* or *western civet;* the back parts of man (according to his division mentioned by the author, page [134]), being the *west.*

[122] *Epist. ad Fam. Trebatio.*

[123] Here is another defect in the manuscript; but I think the author did wisely, and that the matter which thus strained his faculties was not worth a solution; and it were well if all metaphysical cobweb problems were no otherwise answered.

[124] Tacit. [*Annals* vi, 39 and xvi, 18].

[125] A lawyer's coach-hire.

[126] *Cornutus* is either horned or shining, and by this term Moses is described in the vulgar Latin of the Bible.

[127] I cannot conjecture what the author means here, or how this chasm could be filled, though it is capable of more than one interpretation.

[128] This is literally true, as we may observe in the prefaces to most plays, poems, &c.

[129] By dogs, the author means common injudicious critics, as he explains it himself before in his *Digression upon Critics.*

[130] A name of the Rosicrucians.

[131] Nothing is more frequent than for Commentators to force interpretations, which the authors never meant.

[132] This is what the Cabalists among the Jews have done with the Bible, and pretend to find wonderful mysteries by it.

[133] I was told by an eminent divine, whom I consulted on this point, that these two barbarous words, with that of *Acamoth* and its qualities, as here set down, are quoted from Irenæus. This he discovered by searching that ancient writer for another quotation of our author, which he has placed in the title-page, and refers to the book and chapter; the curious were very inquisitive whether those barbarous words, *basima eacabasa, &c.* are really in Irenæus, and upon inquiry, 'twas found they were a sort of cant or jargon of certain heretics, and therefore very properly prefixed to such a book as this of our author.

[134] *Vid. Anima Magica Abscondita.*

Ibid. To the above-mentioned treatise, called *Anthroposophia Theomagica,* there is another annexed, called *Anima Magica Abscondita,* written by the same author, Vaughan, under the name of Eugenius Philalethes, but in neither of those treatises is there any mention of *Acamoth,* or its qualities, so that this is nothing but amusement, and a ridicule of dark, unintelligible writers; only the words, *à cujus lacrymis, &c.* are, as we have said, transcribed from Irenæus, though I know not from what part. I believe one of the author's designs was to set curious men a-hunting through *indexes,* and inquiring for books out of the common road.

[135] By these are meant what the author calls the *true critics.*

[136] The author here lashes those pretenders to purity, who place so much merit in using scripture phrases on all occasions.

[137] The Protestant dissenters use *scripture phrases* in their serious discourses and composures, more than the Church of England men; accordingly, Jack is introduced making *his common talk and conversation to run wholly in the phrase of his WILL.* W. WOTTON.

[138] I cannot guess the author's meaning here, which I would be very glad to know because it seems to be of importance.

[139] The slovenly way of receiving the sacrament among the fanatics.

[140] This is a common phrase to express eating cleanlily, and is meant for an invective against that undecent manner among some people in receiving the sacrament; so in the lines before, 'tis said, Jack *would never say Grace to his Meat,* which is to be understood of the dissenters refusing to kneel at the sacrament.

[141] I cannot well find the author's meaning here, unless it be the hot, untimely, blind zeal of Enthusiasts.

[142] *Vide* Don Quixote.

[143] The villainies and cruelties committed by Enthusiasts and fanatics among us, were all performed under the disguise of religion and long prayers.

[144] They affect differences in habit and behaviour.

[145] They are severe persecutors, and all in a form of cant and devotion.

[146] Cromwell and his confederates went, as they called it, *to seek God,* when they resolved to murder the king.

[147] This is to expose our dissenters' aversion to instrumental music in churches. W. WOTTON.

[148] They quarrel at the most innocent decency and ornament, and defaced the statues and paintings on all the churches in England.

[149] Fanatic preaching, composed either of hell and damnation, or a fulsome description of the joys of heaven; both in such a dirty, nauseous style, as to be well resembled to pilgrim's salve.

[150] The fanatics have always had a way of affecting to run into persecution, and count vast merit upon every little hardship they suffer.

[151] The papists and fanatics, though they appear the most averse to each other, yet bear a near resemblance in many things, as hath been observed by learned men.

Ibid. The agreement of our dissenters and the papists, in that which Bishop Stillingfleet called *the fanaticism of the Church of Rome,* is ludicrously described for several pages together, by Jack's likeness to Peter, and their being often mistaken for each other, and their frequent meeting when they least intended it. W. WOTTON.

[152] *Lib. de aëre, locis, et aquis* [50, 51].

[153] This was King Charles the Second, who at his restoration turned out all the dissenting teachers that would not conform.

[154] Including Scaliger's.

[155] In the reign of King James the Second, the Presbyterians, by the king's invitation, joined with the Papists against the Church of England, and addressed him for repeal of the penal laws and Test. The king, by his dispensing power, gave liberty of conscience, which both Papists and Presbyterians made use of; but upon the Revolution, the Papists being down of course, the Presbyterians freely continued their assemblies by virtue of King James' indulgence, before they had a toleration by law. This I believe the author means by Jack's *stealing* Peter's *protection, and making use of it himself.*

[156] Sir Humphry Edwin, a Presbyterian, was some years ago [1697] Lord Mayor of London, and had the insolence to go in his formalities to a conventicle, with the ensigns of his office.

[157] Custard is a famous dish at a Lord Mayor's feast.

[158] Père d'Orleans.

[159] This was writ before the peace of Ryswick.

[160] Trezenii. Pausan. lib. 2.

A DISCOURSE CONCERNING THE MECHANICAL OPERATION OF THE SPIRIT (1704)

[1] This Discourse is not altogether equal to the two former, the best parts of it being omitted; whether the bookseller's account be true, that he durst not print the rest, I know not; nor indeed is it easy to determine whether he may be relied on in anything he says of this or the former treatises, only as to the time they were writ in, which however appears more from the discourses themselves than his relation.

[2] Some writers hold them for the same, others not.

[3] Macrocephali.

[4] Bernier, *Mem. de Mogol.*

[5] Guagnini Hist. *Sarmat.*

[6] The *snuffling* of men who have lost their noses by lewd courses is said to have given rise to that tone, which our dissenters did too much affect. W. WOTTON.

[7] Herodot.
[8] Diod. Sic. L. 1. Plut. *de Iside et Osiride.*
[9] Herod. L. 2.
[10] Diod Sic. L. 1 and 3.
[11] Id. L. 4.
[12] See the particulars in Diod. Sic. L. 1 and 3.
[13] Dionysia Brauronia.
[14] Vide *Photium in excerptis è Conone.*

A TRITICAL ESSAY UPON THE FACULTIES OF THE MIND (1707)

[1] Could you, my friends, hold back your laughter?
[2] "Because I do not take you in, you take me in." This apocryphal story traces back to Hellenistic times.
[3] "You may drive out Nature with a pitchfork, but she will always hasten back." Horace, *Epistles,* I, x, 24 (imprecisely quoted). The following Latin quotations do little more than repeat the English sentiments immediately preceding them.

THE EXAMINER, NO. 14 (THURSDAY, NOVEMBER 9, 1710)

[1] "Some of these fill their idle ears with conversations; others spread what is told; the story grows, and each new teller adds to what he has heard. Here is Credulity; here heedless Error, vain Joy and confounded Fear, quick Sedition and Whisperings of dubious authority." Ovid, *Metamorphoses,* XII, 56–61.
[2] *The late Earl of* Wharton.

TO THE TRADESMEN, SHOPKEEPERS, FARMERS, AND COMMON-PEOPLE IN GENERAL, OF THE KINGDOM OF IRELAND (1724)

[1] Under the guise of M. B. Drapier, Swift composed a series of pamphlets defending Irish interests against English policy. His immediate provocation is set forth in this, the first, of the papers. For another version, from a later perspective, of the "plain story" the Drapier is about to render, see above, Book III of *Gulliver's Travels,* pp. 145–146. See too the related commentary in *Verses on the Death of Dr. Swift,* lines 165–168, 339–354, 407–430, pp. 553–561.
[2] Vide *one of the preceding Pamphlets, entitled, A Proposal for the Use of* Irish *Manufactures* [also by *Swift—Editors*].
[3] Edward Waters, against whom the Chief Justice of Ireland, William Whitshed (d. 1727), attempted to force a jury to bring in a verdict.

[4] *A sort of Barley in* Ireland.
[5] Turn all arable land into sheep pastures.
[6] Compiled by Andrew Horne; translated into English by William Hughes and published in London in 1646.
[7] Sir Edward Coke, whose *Institutes of the Laws of England* (London, 1628–44) Swift here refers to.

A CHARACTER, PANEGYRIC, AND DESCRIPTION OF THE LEGION CLUB (1736)

[1] *Di quibus imperium est animarum, &c.*
Sit mihi fas audita loqui &c.
[2] *Vestibulum ante ipsum primisque in faucibus Orci*
Luctus et ultrices, &c.
[3] *——Discordia demens,*
Vipereum crinem vittis innexa cruentis.
[4] *Corripit hic subita trepidus, &c.*
——strictamque aciem venientibus offert.
[5] *Et ni docta comes tenues sine corpore vitas.*
[6] *Et centumgeminus Briareus.*

SUGGESTED READING

BLOOM, HAROLD, ED. *Jonathan Swift.* New York: Chelsea House, 1986.

BOYLE, FRANK T. *Swift as Nemesis: Modernity and Its Satirist.* Stanford, CA: Stanford University Press, 2000.

DONOHUE, DENIS. *Jonathan Swift: A Critical Introduction.* Cambridge: Cambridge University Press, 1969.

EHRENPREIS, IRVIN. *Swift: The Man, His Works, and the Age (3 Vols.).* London: Methuen, 1962.

FERGUSON, OLIVER W. *Jonathan Swift and Ireland.* Urbana, IL: University of Illinois Press, 1962.

FOX, CHRISTOPHER, ED. *The Cambridge Companion to Jonathan Swift.* Cambridge: Cambridge University Press, 2003.

LEVINE, JOSEPH M. *The Battle of the Books: History and Literature in the Augustan Age.* Ithaca, NY: Cornell University Press, 1991.

NOKES, DAVID. *Jonathan Swift, A Hypocrite Reversed.* New York: Oxford University Press, 1985.

RAWSON, CLAUDE. *Satire and Sentiment, 1660–1830.* Cambridge: Cambridge University Press, 1994.

STARKMAN, MIRIAM KOSH. *Swift's Satire on Learning in A Tale of a Tub.* New York: Octagon, 1968.

Look for the following titles, available now from The Barnes & Noble Library of Essential Reading.

Visit your Barnes & Noble bookstore, or shop online at *www.bn.com/loer*

NONFICTION

Title	Author	ISBN
Age of Revolution, The	Winston S. Churchill	0760768595
Alexander	Theodore Ayrault Dodge	0760773491
American Democrat, The	James Fenimore Cooper	0760761981
American Indian Stories	Zitkala-Ša	0760765502
Ancient Greek Historians, The	J. B. Bury	0760776350
Ancient History	George Rawlinson	0760773580
Antichrist, The	Friedrich Nietzsche	0760777705
Autobiography of Benjamin Franklin, The	Benjamin Franklin	0760768617
Autobiography of Charles Darwin, The	Charles Darwin	0760769087
Babylonian Life and History	E. A. Wallis Budge	0760765499
Beyond the Pleasure Principle	Sigmund Freud	0760774919
Birth of Britain, The	Winston S. Churchill	0760768579
Boots and Saddles	Elizabeth B. Custer	076077370X
Characters and Events of Roman History	Guglielmo Ferrero	0760765928
Chemical History of a Candle, The	Michael Faraday	0760765227
Civil War, The	Julius Caesar	0760768943
Common Law, The	Oliver Wendell Holmes	0760754985
Confessions	Jean-Jacques Rousseau	0760773599
Conquest of Gaul, The	Julius Caesar	0760768951
Consolation of Philosophy, The	Boethius	0760769796
Conversations with Socrates	Xenophon	0760770441

Creative Evolution	Henri Bergson	0760765480
Critique of Judgment	Immanuel Kant	0760762023
Critique of Practical Reason	Immanuel Kant	0760760942
Critique of Pure Reason	Immanuel Kant	0760755949
Dark Night of the Soul, The	St. John of the Cross	0760765871
Democracy and Education	John Dewey	0760765863
Democracy in America	Alexis de Tocqueville	0760752303
Descent of Man and Selection in Relation to Sex, The	Charles Darwin	0760763119
Dialogues concerning Natural Religion	David Hume	0760777713
Discourse on Method	René Descartes	0760756023
Discourses on Livy	Niccolò Machiavelli	0760771731
Dolorous Passion of Our Lord Jesus Christ, The	Anne Catherine Emmerich	0760771715
Early History of Rome, The	Titus Livy	0760770239
Ecce Homo	Friedrich Nietzsche	0760777721
Edison: His Life and Inventions	Frank Lewis Dyer	0760765820
Egyptian Book of the Dead, The	E. A. Wallis Budge	0760768382
Elements, The	Euclid	0760763127
Emile	Jean-Jacques Rousseau	0760773513
Eminent Victorians	Lytton Strachey	0760749930
Encheiridion	Epictetus	0760770204
Enquiry concerning Human Understanding, An	David Hume	0760755922
Essay concerning Human Understanding, An	John Locke	0760760497
Essays, The	Francis Bacon	0760770182
Essence of Christianity, The	Ludwig Feuerbach	076075764X
Ethics and On the Improvement of the Understanding	Benedict de Spinoza	0760768374
Extraordinary Popular Delusions and the Madness of Crowds	Charles Mackay	0760755825
Fall of Troy, The	Quintus of Smyrna	0760768366
Fifteen Decisive Battles of the Western World	Edward Shepherd Creasy	0760754950
Florentine History	Niccolò Machiavelli	0760756015
From Manassas to Appomattox	James Longstreet	0760759200
From Ritual to Romance	Jessie L. Weston	0760773548
Great Democracies, The	Winston S. Churchill	0760768609
Guide for the Perplexed, The	Moses Maimonides	0760757577
Hannibal	Theodore Ayrault Dodge	076076896X
Happy Hunting-Grounds, The	Kermit Roosevelt	0760755817
History of Atlantis, The	Lewis Spence	076077045X

History of the Conquest of Mexico, The	William H. Prescott	0760759227
History of the Conquest of Peru, The	William H. Prescott	076076137X
History of the Donner Party, The	Charles F. McGlashan	0760752427
History of the English Church and People, The	Bede	0760765510
History of Wales, A	J. E. Lloyd	0760752419
How the Other Half Lives	Jacob A. Riis	0760755892
How to Sing	Lilli Lehmann	0760752311
How We Think	John Dewey	0760770387
Hunting the Grisly and Other Sketches	Theodore Roosevelt	0760752338
Imitation of Christ, The	Thomas À. Kempis	0760755914
In His Steps	Charles M. Sheldon	0760755779
Influence of Sea Power upon History, The, 1660–1783	Alfred Thayer Mahan	0760754993
Interesting Narrative of the Life of Olaudah Equiano, The	Olaudah Equiano	0760773505
Interior Castle, The	St. Teresa of Avila	0760770247
Introduction to Logic	Immanuel Kant	0760770409
Introduction to Mathematical Philosophy	Bertrand Russell	0760773408
Introduction to Mathematics	Alfred North Whitehead	076076588X
Investigation of the Laws of Thought, An	George Boole	0760765847
Kingdom of God is Within You, The	Leo Tolstoy	0760765529
Lady's Life in the Rockies, A	Isabella Bird	0760763135
Leonardo da Vinci and a Memory of His Childhood	Sigmund Freud	0760749922
Letters and Saying of Epicurus	Epicurus	0760763283
Leviathan, The	Thomas Hobbes	0760755930
Life of Johnson	James Boswell	0760773483
Lives of the Caesars, The	Suetonius	0760757585
Manners, Customs, and History of the Highlanders of Scotland	Walter Scott	0760758697
Meditations	Marcus Aurelius	076075229X
Memoirs	William T. Sherman	0760773688
Metaphysics	Aristotle	0760773637
Montcalm and Wolfe	Francis Parkman	0760768358
Montessori Method, The	Maria Montessori	0760749957
Mosby's Memoirs	John Singleton Mosby	0760773726

Myths of North American Indians, The	Lewis Spence	0760770433
Napoleon's Art of War	George C. D'Aguilar	0760773564
New World, The	Winston S. Churchill	0760768587
Nicomachean Ethics	Aristotle	0760752362
Notes on Nursing	Florence Nightingale	0760749949
On Liberty	John Stuart Mill	0760755000
On the Nature of Things	Lucretius	076076834X
On War	Carl von Clausewitz	0760755973
Oregon Trail, The	Francis Parkman	076075232X
Outline of History, The: Volume 1	H. G. Wells	0760758662
Outline of History, The: Volume 2	H. G. Wells	0760758670
Passing of the Armies, The	Joshua L. Chamberlain	0760760527
Personal Memoirs of P. H. Sheridan	Philip H. Sheridan	0760773750
Personal Memoirs of U. S. Grant	Ulysses S. Grant	0760749906
Philosophy of History, The	G. W. F. Hegel	0760757631
Plato and Platonism	Walter Pater	0760765472
Political Economy for Beginners	Millicent Garrett Fawcett	0760754977
Politics	Aristotle	0760768935
Poor Richard's Almanack	Benjamin Franklin	0760762015
Pragmatism	William James	0760749965
Praise of Folly, The	Desiderius Erasmus	0760757607
Principia Ethica	G. E. Moore	0760765464
Principle of Relativity	Alfred North Whitehead	0760765219
Principles of Political Economy and Taxation, The	David Ricardo	0760765367
Problems of Philosophy, The	Bertrand Russell	076075604X
Recollections and Letters	Robert E. Lee	0760759197
Relativity	Albert Einstein	0760759219
Rights of Man, The	Thomas Paine	0760755019
Rough Riders, The	Theodore Roosevelt	0760755760
Russia and Its Crisis	Paul Miliukov	0760768633
Science and Method	Henri Poincare	0760755868
Second Treatise of Government, The	John Locke	0760760950
Sense of Beauty, The	George Santayana	0760770425
Shakespearean Tragedy	A. C. Bradley	0760771693
Social Contract, The	Jean-Jacques Rousseau	0760770212
Subjection of Women, The	John Stuart Mill	076077174X
Tenting on the Plains	Elizabeth B. Custer	0760773718
Theory of Moral Sentiments, The	Adam Smith	0760758689
Totem and Taboo	Sigmund Freud	0760765200
Tractatus Logico-Philosophicus	Ludwig Wittgenstein	0760752354

Tragic Sense of Life	Miguel de Unamuno	0760777764
Travels of Marco Polo, The	Marco Polo	0760765898
Treatise Concerning the Principles of Human Knowledge, A	George Berkeley	0760777691
Treatise of Human Nature, A	David Hume	0760771723
Trial and Death of Socrates, The	Plato	0760762007
Up From Slavery	Booker T. Washington	0760752346
Utilitarianism	William James	0760771758
Vindication of the Rights of Woman, A	Mary Wollstonecraft	0760754942
Violin Playing As I Teach It	Leopold Auer	0760749914
Voyage of the *Beagle*, The	Charles Darwin	0760754969
Wealth of Nations, The	Adam Smith	0760757615
Wilderness Hunter, The	Theodore Roosevelt	0760756031
Will to Believe and Human Immortality, The	William James	0760770190
Will to Power, The	Friedrich Nietzsche	0760777772
Worst Journey in the World, The	Aspley Cherry-Garrard	0760757593
You Know Me Al	Ring W. Lardner	0760758336